Mastering Kotlin for Android 14

Build powerful Android apps from scratch using
Jetpack libraries and Jetpack Compose

Harun Wangereka

Mastering Kotlin for Android 14

Group Product Manager: Rohit Rajkumar
Publishing Product Manager: Vaideeshwari Muralikrishnan
Book Project Manager: Sonam Pandey
Senior Editor: Rakhi Patel
Technical Editor: K Bimala Singha
Copy Editor: Safis Editing
Indexer: Rekha Nair
Production Designers: Alishon Mendonca and Gokul Raj S.T
DevRel Marketing Coordinators: Anamika Singh and Nivedita Pandey

First published: April 2024

Production reference: 1010324

Published by
Packt Publishing Ltd.
Grosvenor House
11 St Paul's Square
Birmingham
B3 1RB, UK

ISBN 978-1-83763-171-1

www.packtpub.com

I extend heartfelt gratitude to my beloved wife for her unwavering encouragement and support in every endeavor, as well as her understanding during the late nights and weekends I dedicated to this book. To my mother: I express deep appreciation for her constant support. I am immensely thankful to my family, friends, and colleagues whose continual motivation propels me toward becoming a better version of myself. Special thanks to the vibrant Android254 and Kotlin Kenya communities, where I found inspiration and ideas through interactions with members and the insightful questions I regularly receive. Lastly, my sincere appreciation goes to the exceptional team at Packt for their dedication and hard work on this book.

—Harun Wangereka

Contributors

About the author

Harun Wangereka is an Android engineer and a Google Developer Expert for Android. He is passionate about creating quality applications and perpetually embraces the journey of continuous learning, contributing to tech communities, and aiding fellow developers in honing their skills. His enthusiasm extends to crafting technical articles centered around Android and Kotlin topics.

He is currently working at Apollo Agriculture. In this role, he helps make financing accessible to small-scale farmers. He collaborates with a cross-functional team to define, design, and ship new features for two apps, namely Agent's App and Agro-Dealers App.

Beyond his professional commitments, Harun is a part of the team that organizes Droidcon Kenya, leading the speakers team. He is an engaged community member at Android254 and Kotlin Kenya, channeling his passion into giving back to the community by sharing knowledge and experiences amassed over time as an Android engineer.

About the reviewers

Dmitrii Ivashchenko is an expert software engineer with over a decade of experience in mobile development and backend systems. Starting as a junior full stack developer, Dmitrii became the lead of a mobile game development team at a major international company. An active member of the International Game Developers Association and the Academy of Interactive Arts & Sciences, Dmitrii has authored articles for Medium and HackerNoon. He has also served as a judge for international awards and often speaks at conferences. Currently, he is the lead software engineer at MY.GAMES, guiding a team dedicated to creating successful and engaging games. Dmitrii is passionate about mentoring and regularly shares his insights within the developer community.

Peter Gichia is a software engineer focused on native Android development and currently working as a freelance Android engineer and an entrepreneur on the side. He enjoys solving problems for his clients whether through code or business strategy. He is also an active contributor to the Android development community through writing and publishing Android-related articles. In the process, he has successfully published a text-based course on building scalable applications with MVVM architecture and is working on publishing another one about clean architecture in collaboration with a leading Edutech company. In his free time, Peter enjoys expanding his knowledge through podcasts and books.

Table of Contents

4

Design with Material Design 3   53

Part 2: Using Advanced Features

5

Architect Your App   79

6

Network Calls with Kotlin Coroutines   99

7

Navigating within Your App   115

8

Persisting Data Locally and Doing Background Work   157

9

Runtime Permissions   193

Part 3: Code Analysis and Tests

10

Debugging Your App   207

11

Enhancing Code Quality   231

12

Testing Your App   249

Part 4: Publishing Your App

13

Publishing Your App   271

Continuous Integration and Continuous Deployment   305

Preface

Kotlin is a programming language created by JetBrains that runs on the **Java Virtual Machine** (**JVM**). It was designed to address issues such as verbosity, null pointer exceptions, concurrency challenges, and the lack of functional support found in Java. Kotlin offers a more modern and concise programming approach while still being compatible with existing Java code and libraries. Google recognized Kotlin as a primary language for building Android apps, leading to significant efforts to support developers. This book adopts an industry-focused approach, preparing you for the role of an Android developer in any company. It follows current best practices recommended by Google's Android team, providing insights based on practical experience.

With practical examples, the book guides you through developing Android apps using Kotlin, imparting hands-on knowledge that is essential for becoming a proficient Android developer. Topics include building apps with Jetpack Compose, incorporating Material Design 3 for a personalized touch, and structuring apps in the MVVM architecture. The guide further demonstrates how to enhance your app's architecture with features such as dependency injection, use Jetpack Libraries such as Room for local data persistence, and implement debugging techniques. It covers testing, identifying code issues using tools such as Ktlint and Detekt, and guides you through the publication process on Google Play Store. Automation of consecutive releases through GitHub Actions and the distribution of test builds using Firebase App Distribution are also explored. Additionally, the book addresses app improvement strategies, including crash reporting tools, tips for boosting user engagement, and insights on securing your app.

Who this book is for

This book is for aspiring Android developers or Android developers working with Java, as they'll learn how to build Android apps with Kotlin from scratch, learn about architecture and other pertinent topics in Android, and finally, know how to publish their apps to Google Play Store. The book is written with current best practices in mind and also guides you to prepare for a role as an Android developer.

What this book covers

Chapter 1, Get Started with Kotlin Android Development, introduces Kotlin as a programming language. It covers features that are useful for Android development and its importance for Android developers. Additionally, it covers how to migrate from Java to Kotlin and some useful tips for developers coming from Java backgrounds.

Chapter 2, Creating Your First Android App, covers how to create Android apps. It familiarizes you with Android Studio, the **Integrated Development Environment** (**IDE**) that you will use to develop Android apps. It also covers some tips, shortcuts, and useful Android Studio features and explores the process of creating a project in Android Studio.

Chapter 3, Jetpack Compose Layout Basics, looks at Jetpack Compose, a declarative way of creating user interfaces for apps. It covers the basics of Jetpack Compose and its layouts.

Chapter 4, Design With Material Design 3, introduces Material 3 and the features that it offers. It also covers how to use Material 3 in Android apps and some of its components.

Chapter 5, Architect Your App, explores the different architectures available for Android projects. It dives deep into the MVVM architecture and its different layers and how to use some of the Jetpack libraries within it. Additionally, it shows you how to use advanced architecture features, such as dependency injection, the Kotlin Gradle DSL, and a version catalog to define dependencies.

Chapter 6, Network Calls with Kotlin Coroutines, discusses how to perform network calls with a networking library, Retrofit. It shows how to consume **Application Programming Interfaces** (**APIs**) using this library. Moreover, it covers how to take advantage of Kotlin coroutines to perform asynchronous network requests.

Chapter 7, Navigating within Your App, explains how to use the Jetpack Compose Navigation library to navigate to different Jetpack Compose screens. It covers the tips and best practices for using this library. Moreover, it covers how to pass arguments as we navigate to screens. Lastly, it covers how to handle navigation on large screens and foldables.

Chapter 8, Persisting Data Locally and Doing Background Work, covers how to save data to a local database, Room, which is part of the Jetpack libraries. It shows how to save items and read from the Room database. Additionally, it covers how to do long-running operations using WorkManager and some of the best practices.

Chapter 9, Runtime Permissions, delves into runtime permissions and how to request runtime permissions.

Chapter 10, Debugging Your App, discusses debugging tips and tricks, how to detect leaks using LeakCanary, how to inspect network requests/responses fired by apps using Chucker, and how to inspect the Room database, network requests, and background tasks using App Inspection.

Chapter 11, Enhancing Code Quality, explores the Kotlin style and the best practices for writing Kotlin code. It also demonstrates how to use plugins such as Ktlint and Detekt to format, lint, and detect code smells early.

Chapter 12, *Testing Your App*, examines how to add tests for the different layers in the MVVM architecture. It covers the importance of adding tests and how to add unit tests, integration tests, and instrumentation tests.

Chapter 13, *Publishing Your App*, delves into how to publish a new app to Google Play Store. It walks through how to create a signed app bundle and topics such as answering questions about the content of our app, creating releases, setting up how users will access the app, either via controlled testing tracks or publicly, and much more. Additionally, it covers some of the Google Play Store policies and how to always stay compliant to avoid apps being removed or accounts being banned.

Chapter 14, *Continuous Integration and Continuous Deployment*, focuses on how to use GitHub Actions to automate some manual tasks, such as deploying new builds to Google Play Store. It also covers how to run tests on CI/CD pipelines and push builds to Google Play Store using GitHub Actions.

Chapter 15, *Improving Your App*, covers the techniques of improving apps by adding analytics, Firebase Crashlytics, and using cloud messaging to increase user engagement in apps. It covers how to send notifications to apps from the Firebase console. Additionally, it covers tips and tricks for securing apps to ensure that a user's data is not compromised.

To get the most out of this book

Software/hardware covered in the book	Operating system requirements
Android Studio Hedgehog or later versions	Windows, macOS, or Linux

Download the example code files

You can download the example code files for this book from GitHub at `https://github.com/PacktPublishing/Mastering-Kotlin-for-Android`. If there's an update to the code, it will be updated in the GitHub repository.

We also have other code bundles from our rich catalog of books and videos available at `https://github.com/PacktPublishing/`. Check them out!

Conventions used

There are a number of text conventions used throughout this book.

`Code in text`: Indicates code words in text, database table names, folder names, filenames, file extensions, pathnames, dummy URLs, user input, and Twitter handles. Here is an example: "We created a class named `PetsRepositoryImpl` that implements the `PetsRepository` interface."

A block of code is set as follows:

```
class PetsViewModel: ViewModel() {
    private val petsRepository: PetsRepository = PetsRepositoryImpl()

    fun getPets() = petsRepository.getPets()
}
```

When we wish to draw your attention to a particular part of a code block, the relevant lines or items are set in bold:

```
[default]
exten => s,1,Dial(Zap/1|30)
exten => s,2,Voicemail(u100)
exten => s,102,Voicemail(b100)
exten => i,1,Voicemail(s0)
```

Any command-line input or output is written as follows:

```
FATAL EXCEPTION: main
Process: com.packt.chapterten, PID: 7168
java.lang.RuntimeException: Unable to start activity
ComponentInfo{com.packt.chapterten/com.packt.chapterten.MainActivity}:
java.lang.RuntimeException: This is a crash
at android.app.ActivityThread.performLaunchActivity(ActivityThread.
java:3645)
at android.app.ActivityThread.handleLaunchActivity(ActivityThread.
java:3782)
```

Bold: Indicates a new term, an important word, or words that you see on screen. For instance, words in menus or dialog boxes appear in **bold**. Here is an example: "Tap on the **New Project** button, which will take us to the **Templates** screen."

> Tips or important notes
> Appear like this.

Get in touch

Feedback from our readers is always welcome.

General feedback: If you have questions about any aspect of this book, email us at customercare@packtpub.com and mention the book title in the subject of your message.

Errata: Although we have taken every care to ensure the accuracy of our content, mistakes do happen. If you have found a mistake in this book, we would be grateful if you would report this to us. Please visit www.packtpub.com/support/errata and fill in the form.

Piracy: If you come across any illegal copies of our works in any form on the internet, we would be grateful if you would provide us with the location address or website name. Please contact us at copyright@packt.com with a link to the material.

If you are interested in becoming an author: If there is a topic that you have expertise in and you are interested in either writing or contributing to a book, please visit authors.packtpub.com.

Share Your Thoughts

Once you've read *Mastering Kotlin for Android 14*, we'd love to hear your thoughts! Scan the QR code below to go straight to the Amazon review page for this book and share your feedback.

https://packt.link/r/1837631719

Your review is important to us and the tech community and will help us make sure we're delivering excellent quality content.

Download a free PDF copy of this book

Thanks for purchasing this book!

Do you like to read on the go but are unable to carry your print books everywhere?

Is your eBook purchase not compatible with the device of your choice?

Don't worry, now with every Packt book you get a DRM-free PDF version of that book at no cost.

Read anywhere, any place, on any device. Search, copy, and paste code from your favorite technical books directly into your application.

The perks don't stop there, you can get exclusive access to discounts, newsletters, and great free content in your inbox daily

Follow these simple steps to get the benefits:

1. Scan the QR code or visit the link below

https://packt.link/free-ebook/9781837631711

2. Submit your proof of purchase
3. That's it! We'll send your free PDF and other benefits to your email directly

Part 1:
Building Your App

In this part, you will embark on a journey into Kotlin, exploring the features that make it an optimal choice for Android development. We will guide you through the process of migrating from Java, offering valuable insights for developers transitioning from a Java background. Step by step, you will delve into constructing your inaugural Android app, including the setting up of your development environment, and becoming acquainted with Android Studio. The focus extends to mastering Jetpack Compose, unraveling the art of crafting intuitive user interfaces. To finish, we will enlighten you on incorporating Material Design 3 into your applications, shedding light on the rich features and components it brings to the development landscape.

This section contains the following chapters:

- *Chapter 1, Get Started with Kotlin Android Development*
- *Chapter 2, Creating Your First Android App*
- *Chapter 3, Jetpack Compose Layout Basics*
- *Chapter 4, Design with Material Design 3*

1

Get Started with Kotlin Android Development

Kotlin is a static programming language that allows you to write concise and typed code. It's the language preferred for Android development by Google.

In this chapter, we'll get to know Kotlin as a programming language. We will cover features that are useful for Android development and their importance for Android developers. Additionally, we'll cover how to migrate from Java to Kotlin and some useful tips for developers coming from Java backgrounds.

In this chapter, we're going to cover the following main topics:

- Introduction to Kotlin
- Kotlin syntax, types, functions, and classes
- Migrating from Java to Kotlin
- Kotlin features for Android developers

Technical requirements

To follow the instructions in this chapter, you'll need to have the following ready:

- IntelliJ IDEA Community Edition (`https://www.jetbrains.com/idea/download/`)
- OpenJDK 11 or higher (`https://openjdk.java.net/install/`)

You can find the code for this chapter at `https://github.com/PacktPublishing/Mastering-Kotlin-for-Android/tree/main/chapterone`

Introduction to Kotlin

Kotlin is a language that runs on the **Java Virtual Machine** (**JVM**) developed by JetBrains. It was developed to overcome the following challenges that Java had:

- **Verbosity**: Java has a very verbose syntax and this leads to developers writing a lot of boilerplate code even for trivial tasks.

- **Null pointer exceptions**: By default, Java allows variables to have null values. This normally results in null pointer exceptions, which has been called **the billion-dollar mistake** in Java as many applications have been affected by this.

- **Concurrency**: Java has threads, but managing concurrency and thread safety can be such a hard task at times. This leads to a lot of performance and memory issues that seriously affect applications that need to do work off the main thread.

- **Slow adoption of features**: The Java release cycle is slow and it is difficult to use the latest Java version to develop Android apps as there's a lot to be done to ensure backward compatibility. This means it's hard for Android developers to easily adopt the new language features and improvements as they're stuck using older versions.

- **Lack of functional support**: Java is not a functional language, which makes it hard for developers to write functional code in Java. It's hard to employ features such as high-order functions or treat functions as first-class citizens.

Over the years, Kotlin has evolved to be multiplatform and server-side and not serviced, and is used in data science as well. Some of the features where Kotlin has an edge over Java are as follows:

- **Conciseness**: The syntax is concise, which in turn reduces the amount of boilerplate code that you write.

- **Null safety**: Many Java developers are very familiar with the famous **Null Pointer Exception** that was a source of many bugs and issues in applications. Kotlin was designed with null safety in mind. Variables that can have null values are indicated when declaring them, and before using these variables, the Kotlin compiler enforces checks for nullability, thereby reducing the number of exceptions and crashes.

- **Coroutines support**: Kotlin has built-in support for Kotlin coroutines. Coroutines are lightweight threads that you can use to perform asynchronous operations. It's easy to understand and use them in your applications.

- **Data classes**: Kotlin has a built-in data class construct that makes it easy to define classes that are used primarily to store data. Data classes automatically generate `equals()`, `hashCode()`, and `toString()` methods, reducing the amount of boilerplate code required.

- **Extension functions**: Kotlin allows developers to add functions to existing classes without inheriting from them, through extension functions. This makes it easier to add functionality to existing classes and reduces the need for boilerplate code.

- **Smart casting**: Kotlin's smart casting system makes it possible to cast variables without the need for an explicit cast. The compiler automatically detects when a variable can be safely cast and performs the cast automatically.

JetBrains is also the company behind IntelliJ IDEA. The language support in this **Integrated Development Environment (IDE)** is also great.

 Kotlin has evolved over the years to support the following different platforms:

- **Kotlin Multiplatform**: This is used to develop applications that target different platforms such as Android, iOS, and web applications

- **Kotlin for server side**: This is used to write backend applications and a number of frameworks to support server-side development

- **Kotlin for Android**: Google has supported Kotlin as a first-class language for Android development since 2017

- **Kotlin for JavaScript**: This provides support for writing Kotlin code that is transpiled to compatible JavaScript libraries

- **Kotlin/Native**: This compiles Kotlin code to native binaries and runs without a **Java Virtual Machine (JVM)**

- **Kotlin for data science**: You can use Kotlin to build and explore data pipelines

In summary, Kotlin provides a more modern and concise approach to programming than Java while still maintaining interoperability with existing Java libraries and code. In addition, you can write Kotlin code and target different platforms.

Now that we have got the gist of Kotlin and its various features, let's move on to the next section where we will understand Kotlin as a programming language and understand Kotlin syntax, types, functions, and classes.

Kotlin syntax, types, functions and classes

In this section, we'll be looking at Kotlin syntax and familiarize ourselves with the language. Kotlin is a strongly typed language. The type of a variable is determined at the time of compilation. Kotlin has a rich type system that has the following types:

- **Nullable types**: Every type in Kotlin can either be nullable or non-nullable. Nullable types are denoted with a question mark operator – for example, `String?`. Non-nullable types are normal types without any operator at the end – for example, `String`.

- **Basic types**: These types are similar to Java. Examples include Int, Long, Boolean, Double, and Char.

- **Class types**: As Kotlin is an object-oriented programming language, it provides support for classes, sealed classes, interfaces, and so on. You define a class using the `class` keyword and you can add methods, properties, and constructors.

- **Arrays**: There is support for both primitive and object arrays. To declare a primitive array, you specify the type and size, as follows:

```
val shortArray = ShortArray(10)
```

The following shows how you define object arrays:

```
val recipes = arrayOf("Chicken Soup", "Beef Stew", "Tuna
Casserole")
```

Kotlin automatically infers the type when you don't specify it.

- **Collections**: Kotlin has a rich collection of APIs providing types such as sets, maps, and lists. They're designed to be concise and expressive, and the language offers a wide range of operations for sorting, filtering, mapping, and many more.

- **Enum types**: These are used to define a fixed set of options. Kotlin has the `Enum` keyword for you to declare enumerations.

- **Functional types**: Kotlin is a functional language as well, meaning functions are treated as first-class citizens. You can be able to assign functions to variables, return functions as values from functions, and pass functions as arguments to other functions. To define a function as a type, you use the `(Boolean) -> Unit` shorthand notation. This example takes a `Boolean` argument and returns a `Unit` value.

We've learned the different types available in Kotlin, and we'll use this knowledge in the next section to define some of these types.

Creating a Kotlin project

Follow these steps to create your first Kotlin project:

1. Open IntelliJ IDEA. On the welcome screen, click on **New Project**. You'll be presented with a dialog to create your new project as shown in the following figure:

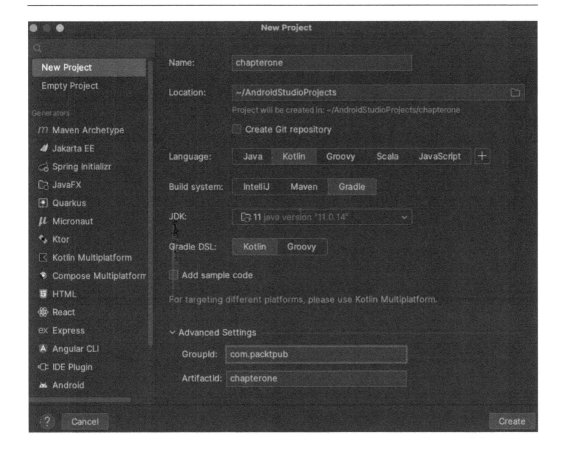

Figure 1.1 – New Project dialog

Let's work through the options in the dialog shown in *Figure 1.1* as follows:

I.   You start by giving the project a name. In this case, it's `chapterone`.

II.   You also specify the location of your project. This is normally where you store your working projects. Change the directory to your preferred one.

III. Next, specify your target language from the options provided. In this case, we opt for **Kotlin**.

IV.   In the next step, specify your build system. We specify **Gradle**.

V.   We also need to specify the Java version that our project is going to use. In this case, it's Java **11**.

VI.   Next, you specify the Gradle DSL to use. For this project, we've chosen to use **Kotlin**.

VII. Lastly, you specify the group and artifact IDs that, when combined, form a unique identifier for your project.

2. Click on **Create** to finalize creating your new project. The IDE will create your project, which might take a few minutes. Once done, you'll see your project as follows:

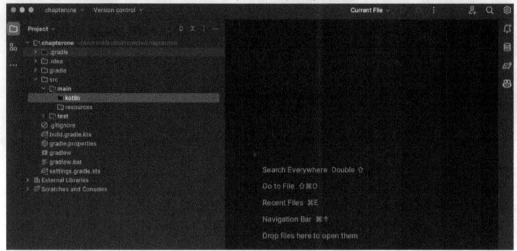

Figure 1.2 – Project structure

The IDE creates the project with the project structure seen in *Figure 1.2*. We are mostly interested in the `src/main/kotlin` package, which is where we'll add our Kotlin files.

3. Start by right-clicking the `src/main/kotlin` package.

4. Select **New** and then **New Kotlin Class/File**. Select the **File** option from the list that appears and name the file `Main`. The IDE will generate a `Main.kt` file.

Now that we've created our first Kotlin project and added a Kotlin file, in the next section, we will create functions in this file.

Creating functions

In Kotlin, a function is a block of code that does a specific task. We use the `fun` keyword to define functions. Function names should be in camel case and descriptive to indicate what the function is doing. Functions can take arguments and return values.

Create the `main()` function in your `Main.kt` file as follows:

```
fun main() {
    println("Hello World!")
}
```

In the preceding code, we've used the `fun` keyword to define a function with the name `main`. Inside the function, we have a `println` statement that prints the message `"Hello Word!"`.

You can run the function by pressing the green run icon to the right of the function. You'll see the console window pop up, displaying the message "Hello World!".

We've learned how to create functions and print output to the console. In the next section, we'll learn how to create classes in Kotlin.

Creating classes

To declare a class in Kotlin, we have the `class` keyword. We're going to create a `Recipe` class as follows:

```
class Recipe {
    private val ingredients = mutableListOf<String>()

    fun addIngredient(name: String) {
        ingredients.add(name)
    }

    fun getIngredients(): List<String> {
        return ingredients
    }
}
```

Let's break down the preceding class:

- We've called the class `Recipe` and it has no constructor.

- Inside the class, we have a member variable, `ingredients`, which is a `MutableList` of Strings. It's mutable to allow us to add more items to the list. Defining variables in a class like this allows us to be able to access the variable anywhere in the class.

- We have `addIngredient(name: String)`, which takes in a name as an argument. Inside the function, we add the argument to our ingredients list.

- Lastly, we have the `getIngredients()` function, which returns an immutable list of strings. It simply returns the value of our ingredients list.

To be able to use the class, we have to modify our main function as follows:

```
fun main() {
    val recipe = Recipe()
    recipe.addIngredient("Rice")
    recipe.addIngredient("Chicken")
    println(recipe.getIngredients())
}
```

The changes can be explained as follows:

- First, we create a new instance of the `Recipe` class and assign it to the `recipe` variable
- Then, we call the `addIngredient` method on the `recipe` variable and pass in the string `Rice`
- Again, we call the `addIngredient` method on the `recipe` variable and pass in the string `Chicken`
- Lastly, we call the `getIngredients` method on the `recipe` variable and print the result to the console

Run the main function again and your output should be as follows:

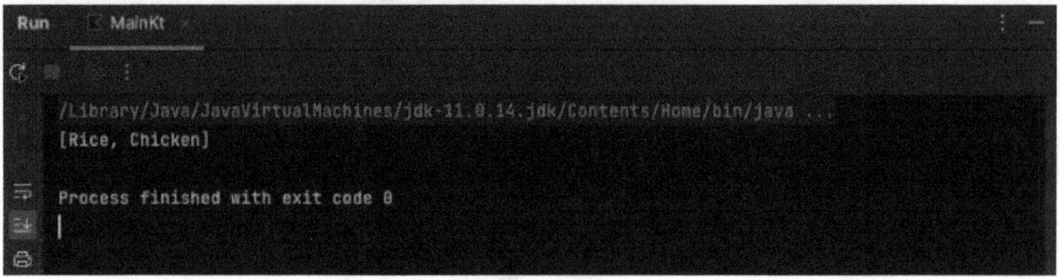

Figure 1.3 – Recipes

As you can see from the preceding screenshot, the output is a list of ingredients that you added! Now you can prepare a nice rice and chicken meal, but in Kotlin!

Kotlin has tons of features and we've barely scratched the surface. You can check out the official Kotlin documentation (`https://kotlinlang.org/docs/home.html`) as well to learn more. You'll also learn more features as you go deeper into this book.

We've learned how to create classes, define top-level variables, and add functions to our class. This helps us understand how classes in Kotlin work. In the next section, we will learn how to migrate a Java class to Kotlin and some of the tools available to use in the migration.

Migrating from Java to Kotlin

Are you a Java developer and have your apps in Java? Are you wondering how you could get started with Kotlin? Worry not, this is your section. Kotlin offers two ways for you:

- **Java-to-Kotlin migration**: The IDE that we are using, IntelliJ IDEA, has a tool for converting existing Java files to Kotlin.
- **Interoperability**: Kotlin is highly interoperable with Java code, meaning you can have both Java and Kotlin code in the same project. You can continue using your favorite Java libraries in your Kotlin projects.

Let's see how to migrate a sample Java class to Kotlin using IntelliJ IDEA:

1. Inside `src/main/kotlin`, open the `Song` class, which has a number of Java functions.

2. Right-click the file and you'll see the **Convert Java to Kotlin** option at the bottom. Select this and you'll be presented the following confirmation dialog:

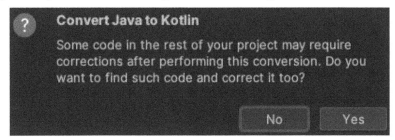

Figure 1.4 – Confirmation dialog

At times after a conversion, you might need to make some corrections and that's why we have this dialog. Click **Yes** to proceed and you'll see your code is now in Kotlin. This is a useful feature that handles a major part of the conversion to Kotlin and you also learn about the syntax.

Now that we've learned how to migrate Java code to Kotlin, in the next section we will cover some of the features of Kotlin that make it useful for Android developers.

Kotlin features for Android developers

Now that you have had an introduction to Kotlin, let's look at why Kotlin is a great language specifically for Android development.

Google announced Kotlin as a first-class language for writing Android apps back in 2017. Since then, there has been lots of work done to make sure that developers have all they need to develop Android apps in Kotlin. Here are some of the features that developers can benefit from:

*   **Improved developer productivity**: Kotlin's concise and expressive syntax can help developers write code faster and with fewer errors, which can ultimately improve developer productivity.

*   **Null safety**: Since Kotlin is written with nullability in mind, it helps us to avoid crashes related to the Null Pointer Exception.

*   **IDE support**: IDE support has been continuously improving. Android Studio, which is built on top of IntelliJ IDEA, has been receiving tons of features such as improved autocompletion support to improve the Kotlin experience.

*   **Jetpack libraries**: Jetpack libraries are available in Kotlin, and older ones are being rewritten with Kotlin. These are a set of libraries and tools to help Android developers write less code. They address common developer pain points and increase developer efficiency.

- **Jetpack Compose**: Jetpack Compose, a new UI framework, is completely written in Kotlin and takes advantage of features of the Kotlin language. It's a declarative UI framework that makes it easy for Android developers to build beautiful UIs for their apps.

- **Kotlin Gradle DSL**: You are now able to write your Gradle files in Kotlin.

- **Coroutine support**: A lot of Jetpack Libraries support coroutines. For example, the `ViewModel` class has `viewModelScope` that you can use to scope coroutines in the lifecycle of the `ViewModel`. This aligns with the Structured Concurrency principles for coroutines. This helps cancel all coroutines when they're no longer needed. Some libraries including Room, Paging 3, and DataStore also support Kotlin coroutines.

- **Support from Google**: Google continues to invest in Kotlin. Currently, there are resources ranging from articles to code labs, documentation, videos, and tutorials from the Android DevRel team at Google to assist you in learning new libraries and architecture for Android Development.

- **Active community and tooling**: Kotlin has a vibrant and active community of developers, which means that there are plenty of unofficial resources, libraries, and tools available to help with Android development.

Summary

In this chapter, we learned about the Kotlin programming language and its features. We explored the Kotlin features that are useful for Android development and why it's important to Android developers. Additionally, we covered how to migrate from Java to Kotlin and some useful tips for developers coming from Java backgrounds.

In the next chapter, we'll learn how to create Android apps with Android Studio. We will explore some of the features that Android Studio offers and learn some tips and shortcuts.

2

Creating Your First Android App

Android, a mobile operating system developed by Google, runs on over two billion devices, such as smartphones, tablets, TVs, watches, and cars, and developers are able to write code that is compatible with these different devices.

In this chapter, we'll create our first Android app. We will also familiarize ourselves with Android Studio, the **Integrated Development Environment (IDE)** that we'll use to develop Android apps. We will also learn some tips, shortcuts, and useful Android Studio features and understand the process of creating a project in Android Studio.

In this chapter, we're going to cover the following main topics:

- Android Studio overview
- Creating your Android app
- Android Studio tips and tricks

Technical requirements

To follow the instructions in this chapter, you will need to have Android Studio Hedgehog or later (`https://developer.android.com/studio/download`) downloaded.

You can find the code for this chapter at `https://github.com/PacktPublishing/Mastering-Kotlin-for-Android/tree/main/chaptertwo`.

Android Studio overview

Developed by Google, Android Studio is the official IDE for creating Android applications. Built upon JetBrains' IntelliJ IDEA, it provides a comprehensive platform for Android app development. It has all the features to enable you to develop Android apps with ease.

Once you download Android Studio from the official site, you need to download SDKs and set everything up for it to be ready for use. Open your newly installed Android Studio. You will see the following welcome screen:

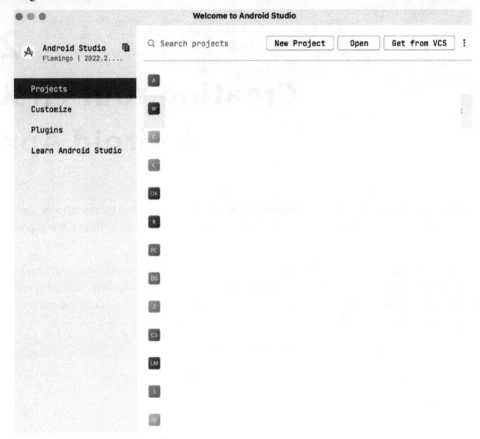

Figure 2.1 – Android Studio welcome screen

On the top right, we have these quick options:

- **New Project**: We use this to create new projects in Android Studio.

- **Open**: We use this when we want to open existing projects using Android Studio.

- **Get from VCS**: **VCS** stands for **version control system**. Examples of VCSs are GitHub, GitLab, and Bitbucket. We can always link our accounts and easily import projects that are hosted on VCS to our Android Studio.

- **More options icon**: This provides us with more options, such as **Profile or Debug APK**, **Import Project**, **Import an Android Code Sample**, **SDK Manager**, and **Virtual Device Manager**. We only use these options as needed, so we are not going to dive deep into them at this point.

Now, let us look at the navigation options on the left:

- **Projects**: This is selected by default. It shows all the projects that you have created with Android Studio if present. If you do not have any, an empty screen will be displayed.

- **Customize**: This provides a settings screen to customize the various aspects of Android Studio, as shown in the following screenshot:

Figure 2.2 – Customize Android Studio screen

From the preceding screenshot, we can see that we can quickly customize the following:

- **Color theme**: We can set the theme to dark (**Dracula**), light (**InteliJ Light**), or high contrast depending on our preferences.

- **IDE font**: Here we set the preferred font size for our IDE.

- **Keymap**: Here we configure what IntelliJ should use for mapping our keyboard and mouse shortcuts. It automatically picks the one for our operating system.

At the bottom of this screen, we can see two more settings options. One is **Import Settings…**, which we use when we want to import settings from either a previous Android Studio installation or a custom file. The other one is **All settings…**, which provides more customization options.

- **Plugins**: Here, we can install external plugins to our Android Studio and also manage our installed plugins. There are several plugins in the Marketplace that we can install depending on the needs.

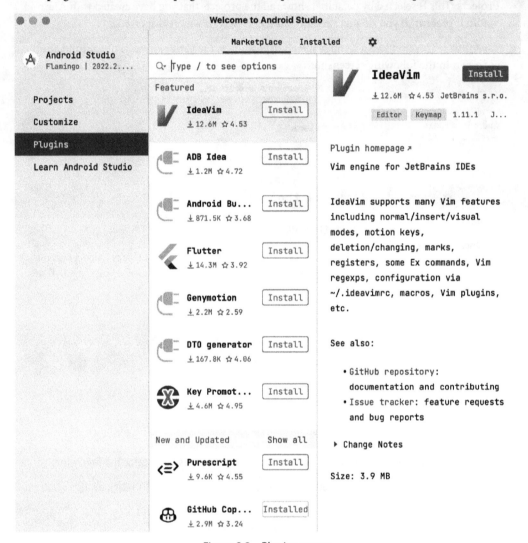

Figure 2.3 – Plugins screen

Now that we have an overview of several essential options on the Android Studio welcome screen, we will use the **New Project** option to create our first Android app in the next section.

Creating your Android app

Follow these steps to create your first Android app:

1. Tap on the **New Project** button, which will take you to the **Templates** screen, as shown in the following figure:

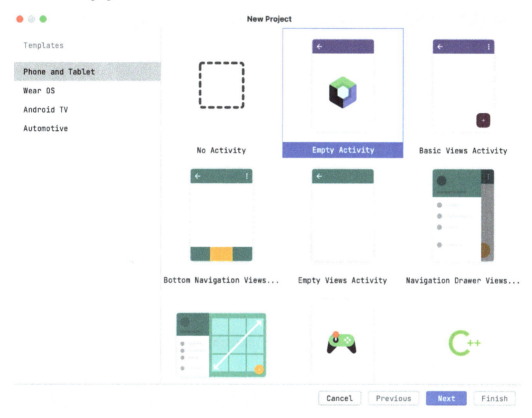

Figure 2.4 – New Project | Templates screen

The IDE presents us with a variety of options to choose from while creating new projects, as seen in *Figure 2.4*. To start with, on the right-hand side, we need to choose the specific form factor that we are targeting. By default, **Phone and Tablet** is selected. We have other options, such as **Wear OS** if we want to target wearables, **Android TV** if we want to develop apps that run on Smart TVs powered by Android OS, and, lastly, **Automotive**, for apps that target Android Auto.

We are going to use the default option since we want to target Android and tablet devices.

Next, we have to choose a template from the options provided. There are several templates that we can use to quickly generate some functionality for our apps. For example, we have **Bottom Navigation View Activity** to generate a project with both UI and Koltin code for displaying bottom tabs.

2. We will choose **Empty Activity** as we want to start from scratch. We use this instead of the **No Activity** option since this comes with some dependencies set up for us.

3. Tap **Next**, and we'll see the screen to configure the project details, as follows:

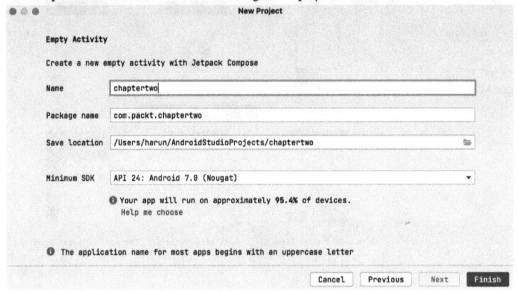

Figure 2.5 – New Project settings

4. As seen in the preceding screenshot, to finalize creating the project, we need to specify the following:

- **Name**: This is the unique name for our project.

- **Package name**: This is a unique identifier for our project. Normally it's a combination of the company website and app name.

- **Save location**: Here we specify the directory that our project will be in.

- **Minimum SDK**: This is the minimum Android version that our Android app will support. Android Studio gives us the percentage of devices using all the versions to help us decide the minimum Android version to support. For our project, we've chosen **API 24: Android 7.0 (Nougat)**, which will run on approximately 94% of devices. It is important to note that choosing a lower minimum SDK version means we will have to make our app compatible across the different device versions, which can be a lot of work. Also, some features are only available in newer SDK versions, so we have to add a fallback mechanism for devices for

5. Lastly, tap **Finish**—this creates our project. It will take a couple of minutes to prepare our project. Once done, we'll be presented with the following screen:

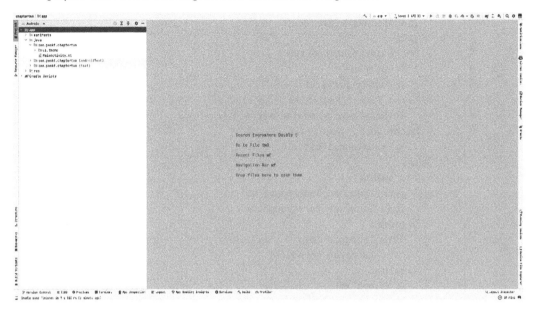

Figure 2.6 – New project

There are a few things about the project structure we need to understand here. We will be diving deep into them in the next section.

Exploring the new project

In this subsection, we are going to look at the whole project structure so that we can understand the different components.

On the left, we have the **project structure** with different directories and packages. On the right is the editor section, which by default does not have anything. When you open any file inside Android Studio, this is where they appear. This is the project structure for our new project:

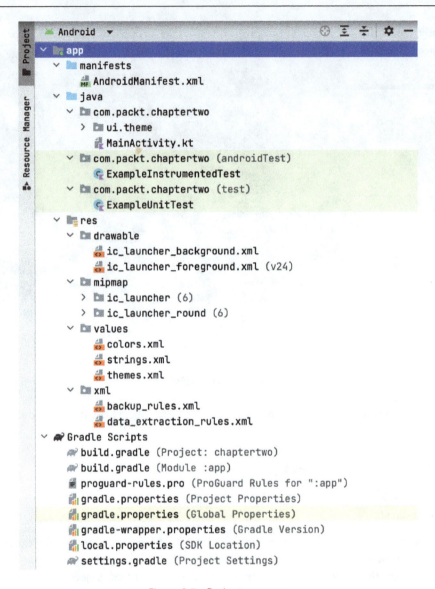

Figure 2.7 – Project structure

On the left, we have the app directory, which is the root directory, which has all files related to the project. From *Figure 2.7*, we can see that inside the app directory, we have the following different directories:

- manifests: This has a single AndroidManifest.xml file, which is essential for our app configuration. A manifest file has a .xml extension and contains the information critical to your app. It communicates this information to the Android system. In this file, we define the permissions needed for our app, the app name, and icons. We also declare activities and services in this file. Without declaring them, it's hard for our app to use them.

- The `java` package: This package, although named `java`, has all the Kotlin files for our project. If we need to add any files, this is where we add them. We can also create packages that help us group files with related functionality together. This directory is further subdivided into the following:

  - `com.packt.chaptertwo`: This is for the Kotlin files in our app

  - `com.packt.chaptertwo (androidTest)`: Here, we add all the files for our instrumentation tests

  - `com.packt.chaptertwo (test)`: Here, we add all the files for our unit tests

- Resources: This directory, normally shortened to `res`, has all the resources needed for our app. These resources can include images, strings, and assets. From *Figure 2.6*, we can see that we have the following subdirectories:

  - `drawable`: This folder contains custom drawables, vector drawables, or PNGs and JPEGs that are used in the app.

  - `mipmap`: This folder is where we place our launcher icons.

  - `values`: This folder is where we place our color, string, style, and theme files. In this folder, we define global values to be used all throughout the app.

  - `xml`: In this folder, we store XML files.

- `Gradle Scripts`: Here, we have all the Gradle scripts and Gradle property files needed for our project. In our new project, we have the following files:

  - `build.gradle (Project: chaptertwo)`: This is the top-level Gradle file where we add configurations that apply all over the project and submodules.

  - `build.gradle (Module: app)`: This is the app module Gradle file. Inside here, we configure the app module. To understand this file, let's look at the one generated for our project:

```
plugins {
    id 'com.android.application'
    id 'org.jetbrains.kotlin.android'
}

android {
    namespace 'com.packt.chaptertwo'
    compileSdk 33
    defaultConfig {
        applicationId "com.packt.chaptertwo"
        minSdk 24
        targetSdk 33
        versionCode 1
        versionName "1.0"
```

```
            testInstrumentationRunner "androidx.test.runner.
AndroidJUnitRunner"
        vectorDrawables {
            useSupportLibrary true
        }
    }
    buildTypes {
        release {
            minifyEnabled false
            proguardFiles getDefaultProguardFile('proguard-
android-optimize.txt'), 'proguard-rules.pro'
        }
    }
    compileOptions {
        sourceCompatibility JavaVersion.VERSION_1_8
        targetCompatibility JavaVersion.VERSION_1_8
    }
    kotlinOptions {
        jvmTarget = '1.8'
    }
    buildFeatures {
        compose true
    }
    composeOptions {
        kotlinCompilerExtensionVersion '1.3.2'
    }
    packagingOptions {
        resources {
            excludes += '/META-INF/{AL2.0,LGPL2.1}'
        }
    }
}

dependencies {
    implementation 'androidx.core:core-ktx:1.10.1'
    implementation 'androidx.lifecycle:lifecycle-runtime-
ktx:2.6.1'
    implementation 'androidx.activity:activity-compose:1.7.2'
    implementation platform('androidx.compose:compose-
bom:2022.10.00')
    implementation 'androidx.compose.ui:ui'
```

```
        implementation 'androidx.compose.ui:ui-graphics'
        implementation 'androidx.compose.ui:ui-tooling-preview'
        implementation 'androidx.compose.material3:material3'
        testImplementation 'junit:junit:4.13.2'
        androidTestImplementation 'androidx.test.ext:junit:1.1.5'
        androidTestImplementation 'androidx.test.espresso:espresso-
core:3.5.1'
        androidTestImplementation platform('androidx.
compose:compose-bom:2022.10.00')
        androidTestImplementation 'androidx.compose.ui:ui-test-
junit4'
        debugImplementation 'androidx.compose.ui:ui-tooling'
        debugImplementation 'androidx.compose.ui:ui-test-manifest'
    }
```

At the very top, we specify the plugins needed by the module. In this case, we have the Android application and Kotlin plugins declared. After the `plugins` block, we have the `android` block. You can see we have the following properties defined inside this block:

* `namespace`: This is used as the Kotlin or Java package name for the generated R and `BuildConfig` classes.

* `compileSDK`: This defines the Android SDK version that will be used by Gradle to compile our app.

* `defaultConfig`: This is a block where we specify the default config for all flavors and build types. Inside this block, we specify properties such as `applicationId`, `minSDK`, `targetSDK`, `versionCode`, `versionName`, and `testInstrumentationRunner`.

* `buildTypes`: This configures different build types for our application, such as `debug` and `release`, or any custom build that we define. Within each build type block, we specify properties such as `minifyEnabled`, `proguardFiles`, or `debuggable`.

* `compileOptions`: We use this block to configure properties related to Java compilation. For example, we have defined `sourceCompatibility` and `targetCompatibility`, which specify the Java version compatibility for our project source code.

* `kotlinOptions`: We use this block to configure options related to Kotlin. A commonly used option is `jvmTarget`, which specifies which Java version to use for Kotlin compilation.

* `buildFeatures`: We use this block to enable and disable specific features in our project. For example, we've enabled `compose` in our project. We can enable or disable other additional features, such as `viewBinding` and `dataBinding`.

* `ComposeOptions`: This block is specific to projects that use Jetpack Compose. For example, inside this block, we can set `kotlinCompilerExtensionVersion`.

- `packagingOptions`: We use this block to customize the packaging options of our project, particularly regarding conflicts and merging.

- `dependencies`: Here we specify the dependencies in our project. We can add different libraries, modules, or external dependencies in this block.

- `proguard-rules.pro`: This is a file where you define rules for ProGuard to use when obfuscating your code. We will dive deep into this later in *Chapter 13*.

- `gradle.properties (Project Properties)`: Here we define properties that apply to the whole project. Some of the properties include setting the Kotlin style and also specifying the memory to be used.

- `gradle.properties (Global Properties)`: This is a global file. We specify settings that we want to apply to all our Android Studio projects.

- `gradle-wrapper.properties (Gradle Version)`: In this file, we specify the Gradle wrapper properties, including the version and the URL from where to download the Gradle wrapper.

- `local.properties (Local Properties)`: In this file, we specify settings that need to apply to our local setup. Normally, this file is never committed to version control, so it means the configurations we add here only apply to our individual setup.

- `settings.gradle (Project Setting)`: We use this file to apply some settings to our project. For example, if we need more modules in our project, this is where they're specified.

When we build the project, Android Studio compiles all the resources and code using the configurations specified in our Gradle files and converts them into an **Android Application Package** (**APK**) or **Android Application Bundle** (**AAB**) that can run on our Android phones or emulators.

In this section, we have explored the newly created project and understood some of the key files and folders generated by Android Studio. In the next section, we are going to see how we can customize some things inside our Android Studio.

Android Studio tips and tricks

In this section, we're going to learn about some useful tips, shortcuts, and features in Android Studio.

We'll start by opening the `MainActivity.kt` file. When you open the file, you'll be presented with the following layout:

```
MainActivity.kt

1      package com.packt.chaptertwo
2
3      import ...
14
15     class MainActivity : ComponentActivity() {
16         override fun onCreate(savedInstanceState: Bundle?) {
17             super.onCreate(savedInstanceState)
18             setContent {
19                 ChaptertwoTheme {
20                     // A surface container using the 'background' color from the theme
21                     Surface(
22                         modifier = Modifier.fillMaxSize(),
23                         color = MaterialTheme.colorScheme.background
24                     ) {
25                         Greeting( name: "Android")
26                     }
27                 }
28             }
29         }
30     }
31
32     @Composable
33     fun Greeting(name: String, modifier: Modifier = Modifier) {
34         Text(
35             text = "Hello $name!",
36             modifier = modifier
37         )
38     }
39
40     @Preview(showBackground = true)
41     @Composable
42     fun GreetingPreview() {
43         ChaptertwoTheme {
44             Greeting( name: "Android")
45         }
46     }
```

Figure 2.8 – MainActivity file

We can now see the code inside the `MainActivity.kt` file, which is Kotlin source code. Above the tab with the filename, we can see a navigation bar, as shown in the following screenshot:

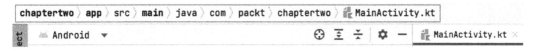

Figure 2.9 – Navigation bar

The navigation bar enables you to navigate easily and quickly between the different project files.

We can also switch to the **project view** to see all the resources in our project. The switch is at the very top of all the directories. By default, it is set to **Android view** and has more options depending on your preference. Switching to project view gives us the following folder structure:

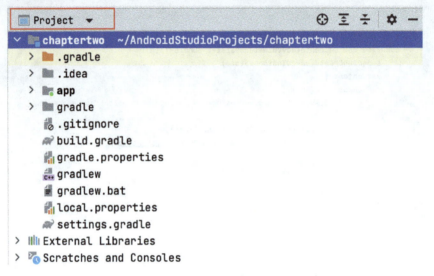

Figure 2.10 – Project view

In *Figure 2.10*, we can see all the resources in our project, and we can easily navigate through the different files and folders.

Android Studio has a variety of different tool windows that provide a variety of options. Let us start with the **Resource Manager** tool window, which is at the top left part below the view switcher tab. Open that window and you will see the following:

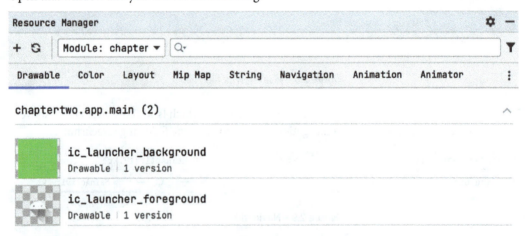

Figure 2.11 – Resource Manager tab

As shown in *Figure 2.11*, the **Resource Manager** tab shows all the resources in your project. We can also quickly add new vector and image assets and drawable files and import drawable here. The good thing is that we can also see a preview of these resources and easily browse the resources that we have in our project. Below this tab, we have the **Project** tab, to switch back to our project view, and below it, there is the **Pull Requests** tab, which enables us to see open pull requests from the project's version control repository. This is especially useful when we are collaborating with other team members or colleagues.

Android Studio allows us to add or remove these tabs or choose which tabs to be shown on either the left, right, or bottom side. To remove a tab, you simply right-click on it and select the **Remove from Sidebar** option. Click on **View**, followed by **Tool Windows**. This action will display all the tool windows currently available for use.

Android Studio provides alternative viewing options in the **View** menu. For example, we can switch to presentation mode while we are doing our presentations. To do this, still, in the **View** menu, tap **Appearance** and then **Enter Presentation Mode**. This brings up a minimized UI, as shown in the following figure:

```
                                                                          ▪Code ▪Split ▪Design
1          package com.packt.chaptertwo
2
3          import ...
14
15      class MainActivity : ComponentActivity() {
16          override fun onCreate(savedInstanceState: Bundle?) {
17              super.onCreate(savedInstanceState)
18              setContent {
19                  ChaptertwoTheme {
20                      // A surface container using the 'background' color from the theme
21                      Surface(
22                          modifier = Modifier.fillMaxSize(),
23                          color = MaterialTheme.colorScheme.background
24                      ) {
25                          Greeting( name: "Android")
26                      }
27                  }
28              }
29          }
30      }
31
32      @Composable
33      fun Greeting(name: String, modifier: Modifier = Modifier) {
34          Text(
35              text = "Hello $name!",
36              modifier = modifier
37          )
38      }
39
40      @Preview(showBackground = true)
41      @Composable
```

Figure 2.12 – Presentation Mode

As shown in *Figure 2.12*, we can see that the font size has increased, and the UI is very minimal. This mode is extremely helpful when doing presentations. To exit this mode, go to **View** and then tap **Exit Presentation Mode**.

At the bottom, we have some more useful tools as shown:

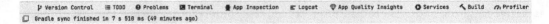

Figure 2.13 – Android Studio bottom tabs

From *Figure 2.13*, let us learn what the tabs do:

- **TODO**: Shows all our to-do items. This is useful for keeping track of things you need to do.

- **Problems**: Shows all the problems in our project. This is useful for keeping track of errors and warnings in our project.

- **Terminal**: Allows us to run terminal commands. This is useful for running commands such as Git or **Android Debug Bridge** (**ADB**) commands.

- **App Inspection**: This allows us to inspect various elements in our app and is useful for debugging our app. It allows us to inspect our background jobs, database, and network requests. For the database, we can see the data in our database, and we can also run queries with the data. For network requests, we can see the network requests and their JSON responses. And for background jobs, we can see the jobs and their status. These are helpful for us to debug and check issues on our app.

- **Logcat**: This shows all our log messages. It is especially useful for debugging errors as they arise.

- **App Quality Insights**: This allows us to view our app quality insights. This enables us to view crashes detected by Firebase Crashlytics inside our Android Studio. We can also see the crash stack trace and the line of code that has the issue, and we can easily navigate to that line from here.

- **Build**: Shows the build output. This is useful for debugging build errors.

- **Profiler**: Allows us to profile our app. For the profiler to work, we must have an instance of our app running. The profiler is useful for debugging performance issues. This provides metrics on how our app is using the CPU, memory, and energy. We can use these metrics to optimize our app.

These tabs can vary in position and at times some might not be shown. You can also easily add or remove them from the sidebar.

Let us now look at some useful shortcuts inside Android Studio.

Some useful shortcuts

Shortcuts help us quickly achieve things inside Android Studio. When well mastered, they can help us boost our productivity. There are many shortcuts available, and you can also customize and create your own. Some of the most common ones include the following:

- *Alt + 7* on Windows or *Command + 7* on Mac: This opens the **Structure** tab. In this tab, you see the various methods and properties available to the class/object or file. For our `MainActivity.kt` file, we can see the following structure:

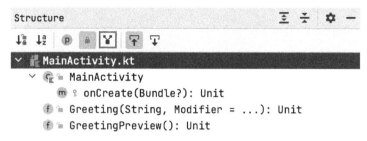

Figure 2.14 – Structure tab

From *Figure 2.14*, we can see that the **Structure** tab lists all the methods in our `MainActivity.kt` file. Clicking on a method from this tab quickly navigates us to the method in our code. There is also an icon, highlighted in red in *Figure 2.14*, that shows the inherited methods. When we click this, it shows all the inherited methods in the file as well.

- *Alt + Enter* on Windows or *Option + Enter* on Mac: This allows us to quickly add imports for packages, files, or dependencies in our project. It also offers more functionality, such as providing quick fixes for errors and allowing us to implement methods.

- Double-press *Shift*: This opens the general search window. Here we can search for classes, symbols, and files all over the project.

- *Ctrl + Shift + F* on Windows or *Command + Shift + F* on Mac: This is helpful for searching text in all files.

- *Ctrl + F6* on Windows or *Command + F6*: This allows us to refactor code. We have renaming, changing method signatures, moving code, and many more.

- *Ctrl + D* on Windows or *Command + D* on Mac: This is for duplicating a line of code or a selected section of code.

- *Ctrl + B* on Windows or *Command + B* on Mac: This allows us to jump to declarations.

We have only covered some of these shortcuts. There are many of them available. If you want to master most of these shortcuts, you can install the Key Promoter X plugin (`https://plugins.jetbrains.com/plugin/9792-key-promoter-x`). The plugins remind you of the shortcut whenever you perform an action that has a shortcut, and it also prompts you to create shortcuts when you repetitively do something that does not have a shortcut.

Summary

In this chapter, we created our first Android app. We familiarized ourselves with Android Studio, the IDE that we use to develop Android apps. We also learned about some tips, shortcuts, and useful Android Studio features and understood the process of creating a project in Android Studio.

In the next chapter, we will be covering Jetpack Compose layout basics. We'll start with an introduction to Jetpack Compose, a declarative way of declaring UIs for our apps.

3

Jetpack Compose Layout Basics

A good UI and user experience are core to our apps. As Android developers, we must be keenly aware of these two areas and learn how to use the different tools provided for us to create UIs. Google introduced **Jetpack Compose**, a modern UI toolkit to help developers create intuitive UIs with ease.

In this chapter, we'll look at Jetpack Compose, a declarative way of creating UIs for our apps. We will learn the basics of Jetpack Compose and layouts in Jetpack Compose.

In this chapter, we're going to cover the following main topics:

- Introduction to Jetpack Compose
- Jetpack Compose layouts

Technical requirements

To follow the instructions in this chapter, you will need to have Android Studio Hedgehog or later (`https://developer.android.com/studio`) downloaded.

You can find the code for this chapter at `https://github.com/PacktPublishing/Mastering-Kotlin-for-Android/tree/main/chapterthree`.

Introduction to Jetpack Compose

Over the years, Android UI development has undergone significant transformations with various frameworks and libraries emerging to simplify the process.

Before Jetpack Compose, this is how we used to write UIs for our apps:

- Views were inflated from XML layout files. XML-based views are still supported alongside Jetpack Compose for backward compatibility and mixed use cases where apps have both XML layouts and Jetpack Compose.

- Themes, styles, and value resources were also defined in XML files.

- For us to be able to access the views from XML files, we used view binding or data binding.

- This method of writing a UI required huge effort, requiring more boilerplate code and being error prone.

Google developed Jetpack Compose as a modern **declarative** UI toolkit. It allows us to create UIs with less code. Layouts created in Jetpack Compose are responsive to different screen sizes and orientations. It is also easier and more productive to write UIs in Compose. With Jetpack Compose, we can reuse components across our code bases. Jetpack Compose also allows us to use code from XML components in our composables.

Jetpack Compose is entirely in Kotlin, meaning it takes advantage of the powerful language features that Kotlin offers. The **view system**, which was used to create UIs before Compose, was more procedural. We had to manage complex life cycles and handle any changes in state manually. Jetpack Compose is a whole other paradigm that uses declarative programming. We describe what the UI should be like based on a state. This enables us to have dynamic content and less boilerplate code and develop our UIs faster.

To understand Jetpack Compose, let us first dive deep into the differences between the declarative and imperative approaches to writing UIs.

Declarative versus imperative UIs

In imperative UIs, we specify step by step the instructions describing how the UI should be built and updated. We explicitly define the sequence of operations to create and modify UI elements. We rely on mutable state variables to represent the current state of the UI. We manually update these state variables as the UI changes and respond to user interactions.

In declarative UIs, we focus on describing the desired outcome rather than specifying the step-by-step instructions. We define what the UI should look like based on the current state, and the framework handles the rest. We define the UI using declarative markup or code. We express the desired UI structure, layout, and behavior by describing the relationships between UI elements and their properties.

The declarative approach puts more emphasis on the immutable state, where the UI state is represented by immutable data objects. Instead of directly mutating the state, we create new instances of the data objects to reflect the desired changes in the UI.

In a declarative UI, the framework takes care of updating the UI based on changes in the application state. We specify the relationships between the UI and the underlying state, and the framework automatically updates the UI to reflect those changes.

Now that we understand both imperative and declarative approaches, let's look at an example of each. Let's create a simple UI for a counter using both the declarative UI in Jetpack Compose (Kotlin) and the imperative UI in XML (Android XML layout). The example will showcase the differences in syntax and the approach between the two. The Jetpack Compose version looks like this:

```kotlin
import android.os.Bundle
import androidx.activity.ComponentActivity
import androidx.activity.compose.setContent
import androidx.compose.foundation.layout.Column
import androidx.compose.foundation.layout.padding
import androidx.compose.material3.*
import androidx.compose.runtime.Composable
import androidx.compose.runtime.remember
import androidx.compose.ui.Modifier
import androidx.compose.ui.unit.dp

class MainActivity : ComponentActivity() {
  override fun onCreate(savedInstanceState: Bundle?) {
    super.onCreate(savedInstanceState)
    setContent {
        MyApp()
    }
  }
}


@Composable
fun MyApp() {
  var count by remember { mutableStateOf(0) }

  Column(
    modifier = Modifier.padding(16.dp)
  ) {
      Text(text = "Counter: $count", style = MaterialTheme.typography.
bodyLarge)
      Spacer(modifier = Modifier.height(16.dp))
      Button(onClick = { count++ }) {
        Text("Increment")
      }
    }
}
```

In the preceding example, we have a MyApp composable function that defines the UI for the app. The UI is defined in a declarative manner, by using composables to define the UI and handling state changes using the remember composable. The UI is defined using a functional approach. Also, we can see that the UI is defined in a more concise manner.

With the imperative approach, we must first create the XML UI, as shown in the following code block:

```xml
<?xml version="1.0" encoding="utf-8"?>
<RelativeLayout xmlns:android="http://schemas.android.com/apk/res/
android"
  xmlns:tools="http://schemas.android.com/tools"
  android:layout_width="match_parent"
  android:layout_height="match_parent"
  android:padding="16dp">

  <TextView
    android:id="@+id/counterTextView"
    android:layout_width="wrap_content"
    android:layout_height="wrap_content"
    android:layout_centerHorizontal="true"
    android:text="Counter: 0"
    android:textSize="20sp" />

  <Button
    android:id="@+id/incrementButton"
    android:layout_width="wrap_content"
    android:layout_height="wrap_content"
    android:layout_below="@id/counterTextView"
    android:layout_centerHorizontal="true"
    android:layout_marginTop="16dp"
    android:text="Increment" />
</RelativeLayout>
```

With the layout file created, we can now create the activity class, which will inflate the layout file and handle the button click:

```
import android.os.Bundle
import android.widget.Button
import android.widget.TextView
import androidx.appcompat.app.AppCompatActivity
```

```
class MainActivity : AppCompatActivity() {

  private var count = 0

  override fun onCreate(savedInstanceState: Bundle?) {
    super.onCreate(savedInstanceState)
    setContentView(R.layout.activity_main)

    val counterTextView: TextView = findViewById(R.id.counterTextView)
    val incrementButton: Button = findViewById(R.id.incrementButton)

    incrementButton.setOnClickListener {
      count++
      counterTextView.text = "Counter: $count"
    }
  }
}
```

In this example, the XML layout is inflated in the onCreate method of the MainActivity class, and UI elements are accessed and manipulated programmatically.

In the preceding examples, the Jetpack Compose code is written in Kotlin and provides a more declarative approach, defining the UI in a functional manner. The XML layout, on the other hand, is written imperatively in XML, specifying the UI structure and properties in a more step-by-step manner using XML and interacting with them imperatively in Kotlin code. Jetpack Compose allows for a more concise and expressive representation of the UI using a declarative syntax.

Now that we have a clear understanding of the imperative and declarative ways of writing UIs, in the next section, we will be diving deep into the building blocks of Jetpack Compose.

Composable functions

As shown in *Figure 3.1*, composable functions are the main building blocks of Jetpack Compose:

```
↥ Harun Wangereka
class MainActivity : ComponentActivity() {
    ↥ Harun Wangereka
    override fun onCreate(savedInstanceState: Bundle?) {
        super.onCreate(savedInstanceState)
        setContent {
            ChapterThreeTheme {
                // A surface container using the 'background' color from the theme
                Surface(
                    modifier = Modifier.fillMaxSize(),
                    color = MaterialTheme.colorScheme.background
                ) {
                    Greeting( name: "Android")
                }
            }
        }
    }
}

↥ Harun Wangereka
@Composable
fun Greeting(name: String, modifier: Modifier = Modifier) {
    Text(
        text = "Hello $name!",
        modifier = modifier
    )
}

↥ Harun Wangereka
@Preview(showBackground = true)
@Composable
fun GreetingPreview() {
    ChapterThreeTheme {
        Greeting( name: "Android")
    }
}
```

Figure 3.1 – Compose UI

A composable function describes how to render a UI. This function must be annotated with the @Composable function. When you annotate a function with this annotation, it means that the function describes how to compose a specific part of the UI. Composable functions are meant to be **reusable**. They can be called multiple times while the UI is active. Whenever the state of the composable changes, it goes through a process of recomposition, which enables the UI to display the latest state.

Composable functions are **pure functions**, meaning they don't have any side effects. They produce the same output when called several times with the same input. This ensures the functions are predictable and efficient in dispatching updates to the UI. However, there are exceptions, for example, launching a coroutine within a composable of calling external methods that do have side-effects, which should be avoided or handled carefully.

Smaller composable functions can be combined to build complex UIs. You can reuse and nest composables inside other composables.

Let's look at an example of a composable function:

```
@Composable
fun PacktPublishing(bookName: String) {
    Text(text = "Title of the book is: $bookName")
}
```

In the preceding code snippet, the `PacktPublishing` function is annotated with the `@Composable` annotation. The function takes a parameter, `bookName`, which is a `String`. Inside the function, we have another composable from the Material Design library. The composable renders some text to our UI.

When designing our UIs, we usually want to see how the UIs look without running our app. Luckily, we have **previews**, which visualize our composable functions. We will be learning about them in the next section.

Previews

In Jetpack Compose, we have the `@Preview` annotation, which generates a preview of our composable function or a group of Compose components inside Android Studio. It has an interactive mode to allow us to interact with our Compose functions. This gives us a way to quickly visualize our designs and easily make changes when needed.

This is how our `PacktPublishing` composable function would look like with a preview:

```
@Preview(showBackground = true)
@Composable
fun PacktPublishingPreview() {
    PacktPublishing("Android Development with Kotlin")
}
```

We have used the `@Preview` annotation to indicate that we want to build a preview for this function. Additionally, we have set the `showBackground` parameter to `true`, which adds a white background to our preview. We have named the function with the `Preview` suffix. The preview is also a composable function.

To be able to see the preview, you need to be in the **split or design mode** in your editor. These options are normally at the top right of Android Studio. We also need to do a build for Android Studio to generate a preview, which will look as follows:

PacktPublishingPreview

Title of the book is: Android Development with Kotlin

Figure 3.2 – Text preview

As seen in *Figure 3.2*, we have a text that displays the string that we passed to the function. The preview also has a white background and its name at the top left.

We can show previews for both dark and light color schemes. We can also configure properties such as the devices and preview windows to be applied.

Previews are great for quick iterations while designing UIs. However, they are not a replacement for actual device/emulator testing, particularly for things such as animations, interactions, or dynamic data.

With an understanding of what previews are and how to create them, let us look into one more Compose feature, **modifiers**, in the next section.

Modifiers

Modifiers allow us to decorate our composable functions by enabling the following:

- Change composables' size, behavior, and appearance
- Add more information
- Process user input
- Add interactions such as clicks and ripple effects

With modifiers, we can change various aspects of our composable, such as size, padding, color, and shape. Most Jetpack Compose components from the library allow us to provide a modifier as a parameter. For example, if we need to provide padding to our preview text, we will have the following:

```
Text(
    modifier = Modifier.padding(16.dp),
    text = "Title of the book is: $bookName"
)
```

We have added the padding modifier to the `Text` composable. This will add `16.dp` padding to the `Text` composable. `16.dp` is a **density-independent** pixel unit in Jetpack Compose. This means it will remain consistent and adjust properly to different screen densities.

We can chain the different modifier functions in one composable. When chaining modifiers, the order of application is crucial. If we don't achieve the desired result, we need to double-check the order. Let's observe this concept in practice:

```
Text(
    modifier = Modifier
        .fillMaxWidth()
        .padding(16.dp)
```

```
        .background(Color.Green),
    text = "Title of the book is: $bookName"
)
```

We have added two more modifiers. The first is the `fillMaxWidth` modifier, which is added to the text composable. This will make the text composable take the full width of the parent. The other one is the background modifier to the `Text` composable. This will add a background color to the text composable. The preview for our text will look as follows:

Figure 3.3 – Text modifier preview

As seen in the preceding screenshot, the text now occupies the whole width of the device and has a green background. It also has a padding of `16dp` all around.

Modifiers do not modify the original composable. They return a new, modified instance. This ensures our composable remains unchanged and immutable. Immutability, a fundamental principle in functional programming, ensures that the state remains unchanged, simplifying state management and reducing side effects. This approach enhances predictability and readability by adhering to the principles of referential transparency. The ability to compose functions, exemplified by chaining modifier functions, facilitates a concise and readable expression of complex UI behavior without altering the original composable. In addition to using the existing modifiers, we can also create our own modifiers when needed.

Now that you have an understanding of what modifiers are, we are going to build on that knowledge by learning about Jetpack Compose layouts in the next section.

Jetpack Compose layouts

Jetpack Compose has a variety of pre-built layouts for us to use. Before looking at the different layouts present, let us first understand how Jetpack Compose transforms state into UI.

Figure 3.4 – How Compose transforms state into UI

From the preceding diagram, we can see that our state is transformed into a UI in the following steps:

1. **Composition**

   This is the initial phase. The Compose compiler creates a tree of UI elements. Each element is a function that represents a UI element. Compose then calls the functions to create the UI tree. The composition step is responsible for determining which composables need updates and which ones can be reused. This happens by comparing a previous tree of composables with the new tree and only updating the ones that have changed. This makes this step very efficient as only elements with updates are updated.

2. **Layout**

   This step happens after the composition phase. Here, the Compose compiler takes the tree generated in the composition phase and determines its size, position, and layout. Each composable is measured and positioned within the layout based on its parent and any constraints set. This phase is responsible for determining the final position and size of each UI element on the screen. It is also responsible for creating the final layout tree used in the drawing phase.

3. **Drawing**

   This is the last phase of transforming our UI to state. In this phase, the Compose compiler takes the final layout tree created in the layout phase and uses it to draw the elements on the screen. This is done by walking through the tree and issuing draw commands to the underlying graphics system. This phase is responsible for rendering the final UI on the screen.

These three phases work together to create our UI in Jetpack Compose. The composition phase builds a tree of composables, the layout phase positions and sizes them, and the drawing phase renders them on the screen. This entire process is optimized, performant, and efficient, allowing for fast and smooth UI rendering in even complex UIs.

Now that we understand how the Compose compiler renders our UI, let us see the layouts that are in Compose.

Jetpack Compose offers the following layouts out of the box:

- `Column`
- `Row`
- `Box`
- Lists

We are going to look at each of these layouts in detail in the next subsections. To begin with, let us look the `Column` layout.

Column

We use `Column` when we want to organize items vertically. An example of the use of `Column` is as follows:

```
Column {
    Text(text = "Android")
    Text(text = "Kotlin")
    Text(text = "Compose")
}
```

In the preceding code, we have created `Column` with three text elements. Adding a preview for this generates the following UI for us:

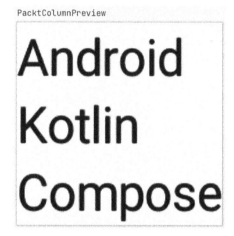

Figure 3.5 – Column preview

As seen from the preceding screenshot, the design is basic. We are going to polish it up a bit by using modifiers since Jetpack Compose also provides support for modifiers in these layouts. Let us add these changes to our column:

```
Column(
    modifier = Modifier
        .fillMaxSize()
        .padding(16.dp),
    verticalArrangement = Arrangement.Center,
    horizontalAlignment = Alignment.CenterHorizontally
) {
    Text(text = "Android")
    Text(text = "Kotlin")
    Text(text = "Compose")
}
```

Here, we have added a `Modifier` to our `Column`. In the modifier parameter, we specify the `fillMaxSize` modifier, which makes our column fill the available space within the parent. This is helpful for building full-view screens for our UIs. We have also added padding of `16.dp` to our column.

Additionally, we have specified two more parameters for our column. One is `verticalArrangement`, which we use to specify the vertical arrangement of the children of this view. In this case, we specify `Arrangement.Center`, which places all the children of our `Column` vertically at the center. The other parameter is `horizontalAlignment`, which is the horizontal alignment of the children of the layout. In this case, we specify the value to be `Alignment.CenterHorizontally`, which will align all the children at the center horizontally. Our preview with the preceding changes will look like this:

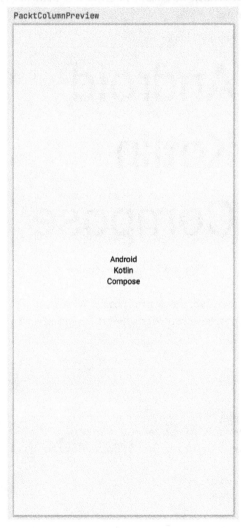

Figure 3.6 – Column modifiers preview

From the preceding screenshot, we can now see our column occupies the whole screen and all the text elements are centered vertically and horizontally within the parent.

Let us now learn about the Row composable in the next section.

Row

We use Row when we want to organize items horizontally. An example of the use of Row is as follows:

```
Row {
    Text(text = "Android")
    Text(text = "Kotlin")
    Text(text = "Compose")
}
```

In the preceding code, the Row composable is used to display three text elements horizontally in a row. The preview for this will look like this:

PacktRowPreview

AndroidKotlinCompose

Figure 3.7 – Row preview

The text elements are all arranged next to each other in a horizontal row. Row, like the composable, supports the addition of modifiers. Let us modify our Row to look as follows:

```
Row(
    modifier = Modifier
        .fillMaxSize()
        .padding(16.dp),
    verticalAlignment = Alignment.CenterVertically,
    horizontalArrangement = Arrangement.SpaceEvenly
) {
    Text(text = "Android")
    Text(text = "Kotlin")
    Text(text = "Compose")
}
```

In the preceding code, we have added modifiers to the Row composable. The `fillMaxSize` modifier makes the row fill the entire available space. The padding modifier adds padding to the Row. The `verticalAlignment` and `horizontalArrangement` modifiers are used to align the children of the Row vertically and horizontally, respectively. Notice that for the `horizontalArrangement` modifier, we use the `Arrangement.SpaceEvenly` option. This makes sure each of the children occupies equal space in the parent. The preview for this looks as follows:

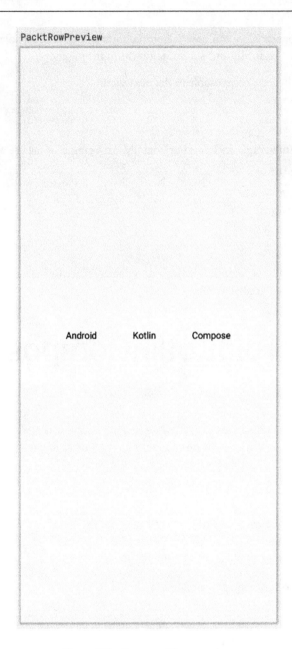

Figure 3.8 – Row modifiers preview

As seen in *Figure 3.8*, the row occupies the whole screen, and the text elements are evenly spaced within the screen width.

In the next section, we will be learning about the Box layout.

Box

The Box layout allows us to position child elements in a flexible way using the X and Y coordinates. Let us see a code example:

```
Box(
    modifier = Modifier
        .size(100.dp),
    contentAlignment = Alignment.Center
) {
    Icon(
        modifier = Modifier
            .size(80.dp),
        imageVector = Icons.Outlined.Notifications,
        contentDescription = null,
        tint = Color.Green
    )
    Text(text = "9")
}
```

In the preceding code, we have a Box composable that has an Icon and Text composable as its children. We have set the size of the Box composable to 100.dp and the Icon composable to 80.dp. The text and icon composables are placed in the center of the Box composable using the contentAlignment parameter. They are placed in the center of the Box composable because we have specified the contentAlignment parameter as Alignment.Center. They are also stacked on top of each other because the Box composable is a layout composable that stacks its children on top of each other. The preview for our Box composable looks as follows:

PacktBoxPreview

Figure 3.9 – Box preview

As we can see from *Figure 3.9*, the notification icon and the text are stacked together. The Box composable enables us to achieve this and much more.

Now let us look at how to display lists in Jetpack Compose in the next section.

Lists

As Android developers, we need to make apps that display lists of items. It can be a list of movies, orders, songs, or books. So, how do we do that in Compose? The good news for us is that Jetpack Compose makes it easier for us to do so. Compose provides the LazyColumn and LazyRow components, which can be used to display a list of items. These components are very efficient and performant. They only render the items that are visible on the screen, rather than rendering all the items at once. LazyColumn displays items vertically, while LazyRow displays items horizontally. LazyColumn and LazyRow are normally optimized for large datasets and at times are not suitable for all use cases. These composable functions allow you to define the contents of the list as a function that returns a single item, and then Compose will automatically generate and render the UI elements for each item in the list as they become visible on the screen.

Let's see an example of LazyColumn:

```
LazyColumn(
    modifier = Modifier
        .fillMaxSize()
        .background(Color.LightGray)
) {
    items(100) {
        Text(
            modifier = Modifier
                .padding(8.dp),
            text = "Item number $it"
        )
    }
}
```

We have LazyColumn with 100 items. Each item is a Text composable. The preview for this looks as follows:

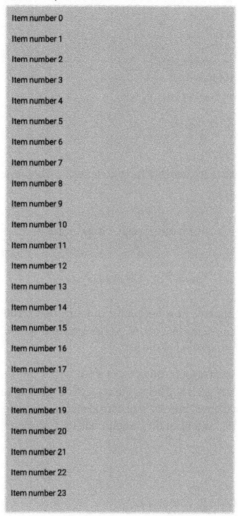

Figure 3.10 – LazyColumn preview

We can see from *Figure 3.10* that we now have a list of items that scroll vertically. As mentioned, it only shows the items that can fit on the screen. If we use interactive mode on our preview, we will be able to scroll through to the bottom of the list.

Let us see the `LazyRow` equivalent as well:

```
LazyRow(
    modifier = Modifier
        .fillMaxWidth()
        .background(Color.LightGray)
```

```
        .padding(8.dp)
) {
    items(100) {
        Text(
            modifier = Modifier
                .padding(8.dp),
            text = "Item number $it"
        )
    }
}
```

We have `LazyRow` with 100 items. Each item is a `Text` composable. The preview for this looks as follows:

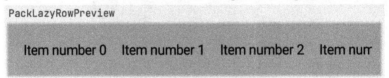

Figure 3.11 – LazyRow preview

We can see from *Figure 3.11* that we now have a list of items that scroll horizontally. Similar to `LazyColumn`, it only shows the items that can fit on the screen. If we use interactive mode on our preview, we can scroll through to the end of the list.

We also have two more types of list layouts, `LazyVerticalGrid` and `LazyHorizontalGrid`. The two layouts are part of the lazy grids and help us to arrange our content in grids. They're commonly used in applications such as galleries, movies, and spreadsheets. `LazyVerticalGrid` creates a vertical list of items in a grid. Let us look at the sample code for `LazyVerticalGrid`:

```
LazyVerticalGrid(
    modifier = Modifier
        .fillMaxSize()
        .background(Color.LightGray)
        .padding(8.dp),
    columns = GridCells.Fixed(3)
) {
    items(100) {
        Text(
            modifier = Modifier
                .padding(8.dp),
            text = "Item number $it"
        )
    }
}
```

We have used the `LazyVerticalGrid` composable. We pass our modifiers as before. Notice we also have the `columns` parameter. This parameter allows us to specify the number of columns and how items are arranged within the columns. In this case, we specified `GridCells` to be `Fixed`. This means the grid will have a fixed number of columns or rows in it is a `LazyHorizontalGrid`. We also have the `Adaptive` type, which defines a grid with as many rows or columns as possible with the condition that every cell has a minimum size and all extra space is distributed evenly. Our preview will look as follows:

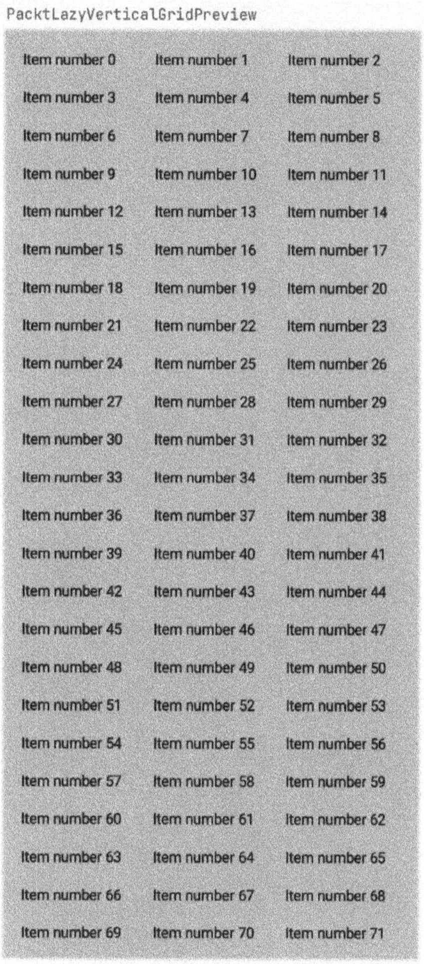

Figure 3.12 – LazyVerticalGrid preview

We have our text elements in a grid of three columns. We are now able to scroll through the items vertically. Let us now look at the code for `LazyHorizontalGrid`:

```
LazyHorizontalGrid(
    modifier = Modifier
```

```
        .fillMaxSize()
        .background(Color.LightGray)
        .padding(8.dp),
    rows = GridCells.Fixed(3)
) {
    items(100) {
        Text(
            modifier = Modifier
                .padding(8.dp),
            text = "Item number $it"
        )
    }
}
```

The code is similar to that for `LazyVerticalGrid`. The only difference is that we are using `LazyHorizontalGrid` and instead of columns, we are now passing `rows` to describe how the cells will form the rows. The preview will look like this:

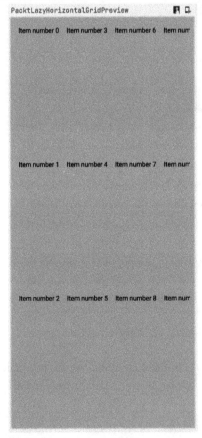

Figure 3.13 – LazyHorizontalGrid preview

As seen in *Figure 3.13*, we now have three rows on the entire screen, and we can also scroll through them horizontally.

In addition to `LazyVerticalGrid` and `LazyHorizontalGrid`, we also have `LazyVerticalStaggeredGrid` and `LazyHorizontalStaggeredGrid`, which are remarkably similar; the only difference is that they adapt to the children's height and width, respectively, meaning they all do not have uniform height or width.

Let us now have a look at `ConstraintLayout` in the next section.

ConstraintLayout

This layout enables us to create responsive layouts. We can create complex layouts with relative positioning. `ConstraintLayout` uses chains, barriers, and guidelines to position child elements relative to each other.

It comes as a separate dependency, and we need to add it to our project. To add it, let us add this dependency to our app `build.gradle` file:

```
implementation 'androidx.constraintlayout:constraintlayout-
compose:1.0.1'
```

This adds the Jetpack Compose dependency to our project. The layout code for the constraint layout is as follows:

```
ConstraintLayout(
  modifier = Modifier
    .padding(16.dp)
) {
    val (icon, text) = createRefs()
      Icon(
          modifier = Modifier
            .size(80.dp)
            .constrainAs(icon) {
                top.linkTo(parent.top)
                bottom.linkTo(parent.bottom)
                start.linkTo(parent.start)
            },
          imageVector = Icons.Outlined.Notifications,
          contentDescription = null,
          tint = Color.Green
      )
    Text(
        modifier = Modifier
          .constrainAs(text) {
              top.linkTo(parent.top)
```

```
                bottom.linkTo(parent.bottom)
                start.linkTo(icon.end) },
        text = "9",
        style = MaterialTheme.typography.titleLarge
    )
}
```

In the preceding code, we used the `ConstraintLayout` composable function to create `ConstraintLayout`. Inside `ConstraintLayout`, we used the `createRefs()` function to create two references, one for the icon and one for the text. We then used the `constrainAs()` function to constrain the icon and the text to the parent. We used the `linkTo()` function to link the icon and the text to the parent. In this case, we have linked the icon to the start, top, and bottom of the parent. For the text, we have linked it to the top and bottom of the parent. We have additionally linked the start of the text to the end of the icon. Our preview will look as follows:

Figure 3.14 – ConstraintLayout preview

From the preceding screenshot, we can see that we have an icon and text to the right of the icon. `ConstraintLayout` helps in positioning items relative to the parent or each other.

Summary

In this chapter, we have introduced ourselves to Jetpack Compose, a declarative way of creating UIs for apps. We have also learned about the different layouts that are in Compose and how the Jetpack Compose compiler renders state into a UI.

In the next chapter, we will be building on top of what we have learned and look at how to design beautiful and intuitive apps with **Material Design 3**. We're going to learn about Material Design 3, its features, and how to add dynamic color to our app.

4

Design with Material Design 3

Material Design is a design system developed by Google. It helps us create beautiful UIs. It provides a set of guidelines and components for us to use as we're developing our Android apps.

In this chapter, we'll introduce ourselves to **Material 3**. We will also cover the features that Material 3 offers. Lastly, we will learn how to use Material 3 in our Android apps and some of the components in Material 3.

In this chapter, we're going to cover the following main topics:

- Material Design 3 and its features
- Using Material Design 3 in our apps
- Building for large screens and foldables
- Making our app accessible

Technical requirements

To follow the instructions in this chapter, you will need to have Android Studio Hedgehog or later (`https://developer.android.com/studio`) downloaded.

You can find the code for this chapter at `https://github.com/PacktPublishing/Mastering-Kotlin-for-Android/tree/main/chapterfour`.

Material Design 3 and its features

The release of **Material Design 3** (**Material 3**) came with lots of new features to help us build UIs for our apps. Here are some of the features of Material Design 3:

- **Dynamic color**: This is a color system that sets the color of our apps to the color of the user's wallpaper. The System UI also adapts to this color. This enables users to have that personalized feel for their apps. Please note that dynamic color only works for Android 12 and above devices.

- **More components**: Material 3 has a new set of improved components that are available for use. Some components have new UIs and others have been added to the APIs.

- **Simplified typography**: Material 3 has a much more simplified naming and grouping for typography. We have the following types: **display**, **headline**, **title**, **body**, and **label**, with each supporting *small*, *medium*, and *large* sizes. This makes it easier for us to define styles all across our apps.

- **Improved color scheme**: The color scheme has undergone a lot of improvements with the addition of more color schemes to fine-grain color customization. It's also way easier for us to support both dark and light color schemes in our apps. In addition to that, they created a new tool, Material Theme Builder (`https://m3.material.io/theme-builder`), which allows us to generate and export dark and light theme colors for our apps.

- **Simplified shapes**: Similar to typography, shapes have also been simplified to the following: **Extra Small**, **Small**, **Medium**, **Large**, and **Extra Large**. All these shapes come with default values, which we can always override to use our own.

The good news for us is that from Android Studio Hedgehog onward, we have project templates that come set up with Material 3, which makes things easier for us. Even the project we created in *Chapter 2* comes with Material 3 set up already.

Material 3 APIs and their predecessors offer a wide range of components for us to use in our apps. In the next subsection, we will be looking at some of the common ones.

Material components

The Material library comes with prebuilt components that we can use to build common UI components. Let us look at some of the commonly used components and some of the updates they had in Material 3.

Top app bars

This is a component displayed at the top of the screen. It has a title and can also have some actions that are related to the screen the user is on. Some of the common actions are the settings icon normally at the top right of the screen. In Material 3, we have four types of top app bars: **center-aligned**, **small**, **medium**, and **large**, as shown in the following figures.

Packt Publishing

Figure 4.1 – Small top app bar

Figure 4.2 – Center-aligned top app bar

Figure 4.3 – Medium top app bar

Figure 4.4 – Large top app bar

As seen in *Figures 4.1* to *4.4*, all the top bars have the same width and only differ in height and positioning of the title text.

Let us look at the sample code for one of these top app bars:

```
@OptIn(ExperimentalMaterial3Api::class)
@Composable
fun PacktCenterAlignedTopBar() {
    CenterAlignedTopAppBar(
        title = {
            Text(text = "Packt Publishing")
        }
    )
}
```

Here, we have our custom composable and, inside it, we are using the `CenterAlignedTopBar` composable from Material 3 and passing in `Text` to the `title` composable. The other three (`LargeTopAppBar`, `MediumTopAppBar`, and `TopAppBar`) are similar; the only difference is the composable that you will use. Notice that we have the `@OptIn` annotation as these components are still experimental.

Next, let us look at the `FloatingActionButton` component.

FloatingActionButton

Most apps use the component to represent a call to action that is frequently used in the app. For example, create a new chat in a chat app. It is normally positioned at the bottom right of the screen or elsewhere, depending on your use case. This is how we create the component:

```
FloatingActionButton(
    onClick = { /*TODO*/ },
    content = {
        Icon(
            imageVector = Icons.Default.Add ,
            contentDescription = "New Chat"
        )
    }
)
```

We use the `FloatingActionButton` component from the Material 3 library. We have the `onclick` argument on the composable and, inside the `content` lambda, we pass in an `Icon` composable that has an *add* icon. The preview should be the following:

Figure 4.5 – FloatingActionButton

The `FloatingActionButton` component has these sizes: large, normal, and small, and you can use whichever fits your purpose.

We have another type of `FloatingActionButton` component known as `ExtendedFloatingActionButton`, which looks like this:

Figure 4.6 – ExtendedFloatingActionButton

As seen in the preceding figure, an `ExtendedFloatingActionButton` component allows us to add more items to our FAB. They are wider than the normal `FloatActionButton` components. In this case, we have a `Text` composable with the text **New Chat** in addition to the icon. You can use it with or without the icon. The implementation for this is as follows:

```
ExtendedFloatingActionButton(
    onClick = { /*TODO*/ },
    content = {
        Icon(
            imageVector = Icons.Default.Add ,
            contentDescription = "New Chat"
        )
        Text(
            modifier = Modifier.padding(10.dp),
            text = "New Chat"
        )
    }
)
```

Here, we used the `ExtendedFloatingActionButton` component and still passed in the same parameters as before. The only difference is that inside the content, we pass in a text since the `content` lambda exposes `RowScope`, which means children composables will be arranged in a row.

Next, let us look at the bottom app bar components.

Bottom app bars

The bottom app bar components display navigation items at the bottom of the screen. They are normally useful for apps that have three to five primary destinations.

Let us look at the code for a bottom app bar:

```
BottomAppBar(
    actions = {
        Icon(imageVector = Icons.Rounded.Home, contentDescription =
"Home Screen")
        Icon(imageVector = Icons.Rounded.ShoppingCart,
contentDescription = "Cart Screen")
        Icon(imageVector = Icons.Rounded.AccountCircle,
contentDescription = "Account Screen")
    }
)
```

We use the `BottomAppBar` component and, inside the `actions` lambda, we pass in three `Icon` composables to represent the items we are supposed to show. This is how the preview of the composable will look:

Figure 4.7 – BottomAppBar

In *Figure 4,7*, we can see we have three icons arranged horizontally.

Additionally, in BottomAppBar, we can also provision a FloatingActionButton component. We are going to use the FloatingActionButton component that we used early on. The updated component code is as follows:

```
BottomAppBar(
    actions = {
        Icon(imageVector = Icons.Rounded.Home, contentDescription =
"Home Screen")
        Icon(imageVector = Icons.Rounded.ShoppingCart,
contentDescription = "Cart Screen")
        Icon(imageVector = Icons.Rounded.AccountCircle,
contentDescription = "Account Screen")
    },
    floatingActionButton = {
        PacktFloatingActionButton()
    }
)
```

In the preceding code, we have used the floatingActionButton parameter and passed in PacktFloatingActionButton() that we created earlier. The updated preview will be as follows:

Figure 4.8 – BottomAppBar with FloatingActionButton

As seen in the preceding figure, our BottomAppBar now has a nice FloatingActionButton to its right. The FAB is automatically positioned for you to the right.

We have looked at the different components in isolation, but what happens when we want to place them on one screen together? Next, we are going to look at Scaffold, which is meant for this.

Scaffold

This is a layout provided by Material Design that helps place all components on your screen in their desired positions with ease.

Let us look at a sample of `Scaffold` that has a top app bar, a floating action button, text center-aligned on the screen, and a bottom navigation bar:

```
Scaffold(
    topBar = {
        PacktSmallTopAppBar()
    },
    bottomBar = {
        PacktBottomNavigationBar()
    },
    floatingActionButton = {
        PacktFloatingActionButton()
    },
    content = { paddingValues ->
      Column(
          modifier = Modifier
              .fillMaxSize()
              .padding(paddingValues)
              .background(Color.Gray.copy(alpha = 0.1f)),
          verticalArrangement = Arrangement.Center,
          horizontalAlignment = Alignment.CenterHorizontally
      ) {
          Text(
              modifier = Modifier.padding(10.dp),
              text = "Mastering Kotlin for Android Development -
Chapter 4",
              textAlign = TextAlign.Center
          )
        }
      }
)
```

A lot is happening here, so let us break it down:

- The `Scaffold` composable is used to create a layout that implements the Material Design guidelines. It is a container that contains the top bar, bottom bar, floating action button, and the content.

- The `topBar` parameter is used to specify the top bar. In this case, we are using the `PacktSmallTopAppBar` composable that we created earlier.

- The `bottomBar` parameter is used to specify the bottom bar. In this case, we are using the `PacktBottomNavigationBar` composable.

- The `floatingActionButton` parameter is used to specify the floating action button. In this case, we are using the `PacktFloatingActionButton` composable.

- The `content` parameter is used to specify the content of the screen. In this case, we are using a `Column` composable that contains a `Text` composable. The text is centered in the column using the `verticalArrangement` and `horizontalAlignment` parameters. Notice that inside `Column`, we are using the `paddingValues` parameter to add padding to the column. This is because the `Scaffold` composable passes the `padding` values to the `content` parameter.

With our `Scaffold` composable ready, let us see how its preview looks:

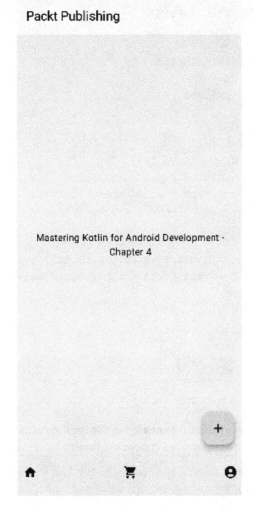

Figure 4.9 – Scaffold

In *Figure 4.9*, we can see that the `Scaffold` composable has added the top bar, bottom bar, and the floating action button to the screen. The components are also placed in the correct positions as per the Material Design guidelines.

We have learned about a bunch of components so far; Material 3 still offers more components out of the box for us. We will be using some of these components in the upcoming chapters of this book. To view the full list of all the components, go to the Material 3 Components website (`https://m3.material.io/components`) to see them and their guidelines.

Now that we understand Material 3 and its features, let us look at how to add it to our apps.

Using Material Design in our apps

To take advantage of the Material 3 features that we looked at in the previous section, we need to add it to our app. Luckily, with Android Studio Hedgehog, we have Material 3 templates. Even the sample apps we have been using already use Material 3. So cool, right? Let us quickly scan the dependencies to understand what is happening:

```
implementation 'androidx.core:core-ktx:1.10.1'
implementation platform('org.jetbrains.kotlin:kotlin-bom:1.8.0')
implementation 'androidx.lifecycle:lifecycle-runtime-ktx:2.6.1'
implementation 'androidx.activity:activity-compose:1.7.2'
implementation platform('androidx.compose:compose-bom:2022.10.00')
implementation 'androidx.compose.ui:ui'
implementation 'androidx.compose.ui:ui-graphics'
implementation 'androidx.compose.ui:ui-tooling-preview'
implementation 'androidx.compose.material3:material3'
testImplementation 'junit:junit:4.13.2'
androidTestImplementation 'androidx.test.ext:junit:1.1.5'
androidTestImplementation 'androidx.test.espresso:espresso-core:3.5.1'
androidTestImplementation platform('androidx.compose:compose-bom:2022.10.00')
androidTestImplementation 'androidx.compose.ui:ui-test-junit4'
debugImplementation 'androidx.compose.ui:ui-tooling'
debugImplementation 'androidx.compose.ui:ui-test-manifest'
```

This dependencies block sets up several for us, including the `compose` dependencies. The most important one is the `androidx.compose.material3:material3` dependency. This is the dependency that contains the Material 3 components. We are using the Compose **Bill of Materials (BOM)** to manage our dependencies. This means that we do not have to specify the version of each dependency. Instead, we specify the version of the BOM, and it will manage the versions of the dependencies for us. This is the recommended way of managing dependencies in Compose. That is why we have not specified the version of each dependency.

With that, our project is ready to take advantage of the Material 3 features. In the next subsection, we will be adding more color schemes to the app.

Adding Material Design 3 color schemes

As mentioned earlier, Material 3 comes with a lot of fine-grained color schemes and introduces **dynamic color**. However, they are not set up with the templates that Android Studio generates. We will be setting them up in the next few steps.

Head over to the `ui/theme` package and open the `Color.kt` file, which has the following code:

```
val Purple80 = Color(0xFFD0BCFF)
val PurpleGrey80 = Color(0xFFCCC2DC)
val Pink80 = Color(0xFFEFB8C8)

val Purple40 = Color(0xFF6650a4)
val PurpleGrey40 = Color(0xFF625b71)
val Pink40 = Color(0xFF7D5260)
```

So far, this file only has a few colors defined. These colors do not cover all the color tokens provided by Material 3. We will add more colors as we need them in the app.

We will be using the **Material Theme Builder** tool to generate these colors. Let us open our browser and go to the Material Theme Builder tool (`https://m3.material.io/theme-builder`). We will be presented with the following screen:

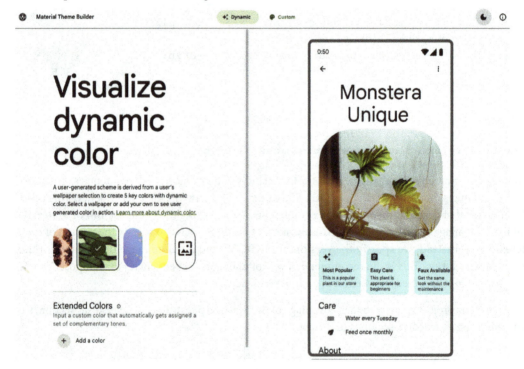

Figure 4.10 – Material Theme Builder tool

This tool helps us visualize the color schemes for our apps and shows how different components will be themed. It makes it easier for us to customize and produce a consistent color scheme for our app. It has two tabs: **Dynamic** and **Custom**. In the **Dynamic** tab, we can select one of the preloaded colors or wallpapers to see how the color changes. One useful feature is that we can also add your own wallpaper and generate the colors based on the wallpaper.

In the **Custom** tab, we can select a color and the tool generates all the complementary colors for us based on the color we select, ensuring a harmonious color palette:

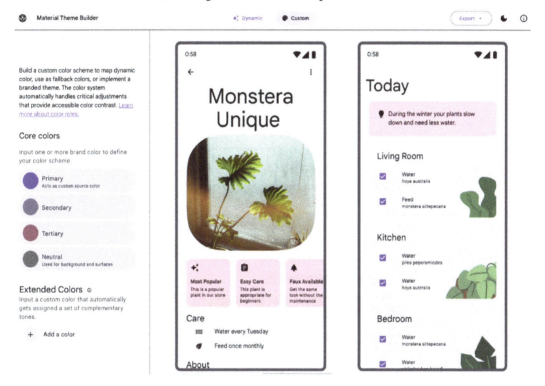

Figure 4.11 – Material Theme Builder tool custom color

On the left, we have the **Core colors** section where we can select either **Primary**, **Secondary**, **Tertiary**, or **Neutral** colors for our app.

We are going to select the **Primary** color option, which opens a **Color Picker** dialog:

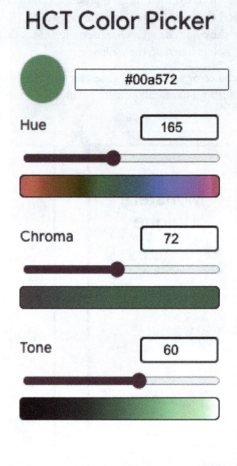

Figure 4.12 – Color Picker

As we are changing the primary color, we will be able to see the visual preview change to match the color we have. Now we have our primary color ready, we are going to export the files so that we can use them in our project:

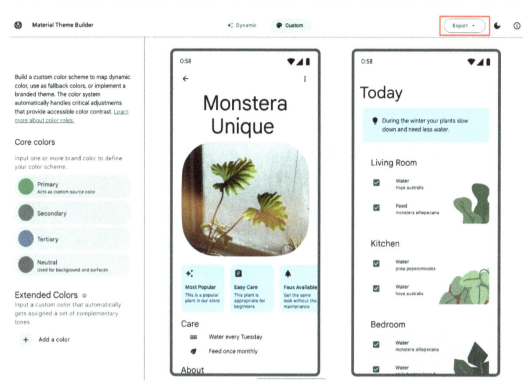

Figure 4.13 – Export option

As seen in *Figure 4.13*, the visual preview has changed to the color we chose. Click on the **Export** option (highlighted in *Figure 4.13*) and, from the dropdown that appears, choose **Jetpack Compose (Theme.kt)**. This will prompt a download of a zipped file. Unzip the file and open the folder. We will now have a `ui` folder that has a `theme` folder inside containing `Color.kt` and `Theme.kt` files.

Let us open the `Color.kt` file, which contains the following code:

```
val md_theme_light_primary = Color(0xFF006C49)
val md_theme_light_onPrimary = Color(0xFFFFFFFF)
val md_theme_light_primaryContainer = Color(0xFF7AFAC0)
val md_theme_light_onPrimaryContainer = Color(0xFF002113)
val md_theme_light_secondary = Color(0xFF4D6357)
val md_theme_light_onSecondary = Color(0xFFFFFFFF)
val md_theme_light_secondaryContainer = Color(0xFFD0E8D8)
val md_theme_light_onSecondaryContainer = Color(0xFF0A1F16)
val md_theme_light_tertiary = Color(0xFF3D6473)
val md_theme_light_onTertiary = Color(0xFFFFFFFF)
val md_theme_light_tertiaryContainer = Color(0xFFC0E9FB)
val md_theme_light_onTertiaryContainer = Color(0xFF001F29)
```

```
val md_theme_light_error = Color(0xFFBA1A1A)
val md_theme_light_errorContainer = Color(0xFFFFDAD6)
val md_theme_light_onError = Color(0xFFFFFFFF)
val md_theme_light_onErrorContainer = Color(0xFF410002)
val md_theme_light_background = Color(0xFFFBFDF9)
val md_theme_light_onBackground = Color(0xFF191C1A)
val md_theme_light_surface = Color(0xFFFBFDF9)
val md_theme_light_onSurface = Color(0xFF191C1A)
val md_theme_light_surfaceVariant = Color(0xFFDCE5DD)
val md_theme_light_onSurfaceVariant = Color(0xFF404943)
val md_theme_light_outline = Color(0xFF707973)
val md_theme_light_inverseOnSurface = Color(0xFFEFF1ED)
val md_theme_light_inverseSurface = Color(0xFF2E312F)
val md_theme_light_inversePrimary = Color(0xFF5CDDA5)
val md_theme_light_shadow = Color(0xFF000000)
val md_theme_light_surfaceTint = Color(0xFF006C49)
val md_theme_light_outlineVariant = Color(0xFFC0C9C1)
val md_theme_light_scrim = Color(0xFF000000)

val md_theme_dark_primary = Color(0xFF5CDDA5)
val md_theme_dark_onPrimary = Color(0xFF003824)
val md_theme_dark_primaryContainer = Color(0xFF005236)
val md_theme_dark_onPrimaryContainer = Color(0xFF7AFAC0)
val md_theme_dark_secondary = Color(0xFFB4CCBD)
val md_theme_dark_onSecondary = Color(0xFF20352A)
val md_theme_dark_secondaryContainer = Color(0xFF364B40)
val md_theme_dark_onSecondaryContainer = Color(0xFFD0E8D8)
val md_theme_dark_tertiary = Color(0xFFA5CDDE)
val md_theme_dark_onTertiary = Color(0xFF063543)
val md_theme_dark_tertiaryContainer = Color(0xFF244C5A)
val md_theme_dark_onTertiaryContainer = Color(0xFFC0E9FB)
val md_theme_dark_error = Color(0xFFFFB4AB)
val md_theme_dark_errorContainer = Color(0xFF93000A)
val md_theme_dark_onError = Color(0xFF690005)
val md_theme_dark_onErrorContainer = Color(0xFFFFDAD6)
val md_theme_dark_background = Color(0xFF191C1A)
val md_theme_dark_onBackground = Color(0xFFE1E3DF)
val md_theme_dark_surface = Color(0xFF191C1A)
val md_theme_dark_onSurface = Color(0xFFE1E3DF)
val md_theme_dark_surfaceVariant = Color(0xFF404943)
val md_theme_dark_onSurfaceVariant = Color(0xFFC0C9C1)
val md_theme_dark_outline = Color(0xFF8A938C)
val md_theme_dark_inverseOnSurface = Color(0xFF191C1A)
```

```
val md_theme_dark_inverseSurface = Color(0xFFE1E3DF)
val md_theme_dark_inversePrimary = Color(0xFF006C49)
val md_theme_dark_shadow = Color(0xFF000000)
val md_theme_dark_surfaceTint = Color(0xFF5CDDA5)
val md_theme_dark_outlineVariant = Color(0xFF404943)
val md_theme_dark_scrim = Color(0xFF000000)
```

As you can now see, we have more color additions. Let us copy these colors to the Color.kt file in our project. Next, let us open the Theme.kt from the unzipped folder.

We will notice it is similar to the Theme.kt file but it defines all the Material 3 color schemes. Copy the contents of this file and paste them into the Theme.kt file in our project. We are going to make minor edits to the code to make sure we maintain the ChapterFourTheme name and dynamic color logic that was in our theme. Next, we need to change the DarkColorScheme variable values to the following:

```
private val DarkColorScheme = darkColorScheme(
    primary = md_theme_light_primary,
    onPrimary = md_theme_light_onPrimary,
    primaryContainer = md_theme_light_primaryContainer,
    onPrimaryContainer = md_theme_light_onPrimaryContainer,
    secondary = md_theme_light_secondary,
    onSecondary = md_theme_light_onSecondary,
    secondaryContainer = md_theme_light_secondaryContainer,
    onSecondaryContainer = md_theme_light_onSecondaryContainer,
    tertiary = md_theme_light_tertiary,
    onTertiary = md_theme_light_onTertiary,
    tertiaryContainer = md_theme_light_tertiaryContainer,
    onTertiaryContainer = md_theme_light_onTertiaryContainer,
    error = md_theme_light_error,
    errorContainer = md_theme_light_errorContainer,
    onError = md_theme_light_onError,
    onErrorContainer = md_theme_light_onErrorContainer,
    background = md_theme_light_background,
    onBackground = md_theme_light_onBackground,
    surface = md_theme_light_surface,
    onSurface = md_theme_light_onSurface,
    surfaceVariant = md_theme_light_surfaceVariant,
    onSurfaceVariant = md_theme_light_onSurfaceVariant,
    outline = md_theme_light_outline,
    inverseOnSurface = md_theme_light_inverseOnSurface,
    inverseSurface = md_theme_light_inverseSurface,
    inversePrimary = md_theme_light_inversePrimary,
```

```
    surfaceTint = md_theme_light_surfaceTint,
    outlineVariant = md_theme_light_outlineVariant,
    scrim = md_theme_light_scrim,
)
```

In the preceding code, we are using the DarkColorScheme function to create a dark color scheme. We are passing the colors that we generated using the Material Theme Builder tool. We will use this color scheme to create a dark theme. The dark color scheme variable is defined in a similar manner, and we can copy the values from the Theme.kt file from the tool and add it there too. Let us now look at our theme composable in wholesome:

```
@Composable
fun ChapterFourTheme(
    darkTheme: Boolean = isSystemInDarkTheme(),
    dynamicColor: Boolean = true,
    content: @Composable () -> Unit
) {
    val colorScheme = when {
        dynamicColor && Build.VERSION.SDK_INT >= Build.VERSION_CODES.S
-> {
            val context = LocalContext.current
            if (darkTheme) dynamicDarkColorScheme(context) else
dynamicLightColorScheme(context)
        }

        darkTheme -> DarkColorScheme
        else -> LightColorScheme
    }
    val view = LocalView.current
    if (!view.isInEditMode) {
        SideEffect {
            val window = (view.context as Activity).window
            window.statusBarColor = colorScheme.primary.toArgb()
            WindowCompat.getInsetsController(window, view).
isAppearanceLightStatusBars = darkTheme
        }
    }

    MaterialTheme(
        colorScheme = colorScheme,
        typography = Typography,
        content = content
    )
}
```

Let us break down the preceding code:

- The `ChapterFourTheme` composable is used to create a theme for our app. It takes three parameters:

  - The `darkTheme` parameter is used to specify whether the theme is dark or light. By default, we are using the system theme.

  - The `dynamicColor` parameter is used to specify whether the theme should use dynamic colors. By default, we are using dynamic colors.

  - The `content` parameter is used to specify the content of the theme. In this case, we are using the `MaterialTheme` composable to create a theme for our app.

- The `colorScheme` variable is used to specify the color scheme to use. We are using a `when` expression to determine the color scheme to use. If the `dynamicColor` parameter is `true` and the device is running Android 12 or higher, we are using the `dynamicDarkColorScheme` or `dynamicLightColorScheme` function to create a dynamic color scheme. When not using dynamic colors, we fall back to the normal themes. If the `darkTheme` parameter is `true`, we are using the `DarkColorScheme` variable to create a dark color scheme. Otherwise, we are using the `LightColorScheme` variable to create a light color scheme.

- The `view` variable is used to get the view that is using the theme.

- The `SideEffect` composable is used to execute a side effect. In this case, we are using it to set the status bar color and the status bar icons' color. We are using the `WindowCompat` class to get `InsetsController` and set the status bar color and the status bar icons' color. We are using the `colorScheme.primary` color to set the status bar color. We are using the `darkTheme` parameter to determine whether the status bar icons' color should be light or dark.

- The `MaterialTheme` composable is used to create a theme for our app. We are using the `colorScheme` parameter to specify the color scheme to use. We are using the `typography` variable to specify the typography to use.

To be able to see the changes we have made, we need to call `PacktScaffold`, which we created earlier inside the `MainActivity.kt` file in the `ChapterFourTheme` block:

```
class MainActivity : ComponentActivity() {
    override fun onCreate(savedInstanceState: Bundle?) {
        super.onCreate(savedInstanceState)
        setContent {
            ChapterFourTheme {
                PacktScaffold()
            }
        }
    }
}
```

Let us build and run the app. We should be able to see the following:

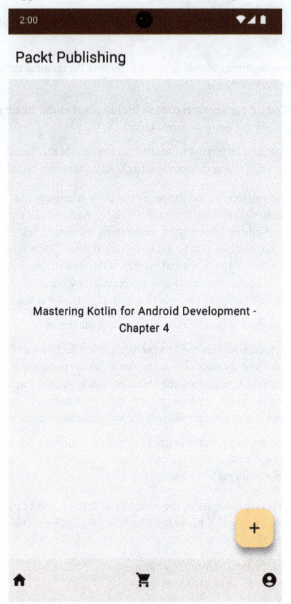

Figure 4.14 – Chapter 4 app

Like me, you might be wondering why the app does not have the greenish color we set on the Material Theme Builder tool. Remember the dynamic color logic in our ChapterFourTheme composable? It is responsible for the brownish color we see. Look at my wallpaper settings:

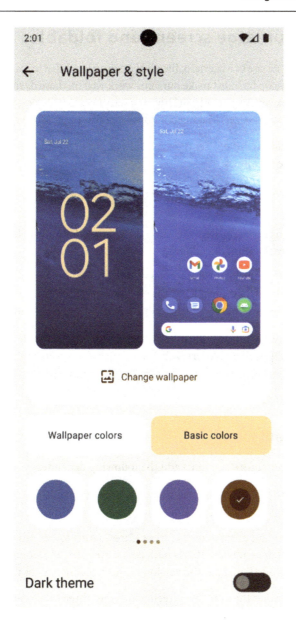

Figure 4.15 – Wallpaper settings

As seen in *Figure 4.15*, my wallpaper has a brown color set. This means our dynamic color logic is working, and our app can adapt well to my wallpaper settings!

We have seen how to use the Material 3 features in our app. In the next section, we will see how we can design UIs that work for large screens and foldables in Jetpack Compose.

Designing UIs for large screens and foldables

In recent years and with the release of Material 3, there has been an increased focus on tablets and foldable devices. As such, we, as developers, must make our apps work well on these devices. In this section, we will look at how we can make our apps work well on large screens and foldables. We need to ensure our apps adapt to the different screen sizes. Making our apps responsive provides a good user experience.

Material 3 offers **canonical layouts** to serve as guidelines for creating UIs for large screens and foldables. These layouts are as follows:

- **List-detail view**: Here, we place a list of items on the left and, on the right, we show the details of a single item.
- **Feed**: Here, we arrange content elements such as cards in a customizable grid, which provides a good view of a large amount of content.
- **Supporting pane**: Here, we organize app content into primary and secondary display areas. The primary area shows the main content while the secondary area shows the supporting content. The primary area occupies most of the screen while the secondary area occupies a smaller portion.

For us to show the different layouts, we must know the screen size of the device the user is using. Luckily for us, Jetpack Compose provides us with a way to get the screen size. We have the Material 3 **WindowSizeClass** to help us determine which layout to show in our app.

We are going to learn how to use `WindowSizeClass` next.

Using WindowSizeClass

For us to use `WindowSizeClass`, we must add the following dependency to our app:

```
implementation 'androidx.compose.material3:material3-window-size-
class'
```

This is the Material 3 dependency that adds `WindowSizeClass` to our project. Notice we are not providing a version for this dependency. This is because we are using the Compose BOM to manage our dependencies. The BOM will manage the version of this dependency for us.

`WindowSizeClass` classifies the available screen width into three categories:

- `Compact`: This is for devices whose width is less than 600 dp. Commonly, these are devices in portrait mode.
- `Medium`: This is for devices whose width is between 600 dp and 840 dp. Devices such as tablets and foldables in portrait mode fall into this category.
- `Expanded`: This is for devices whose width is greater than 840 dp. Devices such as tablets and foldables in landscape mode, phones in landscape mode, and desktops fall into this category.

`WindowSizeClass` uses `widthSizeClass` to get the width of the screen. In addition to `widthSizeClass`, it also has `heightSizeClass` to help us determine the height of the screen.

Let us look at `widthSizeClass` in action:

```
when(calculateWindowSizeClass(activity = this).widthSizeClass) {
    WindowWidthSizeClass.Compact -> {
        CharactersScreen(
            navigationOptions = NavigationOptions.BottomNavigation,
            showDetails = false
        )
    }
    WindowWidthSizeClass.Medium -> {
        CharactersScreen(
            navigationOptions = NavigationOptions.NavigationRail,
            showDetails = true
        )
    }
    WindowWidthSizeClass.Expanded -> {
        CharactersScreen(
            navigationOptions = NavigationOptions.NavigationDrawer,
            showDetails = true
        )
    }
    else -> {
        CharactersScreen(
            navigationOptions = NavigationOptions.BottomNavigation,
            showDetails = false
        )
    }
}
```

Here is an explanation of what the preceding code is doing:

- The `calculateWindowSizeClass` function is used to calculate `WindowSizeClass`. We are passing the activity as the parameter. The function is from the `WindowSizeClass` APIs. It has the `widthSizeClass` and `heightSizeClass` properties, which we can use to get the width and height of the screen, respectively.

- We use `widthSizeClass` to customize our display options:

  - For the `WindowWidthSizeClass.Compact` case, we are using `BottomNavigation` for navigation, and the UI should only show the list of characters

  - For the `WindowWidthSizeClass.Medium` case, we are using `NavigationRail` for navigation, and the UI should show the list of characters and the details of the selected character

- For the `WindowWidthSizeClass.Expanded` case, we are using `NavigationDrawer` for navigation. and the UI should show the list of characters and the details of the selected character

- We have a default case where we are using `BottomNavigation` for navigation, and the UI should only show the list of characters

At a glance, you can see how we take advantage of `WindowSizeClass` to customize our UI and navigation type based on the screen size. This is an immensely powerful feature that we can use to make our apps responsive. This makes sure we take advantage of the screen size and provide a good user experience.

The example shown in this section was a simple one. In *Chapter 7* of this book, we will have a more detailed example where we will use `WindowSizeClass` to customize our UI based on the screen size.

Now that we know how to design and build apps for large screens and foldables, let us look at yet another important topic in this chapter, which is accessibility.

Making our app accessible

Making the apps that we develop accessible is extremely important. It ensures that our apps can be used by everyone. In this section, we will look at how we can make our apps accessible. Jetpack Compose uses **semantics** to make our apps accessible. Semantics are used to describe the UI elements in our apps. They are used by accessibility services to make our apps accessible. Semantics are also used by automated testing tools to test our apps. Some of the best practices for making our apps accessible are as follows:

- We should always ensure that all clickable or touchable elements or those that require user interaction are large enough to be easily tapped or clicked. Most Material components out of the box have a default size that is large enough to be easily tapped or clicked. If we must size by ourselves, we should ensure that the size is at least 48 dp by 48 dp.

- We should add content descriptions to our composables. Components such as `Icon` and `Image` provide this argument to describe visual elements to accessibility services. We should always provide a content description for these components. The following is an example:

```
Icon(
    modifier = Modifier.size(48.dp),
    painter = painterResource(id = R.drawable.ic_launcher_
foreground),
    contentDescription = "Icon"
)
```

You can see in the preceding code that we are using the `contentDescription` parameter to provide a description for `Icon`. This is a good practice that we should always follow.

- We should label our clickable elements. We can pass a clickable label to the clickable modifiers. This enables us to add descriptions to our clickable elements. The following is an example:

```
Text(
    modifier = Modifier
        .clickable(
            onClick = { /*TODO*/ },
            onClickLabel = "Click Me"
        )
        .padding(10.dp),
    text = "Click Me"
)
```

In the preceding example, we are using the `onClickLabel` parameter to add a description to the `Text` composable. This is a good practice that we should always follow.

- By using semantics, we can also describe headers. Headers are used to describe the content that follows them. We can use semantics to add a header to our composables. The following is an example:

```
Text(
    modifier = Modifier
        .semantics { heading() }
        .padding(10.dp),
    text = "Heading One"
)
```

- We can additionally provide information about the state of our composables. For example, we can provide information about the state of a button. We can use semantics to provide this information. The following is an example:

```
Button(
    modifier = Modifier
        .semantics { stateDescription = "Disabled" }
        .padding(10.dp),
    onClick = { /*TODO*/ },
    enabled = false
) {
    Text(text = "Disabled Button")
}
```

This helps us inform our users about the state of our composables.

- For some groups of components, we can also use the `mergeDescendants` parameter to merge the semantics of the children composables. The following is an example:

```
Column(
    modifier = Modifier
        .padding(10.dp)
        .semantics(mergeDescendants = true) { }
) {
    Text(text = "Heading One")
    Text(text = "Heading Two")
    Text(text = "Heading Three")
}
```

Merging descendants is useful when we want to provide a description for a group of composables. In the preceding example, we are using the `mergeDescendants` parameter to merge the semantics of the `Text` composables. However, we should be careful when using this parameter. We should only use it when we want to provide a description for a group of composables. If we use it for a large group of composables, it can lead to performance issues and can also be confusing for the users.

To learn more about accessibility in Jetpack Compose, visit the official documentation (`https://developer.android.com/jetpack/compose/accessibility`).

Summary

In this chapter, we introduced Material 3. We also covered the features that Material 3 offers. We saw how to use Material 3 in our apps. Additionally, we covered how to design and develop our apps for large screens and, finally, we saw how to make our Jetpack Compose UIs accessible.

In the next chapter, we will continue building upon the skills that we've gained from the previous chapters. We will be looking at how to architect our app and the different architectures available. We will learn how to use Jetpack libraries in our apps and how to tackle dependency injection.

Part 2:
Using Advanced Features

Building upon the foundational knowledge gained in *Part 1*, this part propels you into advanced concepts, providing a deeper understanding of Android development. Delving into diverse architectures, the focus shifts toward mastering the MVVM architecture for your applications. Furthermore, you will unravel the intricacies of making network calls by incorporating the Retrofit networking library. Taking it a step further, you will harness the power of Kotlin coroutines to seamlessly execute asynchronous network requests. Your navigational prowess will be honed using the Jetpack Navigation library, exploring techniques for efficient navigation on large screens and foldable devices. The journey continues with insights into handling long-running tasks in the background and leveraging Room for local data storage. Wrapping up, we will demystify runtime permissions, and you will comprehend their significance and master the art of requesting permissions dynamically within your app.

This section contains the following chapters:

- *Chapter 5, Architect Your App*
- *Chapter 6, Network Calls with Kotlin Coroutines*
- *Chapter 7, Navigating within Your App*
- *Chapter 8, Persisting Data Locally and Doing Background Work*
- *Chapter 9, Runtime Permissions*

5

Architect Your App

The process of developing apps needs to be scalable in such a way that you can maintain the app over a long time and easily hand over the development of it to other developers or teams. To be able to do this, we need to properly think about the architecture of our apps. We will be looking at how to build our apps in this chapter.

In this chapter, we will build on what we've learned from the previous chapters. We are going to look at the different architectures available for Android projects. We'll dive deep into **MVVM architecture** and its different layers and how to use some of the Jetpack libraries within their architecture. Additionally, we'll learn how to use advanced architecture features, such as dependency injection and Kotlin Gradle DSL, as well as version catalogs to define dependencies.

In this chapter, we're going to cover the following main topics:

- Introduction to app architecture
- MVVM deep dive
- Jetpack libraries
- Dependency injection
- Migrating to Kotlin Gradle DSL and using version catalogs

Technical Requirements

To follow the instructions in this chapter, you will need to have Android Studio Hedgehog or later (`https://developer.android.com/studio`) downloaded.

You can find the code for this chapter at `https://github.com/PacktPublishing/Mastering-Kotlin-for-Android/tree/main/chapterfive`.

Introduction to app architecture

So far, we have learned how to create apps and designed beautiful UIs with Material 3 and Jetpack Compose. We haven't yet started adopting any architecture for our apps. In this section, we will look at some of the app architectures that we can use to build our apps. We will also look at some of the best practices that we can follow when building our apps. First, let's see some of the benefits of using an app architecture:

- **Separation of concerns**: Using an architecture allows us to separate our code into different layers. Each layer only does one thing. This makes it easy to separate and group our code into different layers. Each layer has its responsibility. This prevents things from being mixed up and makes it easier to maintain our code.

- **Easy testing**: Using an architecture makes it easy to test our code. We can easily test each layer of our code in isolation since things are not tightly coupled.

- **Easy to maintain**: Using an architecture makes it easy to maintain our code. We can easily make changes to our code without affecting other parts of our code. This makes it easy to maintain our code over the long term. We can also swap in and out different parts of the code, and since we have tests, we can test the different implementations and ensure that nothing breaks.

- **Easy to scale**: Using an architecture makes it easy to scale our code. We can easily add new features to our code without affecting other parts of our code.

- **Easy to work in teams**: Using an architecture makes it easy to work in teams. Each team member or team can work on a different layer of the code. It makes it possible to work concurrently on different parts of the codebase.

- **Promotes reusability**: Over time, we can place some of the commonly used code across the projects in common packages or modules, which can then be re-used across the project without having to repeat the code.

When it comes to choosing an architecture for our apps, there are a lot of options that we can choose from. There isn't a particular architecture that fits all the use cases, so it's always recommended that we discuss things with our teams and see which architecture fits the use case. Each architecture has its pros and cons, and we or the whole team have to evaluate which one has more pros than cons. We can architect our app either by feature or by layers. When we architect by feature, we have layers that represent a feature. When we architect by layers, we have layers that represent a layer of our app. An example of architecting by feature is shown in the following points:

- Home feature

- Profile feature

- Settings feature

The preceding example shows how we can architect our app by feature. We have the **Home**, **Profile**, and **Settings** features. Each feature has its layers and all the code related to that feature.

Some of the architectures that we can use to build our apps are the following:

- **Model, View, and ViewModel (MVVM)**: This is the most commonly used architecture and is even recommended by Google to use with our apps. The app has the **Model View** and **ViewModel** layers. The Model layer is responsible for holding the data. The View layer is responsible for displaying the data. The ViewModel layer is responsible for holding the state of the data. It is also responsible for communicating with the Model and View layers. MMVM promotes the clear separation of concerns between the different layers. It also supports **data binding**, which makes it easy to update the UI when the data change. It also supports testing since the different layers are not tightly coupled. It also has less boilerplate code when compared to other architectures. However, it has its downsides, one of them being a large learning curve at times and this can become complex very easily, especially with lots of features.

- **Model View Intent (MVI)**: This has three key layers. The **Model** layer is responsible for holding the data. The **View** layer is responsible for displaying the data. The **Intent** layer represents user actions or events that are dispatched to the model to update a state. MVI promotes unidirectional **data flow**, where data flow in the same direction.

- **Model View Controller (MVC)**: This architecture has three layers. The **Model** layer represents the business logic and holds the data. The **View** layer is responsible for displaying the data. The **Controller** layer is responsible for and acts as an intermediary between the model and the view. It takes care of the user input and updates the view and the model. MVC is very straightforward, especially when starting out, and enables quick iterations and a showcase of app architecture. Its only problem is that it has a tight coupling between the layers, making it hard to test and scale.

- **Model View Presenter (MVP)**: This architecture has three layers. The **Model** layer represents the business logic and holds the data. The **View** layer displays the data and UI components and observes user interactions. The views delegate all UI-related logic to the presenters. The **Presenter** layer contains presentation logic and acts as an intermediary between the model and the view. It processes the user input and updates the view and the model. MVP has a good separation of concerns, and the code is easily testable. However, it has a lot of boilerplate code since every view must have its own presenter. It also has a large learning curve and can become complex very easily.

Now that we understand the different architectures, let us look at MVVM and how we can use it in our apps.

Deep Diving into MVVM

We have already seen the MVVM layers and their pros and cons. In this section, we are going to implement the MMVM architecture in our app step by step. We will start with the model layer, going upwards. Since we all love to have the company of our pets, we are going to use different types of pets as our data.

Let us start by creating a **data** package for our project. We'll do this by right-clicking the `com.packt.` `chapterfive` package; then, we select **New | Package** and name it `data`. Inside this `data` package, let us create a `Pet` data class that will represent our pets:

```
data class Pet(
    val id: Int,
    val name: String,
    val species: String
)
```

The `Pet` data class holds all the data for our pets. Next, we will create a repository interface and its implementation that allows us to get these pets. Create a new file named `PetsRepository` inside the `data` package with the following code:

```
interface PetsRepository {
    fun getPets(): List<Pet>
}
```

This is an interface with one method that returns `List<Pet>`. Next, let us create the implementation class for our interface. While still inside the `data` package, create a new file named `PetsRepositoryImpl` with the following code:

```
class PetsRepositoryImpl: PetsRepository {
    override fun getPets(): List<Pet> {
        return listOf(
            Pet(1, "Bella", "Dog"),
            Pet(2, "Luna", "Cat"),
            Pet(3, "Charlie", "Dog"),
            Pet(4, "Lucy", "Cat"),
            Pet(5, "Cooper", "Dog"),
            Pet(6, "Max", "Cat"),
            Pet(7, "Bailey", "Dog"),
            Pet(8, "Daisy", "Cat"),
            Pet(9, "Sadie", "Dog"),
            Pet(10, "Lily", "Cat"),
        )
    }
}
```

To explain what the preceding code does, please see the following:

- We created a class named `PetsRepositoryImpl`, which implements the `PetsRepository` interface
- We override the `getPets()` method and return a list of pets. Our list has 10 pets with **ID**, **name**, and **species**

We have used a pattern called the **repository pattern** to get our pets. The repository pattern is a pattern that allows us to abstract the data layer from the rest of the app. It allows us to get data from different sources without affecting the rest of the app. For example, we can get data from a local database or a remote server. The class is responsible for merging the data from the two sources and maintaining the source of truth for our data. The repository pattern also allows us to easily test our code since we can easily mock the repository and test the different layers of our app in isolation. Since our app is very simple at the moment, we have already completed the data/model layer of our architecture.

Let us now create a `ViewModel` class for our `ViewModel` layer. Start by creating a `ViewModel` package inside the `com.packt.chapterfive` package. Inside this `ViewModel` package, create a new file named `PetsViewModel` with the following code:

```
class PetsViewModel: ViewModel() {
    private val petsRepository: PetsRepository = PetsRepositoryImpl()

    fun getPets() = petsRepository.getPets()
}
```

To explain what the preceding code does, please see the following:

- We created a class named `PetsViewModel` that extends the `ViewModel` class. This is a class from the **Jetpack libraries**. It helps data persist across configuration changes. It also acts as the intermediary between the View and the Model layers. We use it to expose data to our views, act on user interactions, and update the data in the Model layer.

- We created a private property named `petsRepository` of type `PetsRepository` and initialized it with an instance of `PetsRepositoryImpl`. This is the repository we created earlier.

- We created a method named `getPets()` that returns a list of pets. We called the `getPets()` method from the `petsRepository` property and returned the result.

With this, our `ViewModel` layer is ready to expose data to our views. Our `getPets()` method returns a list of pets. To display the list in **Jetpack Compose**, we use a `LazyColumn` composable. `LazyColumn` follows a lazy-loading approach, meaning that only the items currently visible on the screen are actively composed, reducing resource usage and improving performance. Let us see how a `LazyColumn` works under the hood.

How LazyColumn works

This is how a `LazyColumn` works:

- **On-demand composing**: `LazyColumn` composes only the visible items on the screen. As the user scrolls, it dynamically composes and recomposes items, ensuring that only the necessary elements are rendered at any given time.

- **Recycling items**: Similar to the recycling mechanism in `RecyclerView`, `LazyColumn` reuses composables that move in and out of the viewport, minimizing memory usage and preventing unnecessary recomposition.

- **Optimized for performance**: By lazily loading and recycling items, `LazyColumn` optimizes the rendering process, making it well-suited for displaying large datasets without consuming excessive resources.

Now that we know how `LazyColumn` works, let's see the benefits of using `LazyColumn`.

Benefits of LazyColumn

Some of the benefits of `LazyColumn` are the following:

- **Efficient memory usage**: `LazyColumn` efficiently manages memory by composing only the visible items, ensuring that the app does not unnecessarily store and render all items in a list at once. This is particularly beneficial for long lists or lists with complex UI elements.

- **Improved rendering performance**: The lazy-loading mechanism significantly improves rendering performance, especially when dealing with extensive datasets. It avoids the overhead of rendering and managing all items simultaneously, resulting in smoother scrolling and reduced lag.

- **Simplified UI code**: The declarative nature of Jetpack Compose, coupled with `LazyColumn`, allows us to express UI logic concisely. The code to create and manage large lists becomes more straightforward and readable compared to traditional Android View approaches.

- **Automatic recomposition**: As the data source changes, `LazyColumn` automatically recomposes only the affected items, reducing the need for manual interventions to update the UI.

- **Adaptable for various screen sizes**: `LazyColumn` adapts well to different screen sizes and resolutions, offering a consistent and responsive user experience across various devices.

Now, we're going to create a composable that displays pets.

Creating a composable

Follow these steps to create a composable:

1. Create a new package named `views` inside the `com.packt.chapterfive` package.

2. Inside this `views` package, create a new file named `PetsList` with the following code:

```
@Composable
fun PetList(modifier: Modifier) {
    val petsViewModel: PetsViewModel = viewModel()
    LazyColumn(
        modifier = modifier
```

```
    ) {
        items(petsViewModel.getPets()) { pet ->
            Row(
                modifier = Modifier
                    .fillMaxWidth()
                    .padding(10.dp),
                horizontalArrangement = Arrangement.SpaceBetween
            ) {
                Text(text = "Name: ${pet.name}")
                Text(text = "Species: ${pet.species}")
            }
        }
    }
}
```

Here, we have created a composable named PetList that takes a modifier as a parameter. We then create an instance of PetsViewModel using the viewModel() function from the lifecycle utility library for ViewModel in compose. It helps us easily create an instance of our PetsViewModel. We then use the LazyColumn composable to display the pets. We pass the list of pets from the ViewModel to the items parameter of the LazyColumn. We then use the Row composable to display the name and species of each pet. We have now completed the view layer of our architecture.

3. To finally display our pets, we need to call our PetList composable inside the setContent block of our MainActivity class:

```
ChapterFiveTheme {
    Scaffold(
        topBar = {
            TopAppBar(
                title = {
                    Text(text = "Pets")
                },
                colors = TopAppBarDefaults.
smallTopAppBarColors(
                    containerColor = MaterialTheme.colorScheme.
primary,
                )
            )
        },
        content = { paddingValues ->
            PetList(
                modifier = Modifier
                    .fillMaxSize()
                    .padding(paddingValues)
```

```
                )
            }
        )
    }
```

We are using the Scaffold composable, which we are already familiar with. In our Scaffold, we are passing in a TopAppBar and our PetList composable. We are also passing in paddingValues to our PetList composable. This is because we are using paddingValues to add padding to our PetList composable. We have now completed the MVVM architecture in our app. Let's run the app and see the result:

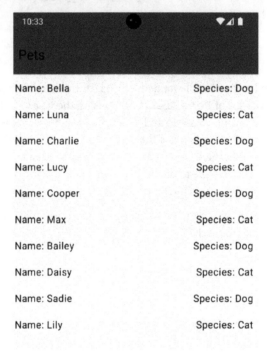

Figure 5.1 – Pet list

As seen from the preceding image, we have our list of pets with their name and species displayed in a list.

We have mentioned **Jetpack libraries** a lot in this section but have not explained what they are. In the next section, we are going to look at Jetpack libraries in detail.

Jetpack libraries

Jetpack Libraries are a collection of libraries and APIs from Google that help us developers create better apps using less code. They are normally created to address some pain points we, as developers, face while creating our apps. Let's look at some of these pain points and some of the Jetpack libraries that were created to address them:

- **Storing data locally and observing changes to the data**: We had to use **SQLite** to store data locally. Even for simple **Create**, **Read**, **Update**, and **Delete** (**CRUD**) operations, we had to write a lot of boilerplate code. We also had to write a lot of code to observe changes to the data. This is a lot of work for a simple task. Jetpack libraries, such as **Room** and **LiveData**, were created to address this pain point. Room is a library that allows us to easily store data locally. It also allows us to easily observe changes to the data. LiveData is a library that allows us to observe changes to data easily. It is also lifecycle-aware. This means it automatically stops observing data changes when the lifecycle of the component observing the data ends. This helps us avoid memory leaks in our apps. Room also has support for **Kotlin Coroutines**, which we will be looking at deeply in *Chapter 6*. This makes it easy to store and access data locally with less boilerplate code.

- **Navigation was a challenging thing to achieve perfectly in our apps**: Lots of open-source libraries were created to solve this pain point. It also required a lot of boilerplate code to navigate between activities and fragments and maintain consistent and predictable back behavior. **Jetpack Navigation** was created to address this pain point. It allows us to navigate between screens in our app easily. It also allows us to easily maintain consistent and predictable back behavior. It also allows us to pass data between screens in our app. It also has support for Jetpack Compose and functions, such as deep links, which are supposed to open a specific screen in our app when a user clicks on a link.

- **Handling lifecycle in activities and fragments**: In Android, both activities and fragments have their own lifecycle, and it is particularly important for us to be aware of these lifecycles so that we can be able to do operations in the right lifecycle. For example, we should be observing data in our views when the lifecycle is in the started state and free up resources when the lifecycle is either in the stopped or destroyed state. Doing this was harder and required a lot of code, which could be bug-prone. The team at Google came up with the **lifecycle** library to help us manage lifecycles in our activities and fragments. Additionally, we have classes, such as the **ViewModel**, which we created earlier on, that allow your data to persist across configuration changes. Most of the Jetpack libraries are also lifecycle-aware, which makes it easy to use them in our apps. Taking the ViewModel as an example, it survives beyond the lifecycle of the activity or fragment that created it. This makes it easy for data to persist across configuration changes. It also makes it easy to share data between fragments and activities.

- **Loading infinite lists**: Most apps that we developers work on have a list of items that we want to show to our users. Often, this list of items can be large, and we cannot display all of them at once. We are supposed to display them in batches, which is called **pagination**. To achieve this by ourselves, we had to do several workarounds, such as observing the scroll position and fetching the next or previous batch of items when a user reaches the top or bottom of the list. Again, this was quite a bit of work, and the team at Google introduced the **Paging** library to help us achieve this. It allows us to load data in batches easily and display it to our users. It also has support for Jetpack Compose and Kotlin Coroutines. It makes it easy to display infinite lists in our apps.

- **Handling background jobs**: Performing lengthy background tasks for apps proved to be somewhat challenging. The common issue was that some of the background jobs did not run due to the different restrictions that phone manufacturers add to the phones to improve their performance of the phone. The team at Google introduced the **WorkManager** library to help us achieve this. It allows us to schedule background jobs in our apps easily. It also supports periodic background jobs and ensures that our jobs run irrespective of the phone brand that the user is using.

- **Performance**: There was no clear guidance on how best we developers can improve the performance of our apps. That is not the case anymore; we have several Jetpack libraries to help us detect performance issues and improve the performance of our apps. A good example of this is the **baseline profiles**, which help improve app start-up time and make app interactions much smoother.

There are a lot of Jetpack libraries. You can explore all the available Jetpack libraries here: `https://developer.android.com/jetpack/androidx/explorer`. The following are some of the benefits of using Jetpack libraries:

- We can follow the best practices
- We can write less boilerplate code
- We reduce fragmentation
- The APIs work well together

We have already seen how to use a `ViewModel` class in this chapter. We will also be using other Jetpack libraries in the later chapters of this book.

We have looked at how the Jetpack Libraries fit in with the different layers of our architecture. In the next section, we are looking at an important topic in architecture, which is **dependency injection**.

Dependency injection

Dependency injection is a way for us to manage and provide dependencies that a class needs to do its work without the class having to create the dependencies itself. In this book, we will be using Koin (`https://insert-koin.io/`) as our dependency injection library.

Our `PetsViewModel` class creates the `PetsRepository` class by itself. This is a suitable candidate for dependency injection. We will be refactoring this to use dependency injection. Let's start by adding the Koin dependency to our app. Open the `build.gradle` file for the app module and add the following dependency:

```
implementation 'io.insert-koin:koin-core:3.4.3'
implementation 'io.insert-koin:koin-android:3.4.3'
implementation 'io.insert-koin:koin-androidx-compose:3.4.6'
```

We are adding the Koin `core`, `android`, and `compose` dependencies as well, which will be used in our project to provide the dependencies.

After adding this to our project and syncing the project, we need to create Koin **modules** for our dependencies. Modules are used to declare dependencies. We will create a module for our `PetsRepository` class. Create a new package named `di` inside the `com.packt.chapterfive` package. Inside this `di` package, create a new file named `Modules` and add the following code:

```
val appModules = module {
    single<PetsRepository> { PetsRepositoryImpl() }
}
```

In the preceding code above, we are creating a new variable named `appModules` of the type module. We are using the `module` function from the Koin library to create a module. We are using the `single` function to create a single instance of the `PetsRepository` class. Koin has dependency injection scopes, such as `single`, `factory`, and `scoped`, that govern the lifecycle and visibility of dependency instances within the container. The `single` scope creates singleton instances that persist throughout the entire application, making it suitable for objects requiring a globally shared state, such as database instances. `Factory` scope generates new instances each time they are requested, fitting stateless utility classes or objects that don't need to maintain a persistent state. The `scoped` scope ties instances to specific contexts, such as activity or fragment lifecycles, allowing them to be shared within a designated scope but recreated for different contexts. The `single` scope is particularly useful for managing global or long-lived dependencies efficiently, ensuring a single instance is shared consistently across various components of the application, thereby optimizing resource usage and maintaining a unified state. This is why we are using `single` to create an instance of our `PetsRepository` class. We are using the `PetsRepositoryImpl` class as the implementation of the `PetsRepository` interface.

Next, we will refactor our `PetsViewModel` class to use dependency injection. Open the `PetsViewModel` class and update it as shown in the following code snippet:

```
class PetsViewModel(
    private val petsRepository: PetsRepository
): ViewModel() {

    fun getPets() = petsRepository.getPets()
}
```

In the preceding code, we have removed the instantiation of the PetsRepository class from the PetsViewModel class. We have, instead, added a constructor that takes a PetsRepository parameter. We also need to create a new dependency for ViewModel, just below the PetsRepository dependency in our appModules variable. Let us add the following code:

```
single { PetsViewModel(get()) }
```

Here, we are creating a single instance of the PetsViewModel class. We are using the get() function to get the PetsRepository dependency. We are passing it to the constructor of the PetsViewModel class. With this, our app is ready to use these dependencies. We will also change the way we create the PetsViewModel instance in our PetList composable. Open the PetList composable and update the initialization of PetsViewModel, as shown here:

```
val petsViewModel: PetsViewModel = koinViewModel()
```

Instead of using the ViewModel() function from the lifecycle library, we are using the koinViewModel() function from the Koin library. This function helps us create an instance of the PetsViewModel class. This now returns an instance of PetsViewModel that has the PetsRepository dependency injected.

The last step in ensuring our app has dependency injection setup is to initialize Koin in our app. We will create a class that extends the Application class and initialize Koin in the onCreate() method. Create a new file named ChapterFiveApplication and add the following code:

```
class ChapterFiveApplication: Application() {
    override fun onCreate() {
        super.onCreate()
        startKoin {
            modules(appModules)
        }
    }
}
```

Our ChapterFiveApplication class extends the Application class. We are overriding the onCreate() method and calling the startKoin() function. We are using the modules parameter to pass in the appModules variable that we created earlier on. This initializes Koin in our app. We also need to update the AndroidManifest.xml file to use our ChapterFiveApplication class. Open the AndroidManifest.xml file and update the application tag with the name attribute, as shown here:

```
android:name=".ChapterFiveApplication"
```

We are passing the name of our ChapterFiveApplication class to the name attribute. Now, if you run the app, it still runs as before, but this time, it uses dependency injection.

Now that we understand what dependency injection is and how to use it in our apps, let us look at **Kotlin Gradle DSL** and how we can use **version catalogs** to manage our dependencies.

Migrating to Kotlin Gradle DSL and using version catalogs

In *Chapter 1*, one of the advantages of using Kotlin that we listed is that we can also write our Gradle files in Kotlin. In this section, we will look at how we can migrate our Gradle files to Kotlin Gradle DSL. We will also look at how we can use a version catalog to manage our dependencies.

Before we migrate, let's see some of the benefits we get from using Kotlin Gradle DSL:

- **Code autocompletion**: We get hints about the completion of our code in Gradle files as we are using Kotlin.

- **Type safety**: We get compile time errors when we make mistakes in our Gradle files.

- **Function calls and variable assignments**: We can use functions and variables in our Gradle files the same way we use them in our Kotlin code. It makes it even easier for us to write and understand.

- **Compile time errors**: We get errors at compile time when we make mistakes in our Gradle files. This helps us avoid runtime errors when building our apps.

- **Official Android Studio Support**: From Android Studio Giraffe onwards, Kotlin Gradle DSL is the recommended way of creating our Gradle files. It is also the default way of creating our Gradle files in Android Studio Giraffe onwards.

So many benefits, right? Let's now migrate our app so as to use Kotlin Gradle DSL.

Migrating our app to Kotlin Gradle DSL

> **Important note**
> If your apps already use Kotlin Gradle DSL, you can skip this section.

Follow these steps to migrate your app to Kotlin Gradle DSL:

1. First, we have to rename all our Gradle files to have a `.kts` extension, which allows our IDE to recognize them as Kotlin Gradle files. Rename the `build.gradle(Project : chapterfive)`, `build.gradle(Module: app)`, and `settings.gradle` files to `build.gradle.kts(Project: chapterfive)`, `build.gradle.kts(Module: app)`, and `settings.gradle.kts`, respectively. This allows us to use Kotlin in our Gradle files now.

2.   After renaming the files, we have to update their content to use Kotlin Gradle DSL. Let's start with the `settings.gradle.kts` file. Open the `settings.gradle.kts` file and update it, as shown in the following code:

```
pluginManagement {
    repositories {
        google()
        mavenCentral()
        gradlePluginPortal()
    }
}
dependencyResolutionManagement {
    repositoriesMode.set(RepositoriesMode.FAIL_ON_PROJECT_REPOS)
    repositories {
        google()
        mavenCentral()
    }
}
rootProject.name = "chapterfive"
include(":app")
```

3.   Next, update the `build.gradle.kts` (`Module: app`) file, as shown in the following code:

```
plugins {
    id("com.android.application")
    id("org.jetbrains.kotlin.android")
}

android {
    namespace = "com.packt.chapterfive"
    compileSdk = 33

    defaultConfig {
        applicationId = "com.packt.chapterfive"
        minSdk = 24
        targetSdk = 33
        versionCode = 1
        versionName = "1.0"
        testInstrumentationRunner = "androidx.test.runner.
AndroidJUnitRunner"
        vectorDrawables {
            useSupportLibrary = true
        }
    }

    buildTypes {
```

```
        release {
            isMinifyEnabled = false
            setProguardFiles(
                listOf(
                    getDefaultProguardFile("proguard-android.
txt"),
                    "proguard-rules.pro"
                )
            )
        }
    }
    compileOptions {
        sourceCompatibility = JavaVersion.VERSION_1_8
        targetCompatibility = JavaVersion.VERSION_1_8
    }
    kotlinOptions {
        jvmTarget = "1.8"
    }
    buildFeatures {
        compose = true
    }

    composeOptions {
        kotlinCompilerExtensionVersion = "1.4.6"
    }

    packagingOptions {
        resources {
            pickFirsts.add("META-INF/AL2.0")
            pickFirsts.add("META-INF/LGPL2.1")
        }
    }
}

dependencies {
    implementation("androidx.core:core-ktx:1.10.1")
    implementation(platform("org.jetbrains.kotlin:kotlin-
bom:1.8.0"))
    implementation("androidx.lifecycle:lifecycle-runtime-
ktx:2.6.1")
    implementation("androidx.activity:activity-compose:1.7.2")
    implementation(platform("androidx.compose:compose-
bom:2022.10.00"))
    implementation("androidx.compose.ui:ui")
```

```
        implementation("androidx.compose.ui:ui-graphics")
        implementation("androidx.compose.ui:ui-tooling-preview")
        implementation("androidx.compose.material3:material3")
        implementation("androidx.lifecycle:lifecycle-viewmodel-
compose")
        implementation("io.insert-koin:koin-core:3.4.3")
        implementation("io.insert-koin:koin-android:3.4.3")
        implementation("io.insert-koin:koin-androidx-compose:3.4.6")
        testImplementation("junit:junit:4.13.2")
        androidTestImplementation("androidx.test.ext:junit:1.1.5")
        androidTestImplementation("androidx.test.espresso:espresso-
core:3.5.1")
        androidTestImplementation(platform("androidx.
compose:compose-bom:2022.10.00"))
        androidTestImplementation("androidx.compose.ui:ui-test-
junit4")
        debugImplementation("androidx.compose.ui:ui-tooling")
        debugImplementation("androidx.compose.ui:ui-test-manifest")
}
```

4. Lastly, update the `build.gradle.kts (Project: chapterfive)` file, as shown in the following snippet:

```
plugins {
    id("com.android.application") version "8.1.0" apply false
    id("com.android.library") version "8.1.0" apply false
    id("org.jetbrains.kotlin.android") version "1.8.20" apply
false
}
```

After updating the files, we have to sync the project. We can do this by clicking on the Sync prompt that appears in the top right corner of the IDE. After syncing the project, we can now run the app, and it should run as before. We have now successfully migrated our app to use Kotlin Gradle DSL. You can also see that the syntax highlighting and the colors of the functions, methods, and variables change to reflect the Kotlin syntax. Some key changes about this migration to highlight are the following:

*   To assign values to properties, we have to use the = operator specifically. For example, `minSdk` 24 changes to `minSdk = 24`.

*   In our `android` config block, `namespace 'com.packt.chapterfive'` changes to `namespace = "com.packt.chapterfive"`. In Kotlin, we define strings using double quotes; that's why we have to change the single quotes to double quotes in all the places we have strings.

*   In defining our dependencies, we have to use double quotes too. For example, `implementation 'androidx.activity:activity-compose:1.7.2'` changes to `implementation("androidx.activity:activity-compose:1.7.2")`.

- Similarly, defining our plugins in the `plugins` block changes. For example, id `'org.jetbrains.kotlin.android'` changes to `id("org.jetbrains.kotlin.android")`.

Our project had minimal Gradle configurations, so if you have a complex project, you might need to do more migration; you can have a look at the Migrate to Kotlin DSL official documentation (`https://developer.android.com/build/migrate-to-kotlin-dsl`) for more examples.

We have now migrated our app to use Kotlin Gradle DSL. In the next subsection, let's look at how we can use a **versions catalog** to manage our dependencies.

Using a versions catalog

Quoting from the official documentation (`https://docs.gradle.org/current/userguide/platforms.html`), a version catalog is a list of dependencies, represented as dependency co-ordinates, that a user can pick from when declaring dependencies in a build script. It helps us easily manage our dependencies and their versions in one central place. Currently, you can see that we define all our dependencies and their versions in our app-level `build.gradle.kts` file. Over time, and as you add more modules to your app, it becomes hard to share these dependencies, and we can find ourselves in situations where different modules have different versions of a similar dependency. This is where version catalogs come in to help us. Let's see all the benefits that they offer:

- They provide a central place to manage all our dependencies and their versions. They make it easier to share the dependencies across the project

- They have a simple and easy-to-use syntax

- They show hints for dependencies that need to be updated

- They make it easier to make changes, and these changes do not recompile the whole project, meaning the builds are faster

- We can bundle dependencies together and share them across the project

- They have official support and are recommended by Google to be used from Android Studio Giraffe going forward

Let's now see how we can use a version catalog in our app. In the `gradle` folder, create a new file named `libs.versions.toml`. In this file, here are some basic rules that we will follow:

- We can use separators, such as -, _v, and ., that will be normalized by Gradle to "." in the Catalog, allowing us to create subsections.

- We define variables using **CamelCase**.

- For libraries, we normally check if we can add them to any existing bundles. For new libraries that are normally used together, we can create a new bundle for them.

We will start by defining the versions for our dependencies as follows:

```
[versions]
coreKtx = "1.10.1"
lifecycle = "2.6.1"
activity = "1.7.2"
composeBom = "2022.10.00"
koin = "3.4.3"
koinCompose = "3.4.6"
junit = "4.13.2"
junitExt = "1.1.5"
espresso = "3.5.1"
```

Here, we are defining all the versions for the libraries that are in our app. We use the **versions** keyword to define the versions. We then define the versions for each library. As we edit this file, you will notice that the IDE prompts you to do a Gradle sync for our changes to be added to the project. For now, we can ignore this and continue editing the file. Next, we will define the bundles for our dependencies:

```
[libraries]
core-ktx = { module = "androidx.core:core-ktx", version.ref =
"coreKtx" }
lifecycle = { module = "androidx.lifecycle:lifecycle-runtime-ktx",
version.ref = "lifecycle" }
activity-compose = { module = "androidx.activity:activity-compose",
version.ref = "activity" }
compose-bom = { group = "androidx.compose", name = "compose-bom",
version.ref = "composeBom" }
compose-ui = { group = "androidx.compose.ui", name = "ui" }
compose-ui-graphics = { group = "androidx.compose.ui", name = "ui-
graphics" }
compose-ui-tooling = { group = "androidx.compose.ui", name = "ui-
tooling" }
compose-material3 = { group = "androidx.compose.material3", name =
"material3" }
compose-manifest = { group = "androidx.compose.ui", name = "ui-test-
manifest" }
compose-viewmodel = { module = "androidx.lifecycle:lifecycle-
viewmodel-compose", version.ref = "lifecycle" }
koin-core = { module = "io.insert-koin:koin-core", version.ref =
"koin" }
koin-android = { module = "io.insert-koin:koin-android", version.ref =
"koin" }
koin-android-compose = { module = "io.insert-koin:koin-androidx-
compose", version.ref = "koinCompose" }
```

```
test-junit = { module = "junit:junit", version.ref = "junit" }
test-junitExt = { module = "androidx.test.ext:junit", version.ref =
"junitExt" }
test-espresso = { module = "androidx.test.espresso:espresso-core",
version.ref = "espresso" }
test-compose-junit4 = { group = "androidx.compose.ui:ui-test-junit4",
name = "ui-test-junit4" }
```

Here, we have defined all the dependencies in our project using the **libraries** keyword.

Next, let's use the **bundles** keyword to create a bundle for Koin and compose dependencies as follows:

```
[bundles]
compose = ["compose.ui", "compose.ui.graphics", "compose.ui.tooling",
"compose.material3", "compose.viewmodel"]
koin = ["koin-core", "koin-android", "koin-android-compose"]
```

The bundles keyword allows us to group dependencies and use them as one. Now, we can sync the project. The last step is to update our app-level build.gradle.kts file to use the version catalog. Open the app-level build.gradle.kts file and update the dependencies block as follows:

```
dependencies {
    implementation(libs.core.ktx)
    implementation(libs.lifecycle)
    implementation(libs.activity.compose)
    implementation(platform(libs.compose.bom))
    implementation(libs.bundles.compose)
    implementation(libs.bundles.koin)
    testImplementation(libs.test.junit)
    androidTestImplementation(libs.test.junitExt)
    androidTestImplementation(libs.test.espresso)
    androidTestImplementation(platform(libs.compose.bom))
    androidTestImplementation(libs.test.compose.junit4)
    debugImplementation(libs.compose.ui.tooling)
    debugImplementation(libs.compose.manifest)
}
```

We can now access the dependencies from our versions catalog file. Notice we must start with the **libs** keyword, and the next part is the names of the bundles or the dependencies, as per our version catalog. After adding these changes, we can now do Gradle sync. Build and run the app. The app displays a list of pets, as before, and nothing changes since we were only refactoring the dependencies.

Summary

In this chapter, we have built on what we learned from the previous chapters. We looked at the different architectures available for Android projects. We dived deep into MVVM architecture and its different layers and how to use some of the Jetpack libraries in this architecture. Additionally, we learned how to use advanced architecture features such as dependency injection and Kotlin Gradle DSL, as well as using Gradle version catalogs to define our dependencies.

As we were creating the MVVM architecture, we used dummy pet data for our data layer. In the next chapter, we are going to learn how to make network calls to fetch data and display it in our app.

6

Network Calls with Kotlin Coroutines

Most of the apps we use on our phones fetch data that is hosted online on a server. As such, we developers have to understand how to request and send data to the servers too. In this chapter, we will learn how to send and request data that is hosted online and display it in our apps.

In this chapter, we will learn how to perform network calls with a networking library, **Retrofit**. We will learn how to consume **application programming interfaces** (**APIs**) using this library. Moreso, we will learn how to take advantage of **Kotlin coroutines** to perform asynchronous network requests in our app.

In this chapter, we're going to cover the following main topics:

- Setting up Retrofit

- Introduction to Kotlin coroutines

- Using Kotlin coroutines for network calls

Technical requirements

To follow the instructions in this chapter, you will need to have Android Studio Hedgehog or later (`https://developer.android.com/studio`) downloaded.

You can find the code for this chapter at `https://github.com/PacktPublishing/Mastering-Kotlin-for-Android/tree/main/chaptersix`.

Setting up Retrofit

Retrofit is a type-safe REST client for Android, Java, and Kotlin developed by Square. The library provides a powerful framework for authenticating and interacting with APIs and sending network requests with OkHttp. In this book, we will be using Retrofit to perform our network requests.

To begin with, we will add the Retrofit dependencies using our newly created version catalog. Let's define the versions in the `libs.versions.toml` file as follows:

```
retrofit = "2.9.0"
retrofitSerializationConverter = "1.0.0"
serializationJson = "1.5.1"
coroutines = "1.7.3"
okhttp3 = "4.11.0"
```

Next, let's define the libraries in the `libs.versions.toml` file in the libraries section of our versions catalog as follows:

```
retrofit = { module = "com.squareup.retrofit2:retrofit" , version.ref
= "retrofit" }
retrofit-serialization = { module = "com.jakewharton.
retrofit:retrofit2-kotlinx-serialization-converter", version.ref =
"retrofitSerializationConverter" }
coroutines = { module = "org.jetbrains.kotlinx:kotlinx-coroutines-
core" , version.ref = "coroutines" }
coroutines-android = { module = "org.jetbrains.kotlinx:kotlinx-
coroutines-android" , version.ref = "coroutines" }
serialization-json = { module = "org.jetbrains.kotlinx:kotlinx-
serialization-json", version.ref = "serializationJson" }
okhttp3 = { module = "com.squareup.okhttp3:okhttp", version.ref =
"okhttp3" }
```

We are adding these dependencies to our project:

- **Retrofit**: As mentioned earlier, we will use Retrofit to perform our network requests.

- **Retrofit serialization**: This is a converter that uses **Kotlinx serialization** to convert Kotlin objects to and from JSON.

- **Coroutines**: We will use Kotlin coroutines to perform our network requests asynchronously. We will be learning more about coroutines shortly.

- **Kotlinx serialization JSON**: This is a Kotlin serialization library for JSON. We will use this to parse our JSON responses. We have other serialization libraries, such as Moshi and Gson, but we used the Kotlinx serialization library for the following reasons:

  - **Kotlin-centric development**: Kotlinx serialization is designed with Kotlin in mind, providing seamless integration and native support for Kotlin serialization.

  - **Declarative syntax**: Kotlinx serialization uses a declarative syntax, leveraging Kotlin's language features for concise and readable serialization code.

  - **Compile-time safety**: Compile-time safety is a key feature, catching serialization-related errors during the compilation phase and reducing the likelihood of runtime errors.

- **Custom serialization strategies**: We have the flexibility to define custom serialization strategies for specific types or scenarios, offering fine-grained control over the serialization process.

- **Seamless integration with Kotlin ecosystem**: Being part of the Kotlin ecosystem, Kotlinx serialization integrates seamlessly with other Kotlin libraries and frameworks, contributing to a cohesive development experience.

- **OkHttp**: This is an HTTP client that is used to make network requests. It provides some utilities for working with Retrofit.

All these dependencies will be added together, so this is a chance for us to group them in our **bundles** section. In our `libs.versions.toml` file, add this bundle below our Koin bundle:

```
networking = ["retrofit", "retrofit-serialization", "serialization-
json", "coroutines", "coroutines-android"]
```

Here, we create a new bundle called `networking` and add all the dependencies that we specified earlier on. We have to sync the project for our changes to be added to the project. Tap on **Sync Now** in the notification that appears at the top when you edit the `libs.versions.toml` file. After syncing, let us start setting up the plugins and dependencies.

First, in our project-level `build.gradle.kts` file, we need to add the Kotlinx serialization plugin. Open the project-level `build.gradle.kts` file and on the plugins block add the following:

```
id("org.jetbrains.kotlin.plugin.serialization") version "1.8.20" apply
false
```

We define the Kotlinx serialization plugin and specify the version to use. This will set up the Kotlinx serialization plugin for us. The plugin generates Kotlin code for serializable classes. We will use this plugin to generate our models. Next, let us set up the plugin in our app module. Open the app-level `build.gradle.kts` file and add the following in the plugins block:

```
id("kotlinx-serialization")
```

This ensures our module is set up to use the Kotlinx serialization plugin. Next, we will add our `networking` bundle to our app module. In the app-level `build.gradle.kts` file, add the following:

```
implementation(libs.bundles.networking)
```

This will add all the dependencies that we have specified in our `networking` bundle. Having done all these, our project is set up to use Retrofit. We will be using Koin to create a Retrofit instance that will be injected into classes that need it. Let us head over to the `Module.kt` file and add the `PetsViewModel` definition:

```
single {
    Retrofit.Builder()
        .addConverterFactory(
            Json.asConverterFactory(contentType = "application/json".
toMediaType())
        )
        .baseUrl("https://cataas.com/api/")
        .build()
}
```

In the preceding code, we created a Retrofit instance using the Retrofit builder. We also added a converter factory that uses Kotlinx serialization to convert Kotlin objects to and from JSON. We also specified the base URL for our API. We are using the **Cat as a Service API** (`https://cataas.com/`), which returns cat images. We will use this instance to create our API class, which is a class with methods that will be used to make network requests. Let us create this class. Create a new Kotlin interface inside the data package called `CatsAPI.kt` and add the following method:

```
@GET("cats")
suspend fun fetchCats(
    @Query("tag") tag: String,
): Response<List<Cat>>
```

In the preceding code, we use the `@GET` annotation to specify that we will be using the `GET` HTTP method for this request. Inside the method, we are also specifying a path that will be appended to our base URL to make the full URL for our request. Using the `GET` method means our method will only request data. We have the following built-in HTTP annotations:

- `POST`: This is used when we want to send data to the server
- `PUT`: This is used when we want to update data on the server
- `DELETE`: This is used when we want to delete data from the server
- `HEAD`: This method asks for a response identical to the one that would correspond to a `GET` request but without the response body
- `PATCH`: This is used when we want to update data partially on the server
- `OPTIONS`: This method requests permitted communication options for the target resource

Back to our `fetchCats()` function, you can notice that we use the `@Query` annotation to specify the query parameter for our request. We use the `tag` query parameter to specify the type of cat we want to fetch. We also use the `suspend` keyword to specify that this method will be called from a coroutine or another `suspend` function. We will learn more about coroutines shortly in the *Introduction to Kotlin coroutines* section of this chapter. We also use the `Response` class to wrap up our response. This class is provided by Retrofit and it contains the HTTP response metadata such as response code, headers, and the raw response body. We also specify that the response will be a list of `Cat` objects. Retrofit will map the response to a list of `Cat` objects. To resolve the error for the `Cat data class`, let us create it. Create a new Kotlin data class inside the data package called `Cat.kt` and add the following:

```
@Serializable
data class Cat(
    @SerialName ("createdAt")
    val createdAt: String,
    @SerialName("_id")
    val id: String,
    @SerialName("owner")
    val owner: String,
    @SerialName("tags")
    val tags: List<String>,
    @SerialName("updatedAt")
    val updatedAt: String
)
```

The `Cat` data class has the fields that correspond to the JSON response from the Cat as a Service API. It is also annotated with the `@Serializable` annotation. This annotation is provided by Kotlinx Serialization and it is used to mark a class as serializable. This annotation is required for all the classes that we want to serialize or deserialize. We have used the `@SerialName` annotation before each variable in our data class. The `@SerialName` is an annotation used to customize the mapping between Kotlin property names and the corresponding names used in the serialized form, such as JSON or other data interchange formats. This annotation allows you to specify a different name for a property when it is serialized or deserialized, providing flexibility in handling naming conventions.

In our project, we are using Koin for dependency injection. So, we now need to create an instance of our `CatsAPI` class in our Koin modules. Let us head back to the `Module.kt` file and below the Retrofit instance add the following:

```
single { get<Retrofit>().create(CatsAPI::class.java) }
```

Here, we get our Retrofit instance and use it to create an instance of our `CatsAPI` class, which we use to make the actual network requests. With that, our project is ready to make the network requests. But before that, let us learn more about Kotlin coroutines as we are going to modify our repository to use coroutines.

Introduction to Kotlin coroutines

Coroutines, introduced by JetBrains for Kotlin, provide a way to write asynchronous code in a more readable and synchronous manner. We can use them to perform background tasks and they are a great way to perform network requests and long-running tasks such as reading and writing to a database. They do these tasks off the main thread and ensure that we don't block our main thread while performing these operations. The main benefits of using coroutines are as follows:

- They are lightweight and easy to use.
- They have built-in cancellation support.
- They lower the chances of apps having memory leaks.
- As mentioned in earlier chapters, Jetpack libraries also support and use coroutines.

We have already added the core and Android coroutines libraries in our app. Let us understand some coroutines basics before proceeding to use coroutines in our project.

Coroutine basics

In this section, we will be looking at different terms and concepts used in Kotlin coroutines:

- `suspend`: This is a keyword that is used to mark a function. A `suspend` function is a function that can be paused and resumed at a later time. We have already used this keyword in our `CatsAPI` class to mark the `fetchCats()` function as a `suspend` function. A `suspend` function can only be called from another `suspend` function or from a coroutine.

- **Coroutine builders**: These are functions that are used to create coroutines. We have the `launch` and `async` coroutine builders. `launch` is used to create a coroutine that does not return a result while `async` is used to create a coroutine that returns a result. The result is a `Deferred` object and we can use the `await()` method to get the result. Both of these builders return a `Job` object that we can use to check if the coroutine is still active or if it has been canceled. We can also use the job to wait for the coroutine to finish. A job ends when it's completed or canceled.

- **Jobs**: A job is a coroutine instance with a **life cycle** and can be canceled. We can use the job to check if the coroutine is still active or if it has been canceled. We can also use the job to wait for the coroutine to finish. A job ends when it's completed or canceled. As mentioned earlier, both the `launch` and `async` coroutine builders return a `Job` object which we use to manage the coroutine life cycle. We have a normal `Job` and `SupervisorJob`. A normal `Job` is canceled when any of its children fail. `SupervisorJob` is not canceled when any of its children fail. It is recommended to use `SupervisorJob` when we have multiple coroutines running concurrently.

- **Coroutine scope**: This keeps track of all the coroutines we create using the `launch` or `async` builders. It is responsible for knowing how long a coroutine will live. Every coroutine builder is defined as an extension function of scope. Coroutines cannot be launched without a scope. We have `GlobalScope`, which is a scope that is not tied to any life cycle. It is not recommended to use this scope as it can lead to memory leaks. In Android, the KTX libraries provide `viewModelScope`, which is a scope that is tied to `ViewModel`. We can use this scope to launch coroutines that will be canceled when `ViewModel` is destroyed. We also have `lifecycleScope`, which is a scope that is tied to an activity or fragment life cycle. We can use this scope to launch coroutines that will be canceled when the life cycle is destroyed. We can also create our own custom scopes if we want to launch coroutines that will be canceled when a custom life cycle is destroyed.

- **Coroutine context**: This is a collection of many elements. `CoroutineContext` defines the behavior of our coroutines using elements such as the following:

  - `Job`: This manages the life cycle of the coroutine.

  - `CoroutineDispatcher`: This defines the thread on which the coroutine will run.

  - `CoroutineName`: This defines the name of the coroutine.

  - `CoroutineExceptionHandler`: This handles uncaught exceptions in the coroutine.

- **Dispatchers**: These specify which thread the coroutines will run on. We have the following dispatchers:

  - `Dispatchers.Main`: This is the main thread. It is used when we need to interact with the UI in our coroutines.

  - `Dispatchers.IO`: This is a thread pool that is optimized for IO tasks such as reading and writing to a database or making network requests.

  - `Dispatchers.Default`: This is a thread pool that is optimized for CPU-intensive tasks.

  - `Dispatchers.Unconfined`: This is a dispatcher that is not confined to any thread. It is used to create a coroutine that inherits the context of the parent coroutine.

  Inside coroutines, we can use the `withContext()` function to switch between different dispatchers. `withContext()` is a `suspend` function that switches the context of the coroutine.

- **Flows**: Suspend functions only return single values. Flows are a type of asynchronous data stream that can return multiple values. We can use flows to return multiple values from a `suspend` function. We can also use flows to perform asynchronous operations. Flows are **cold streams**. This means that they only start emitting values when they are collected. We can use the `collect()` function to collect values from a flow. We have `StateFlow` and `SharedFlow`, which are types of flows. `StateFlow` is a flow that emits the current value to new collectors and emits new values to existing collectors. `SharedFlow` is a flow that emits new values to all collectors. We will be learning more about flows in the next chapter. In Android, we will normally use the two types of flows to emit data to our UI. We will see the usage of `StateFlow` in `ViewModel` as we refactor it to use coroutines.

With this understanding of the basics, in the next section, we will be refactoring our repository to use coroutines.

Using Kotlin coroutines for network calls

In this section, we will refactor our repository to use coroutines. We will use `StateFlow` to emit data from `ViewModel` to the view layer. We will also use the `Dispatchers.IO` dispatcher to perform our network requests on a background thread.

Let us start by creating a `NetworkResult sealed class`, which will represent the different states of our network request:

```
sealed class NetworkResult<out T> {
    data class Success<out T>(val data: T) : NetworkResult<T>()
    data class Error(val error: String) : NetworkResult<Nothing>()
}
```

The `NetworkResult` class is a sealed class that has two subclasses. We have the `Success` data class that will be used to represent a successful network request. It has a data property that will be used to hold the data returned from the network request. We also have the `Error` class, which will be used to represent a failed network request. It has an `error` property that will be used to hold the error message returned from the network request. The sealed class encapsulates a generic data type `T`, which makes it easier for us to reuse the class in all our network calls. The `Success` data class also has a generic parameter for the same purpose.

Next, let us modify `PetsRepository` as follows:

```
interface PetsRepository {
    suspend fun getPets(): NetworkResult<List<Cat>>
}
```

We have updated the interface to use the `NetworkResult` class. We have also marked the `getPets()` function as a `suspend` function. We will use this method to fetch the cats from the API. Next, let us modify `PetsRepositoryImpl` to add the changes from `PetsRepository`:

```
class PetsRepositoryImpl(
    private  val catsAPI: CatsAPI,
    private val dispatcher: CoroutineDispatcher
): PetsRepository {
    override suspend fun getPets(): NetworkResult<List<Cat>> {
        return withContext(dispatcher) {
            try {
                val response = catsAPI.fetchCats("cute")
                if (response.isSuccessful) {
```

```
                        NetworkResult.Success(response.body()!!)
                } else {
                        NetworkResult.Error(response.errorBody().
toString())
                }
        } catch (e: Exception) {
            NetworkResult.Error(e.message ?: "Unknown error")
        }
      }
    }
}
```

We have changed a number of things here:

- First, we added a constructor that takes in an instance of our `CatsAPI` class, which we will use to make our network requests. It also has a `dispatcher` parameter, which will be used to specify the dispatcher that we will use to perform our network requests. We will use the `Dispatchers.IO` dispatcher to perform our network requests on a background thread.

- We have also changed the return type of the `getPets()` function to `NetworkResult<List<-Cat>>`. This is because we will return a `NetworkResult` object from this method.

- We use the `withContext()` function to switch the context of the coroutine to the `Dispatchers.IO` dispatcher. This ensures that the network request is performed on a background thread.

- We have also wrapped our network request in a `try-catch` block. This is to ensure we catch all the errors that might occur during the network request.

- Inside our `try` block, we are making the network request using our `CatsAPI` instance. We use the `fetchCats()` method to make the request. We pass in the `cute` tag to specify the type of cats we want to fetch. We check if the response is successful. If it is, we return a `NetworkResult.Success` object with the response body. If it is not, we return a `NetworkResult.Error` object with the error message.

- Lastly, we catch all the exceptions that might occur during the network request and return a `NetworkResult.Error` object with the error message.

In our Koin modules, we also need to change how we instantiate our repository. Let us head over to `Module.kt` and update the `PetsRepository` definition as follows:

```
single<PetsRepository> { PetsRepositoryImpl(get(), get()) }
single { Dispatchers.IO }
```

We inject the CatsAPI instance and the dispatcher into our repository. We also declare the dispatcher as a single instance. Now we need to modify our PetsViewModel to accommodate these changes. To begin with, we need to create a state class that holds the state of our network request and exposes it to our view. Create a new Kotlin data class inside the view package called PetsUIState.kt:

```
data class PetsUIState(
    val isLoading: Boolean = false,
    val pets: List<Cat> = emptyList(),
    val error: String? = null
)
```

The PetsUIState class is a data class that holds the state of our network request. It has three properties:

- isLoading: This is a Boolean that is used to indicate whether the network request is loading or not.

- pets: This is a list of cats that will be returned from the network request.

- error: This is a string that will be used to hold the error message returned from the network request.

Next, in PetsViewModel, let us create a variable that will hold the state of our network request:

```
val petsUIState = MutableStateFlow(PetsUIState())
```

We use the MutableStateFlow class to hold the state of our network request. MutableStateFlow allows us to update the value of the state. We initialize it with an empty PetsUIState object. Next, let us update the getPets() method as follows:

```
private fun getPets() {
    petsUIState.value = PetsUIState(isLoading = true)
    viewModelScope.launch {
        when (val result = petsRepository.getPets()) {
            is NetworkResult.Success -> {
                petsUIState.update {
                    it.copy(isLoading = false, pets = result.data)
                }
            }
            is NetworkResult.Error -> {
                petsUIState.update {
                    it.copy(isLoading = false, error = result.error)
                }
            }
        }
    }
}
```

```
        }
    }
```

Here, we will break down the preceding code:

- We update the value of the `petsUIState` variable to indicate that the network request is loading.

- We use `viewModelScope` to launch a coroutine. This ensures that the coroutine is canceled when the `ViewModel` is destroyed.

- There is a when statement, which is a Kotlin pattern-matching feature to check the result of the network request. If the result is a `NetworkResult.Success` object, we update the value of `petsUIState` to indicate that the network request was successful and passed in the list of cats. If the result is a `NetworkResult.Error` object, we update the value of `petsUIState` to indicate that the network request failed and pass in the error message.

In `PetsViewModel`, let us add a new `init` block that will call the `getPets()` function:

```
init {
    getPets()
}
```

This will ensure that the `getPets()` function is called when `ViewModel` is created. We now need to update our `PetList` composable to accommodate these changes, too. We will also add more UI components since we need to show the loading state, images, and error messages. Let us start by adding a library that allows us to load images from a URL. We will use Coil (`https://coil-kt.github.io/coil/`), which is an image-loading library. In the versions catalog, let's add the following:

```
coil-compose = "io.coil-kt:coil-compose:2.4.0"
```

We will also add the `coil-compose` dependency to our `compose` bundle so that it can be provided alongside other compose libraries. The updated compose bundle will be as follows:

```
compose = ["compose.ui", "compose.ui.graphics", "compose.ui.tooling",
"compose.material3", "compose.viewmodel", "coil-compose"]
```

Let us now create a new composable that displays an image and tags for each cat inside the `view` package called `PetListItem.kt` and add the following:

```
@OptIn(ExperimentalLayoutApi::class)
@Composable
fun PetListItem(cat: Cat) {
    ElevatedCard(
        modifier = Modifier
            .fillMaxWidth()
            .padding(6.dp)
```

```
    ) {
        Column(
            modifier = Modifier
                .fillMaxWidth()
                .padding(bottom = 10.dp)
        ) {
            AsyncImage(
                model = "https://cataas.com/cat/${cat.id}",
                contentDescription = "Cute cat",
                modifier = Modifier
                    .fillMaxWidth()
                    .height(200.dp),
                contentScale = ContentScale.FillWidth
            )
            FlowRow(
                modifier = Modifier
                    .padding(start = 6.dp, end = 6.dp)
            ) {
                repeat(cat.tags.size) {
                    SuggestionChip(
                        modifier = Modifier
                            .padding(start = 3.dp, end = 3.dp),
                        onClick = { },
                        label = {
                            Text(text = cat.tags[it])
                        }
                    )
                }
            }
        }
    }
}
```

This composable takes in a `Cat` object and displays the image and tags for the cat. We use the `AsyncImage` composable from the Coil library to load the image from the URL. We also use the `FlowRow` composable to display the tags for the cat. We use the `SuggestionChip` composable to display each tag. We display the image and tags in the `ElevatedCard` composable.

Next, let us update our `PetList` composable to accommodate these changes. In the `PetList.kt` file, update the `PetList` composable as follows:

```
@Composable
fun PetList(modifier: Modifier) {
    val petsViewModel: PetsViewModel = koinViewModel()
    val petsUIState by petsViewModel.petsUIState.
collectAsStateWithLifecycle()

    Column(
        modifier = modifier
            .padding(16.dp),
        verticalArrangement = Arrangement.Center,
        horizontalAlignment = Alignment.CenterHorizontally
    ) {
        AnimatedVisibility(
            visible = petsUIState.isLoading
        ) {
            CircularProgressIndicator()
        }

        AnimatedVisibility(
            visible = petsUIState.pets.isNotEmpty()
        ) {
            LazyColumn {
                items(petsUIState.pets) { pet ->
                    PetListItem(cat = pet)
                }
            }
        }
        AnimatedVisibility(
            visible = petsUIState.error != null
        ) {
            Text(text = petsUIState.error ?: "")
        }
    }
}
```

The following is the breakdown of the preceding code:

- Same as before, we use the `koinViewModel()` function to get an instance of `PetsViewModel`.

- We use the `collectAsStateWithLifecycle()` function to collect the state of our network request. This function is provided by the `lifecycle-runtime-compose` library. It is used to collect the state of a flow and automatically cancel the collection when the life cycle is destroyed. We use the `petsUIState` property of `PetsViewModel` to get the state of our network request.

- We have a `Column` composable that contains three `AnimatedVisibility` composables. The first one is used to display a `CircularProgressIndicator` when the network request is loading. The second one is used to display the list of cats when the network request is successful. The last one is used to display an error message when the network request fails.

The `collectAsStateWithLifecycle()` shows an error since we have not added its dependency. Let us add it to our libraries section in the versions catalog as follows:

```
compose-lifecycle = { module = "androidx.lifecycle:lifecycle-runtime-
compose", version.ref = "lifecycle" }
```

We will also add it to our `compose` bundle so that it can be provided alongside other compose libraries. The updated compose bundle will be as follows:

```
compose = ["compose.ui", "compose.ui.graphics", "compose.ui.tooling",
"compose.material3", "compose.viewmodel", "coil-compose", "compose-
lifecycle"]
```

Do a Gradle sync and the IDE will prompt you to add imports for the `collectAsStateWith-Lifecycle()` function.

We have completed updating all our layers to use the new coroutines approach. Good work so far! One last thing: since our app is now fetching these items from an API hosted online, we need to add the `INTERNET` permission to our app. Open the `AndroidManifest.xml file` and add the following:

```
<uses-permission android:name="android.permission.INTERNET" />
```

Run the app and see if everything is working as expected. We can see a list of cute cats with their tags being displayed. We can also see the loading indicator when the network request is loading and the error message when the network request fails. We have successfully refactored our app to use coroutines.

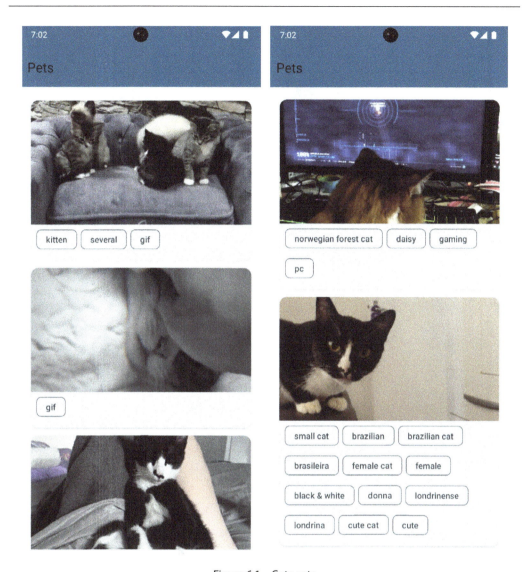

Figure 6.1 – Cute cats

Summary

In this chapter, we learned how to perform network calls with Retrofit. Moreso, we learned how to take advantage of Kotlin coroutines to perform asynchronous network requests in our app and refactored our app to fetch some cute cats with Kotlin coroutines.

In the next chapter, we will be looking at another Jetpack library, **Jetpack Navigation**, to handle navigation in our app.

7

Navigating within Your App

The apps we make need to move from one screen to the other, showing different content on these screens. So far, we have been making apps with only one screen. In this chapter, we will learn how to move from one screen to the other. We will learn how to use the **Jetpack Compose Navigation** library to navigate to different Jetpack Compose screens within our app. We will learn the tips and best practices for using this library. Also, we will cover how to pass arguments as we navigate to screens. Lastly, we will build on what we learned in *Chapter 4*, by handling navigation on large screens and foldables.

In this chapter, we're going to cover the following main topics:

- Jetpack Navigation overview
- Navigating to Compose destinations
- Passing arguments to destinations
- Navigation in foldables and large screens

Technical requirements

To follow the instructions in this chapter, you will need to have Android Studio Hedgehog or later (`https://developer.android.com/studio`) downloaded.

You can use the previous chapter's code to follow the instructions in this chapter. You can find the code for this chapter at `https://github.com/PacktPublishing/Mastering-Kotlin-for-Android/tree/main/chapterseven`.

Jetpack Navigation overview

The Jetpack Navigation library provides an API for handling **complex navigation** with ease while also following the principles of Android Jetpack. The library is available for both the old view system, which uses XML (https://developer.android.com/guide/navigation), and Jetpack Compose (https://developer.android.com/jetpack/compose/navigation). We will be learning about the latter in this chapter.

Still building on the Pets app we used in the previous chapter, we are going to navigate to a details screen that has a back button to the previous screen. We will also be passing data to the details screen.

To start with, we need to add the Jetpack Navigation Compose dependency to our project. Let's add the following library inside the `versions` section in our `libs.versions.toml` file:

```
compose-navigation = "androidx.navigation:navigation-compose:2.7.2"
```

Next, we need to add the dependency to our app module's `build.gradle.kts` file:

```
implementation(libs.compose.navigation)
```

Do a Gradle sync to add the library to our project. The next step is to create `NavController` and `NavHost`. `NavController` is a class that manages app navigation within `NavHost`. `NavHost` is a container that hosts composables and handles navigation between them. Let's create a new package called `navigation` and create a new sealed class called `Screens.kt`. Inside the file, let us add the following code:

```
sealed class Screens(val route: String) {
    object PetsScreen : Screens("pets")
    object PetDetailsScreen : Screens("petDetails")
}
```

This is a sealed class that has two objects. A sealed class is used to represent restricted class hierarchies wherein the object or value can only have a value among one of the types defined in the sealed class. The first object is `PetsScreen`, which will be the first screen we will see when we launch the app. The second object is `PetDetailsScreen`, which will be the screen we will navigate to when we click on a pet item in `PetsScreen`. Every time we need to add a new destination screen, we will add a new object to the sealed class.

Next, let us create a new file inside the `navigation` package called `AppNavigation.kt`. Inside the file, let us add the following code:

```
@Composable
fun AppNavigation() {
    val navController = rememberNavController()

    NavHost(
```

```
        navController = navController,
        startDestination =  Screens.PetsScreen.route
    ) {
        composable(Screens.PetsScreen.route) {
            PetsScreen()
        }
    }
}
```

Let's explain the preceding code:

- We create `NavController` using the `rememberNavController()` function. This function is used to create `NavController` that will be remembered across recompositions. This is important because we need to be able to navigate to different screens in our app.

- We create a `NavHost` composable that takes in `navController` and `startDestination`. `startDestination` is the first screen we want to see when we launch the app. In our case, it is `PetsScreen`.

- We add the `PetsScreen` composable. This composable has an error because we have not created it yet. We will do that shortly.

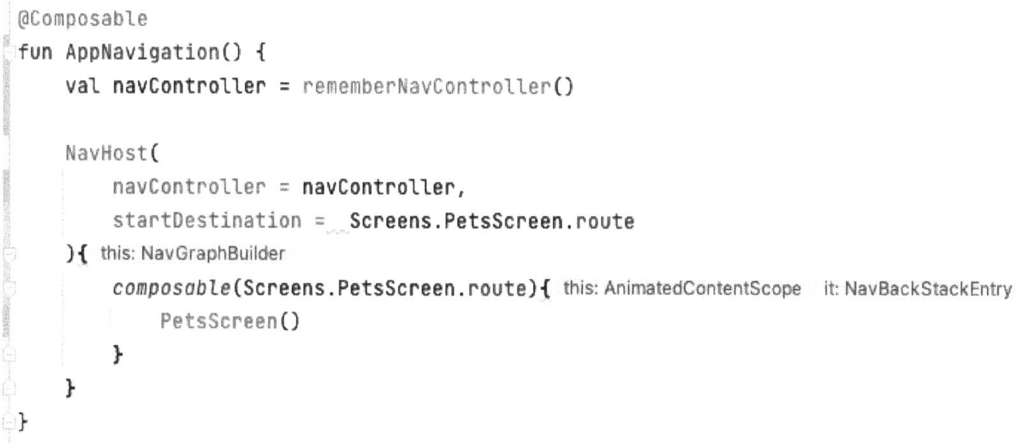

```
@Composable
fun AppNavigation() {
    val navController = rememberNavController()

    NavHost(
        navController = navController,
        startDestination =  Screens.PetsScreen.route
    ){ this: NavGraphBuilder
        composable(Screens.PetsScreen.route){ this: AnimatedContentScope    it: NavBackStackEntry
            PetsScreen()
        }
    }
}
```

Figure 7.1 – PetsScreen error

As seen in the preceding screenshot, the `PetsScreen` composable is highlighted in red because we have not created the composable yet. We will refactor our code a bit. Let us create a new file called `PetsScreen.kt`. Inside the file, let's add the following code:

```
@OptIn(ExperimentalMaterial3Api::class)
@Composable
fun PetsScreen(onPetClicked: (Cat) -> Unit) {
```

```
    Scaffold(
        topBar = {
            TopAppBar(
                title = {
                    Text(text = "Pets")
                },
                colors = TopAppBarDefaults.smallTopAppBarColors(
                    containerColor = MaterialTheme.colorScheme.
primary,
                )
            )
        },
        content = { paddingValues ->
            PetList(
                modifier = Modifier
                    .fillMaxSize()
                    .padding(paddingValues),
                onPetClicked = onPetClicked
            )
        }
    )
}
```

The `PetsScreen` composable displays a list of pets. We have added a `Scaffold` composable as the root element. Inside the `Scaffold` composable, we have added a `TopAppBar` composable. We have also added a `PetList` composable as the content of the `Scaffold` composable. We have added a new `onPetClicked` callback to the `PetList` composable. We will be using this callback to navigate to `PetDetailsScreen` when we click on a pet item in the list.

With this, our navigation graph is ready. We can now add the `AppNavigation` composable to our `MainActivity.kt` file. Let's replace all the code inside the `ChapterSevenTheme` block with the following:

```
ChapterSevenTheme {
    AppNavigation()
}
```

Build and run the app. The app still displays a list of cute pets as before, but now we are using the Jetpack Navigation library to handle our navigation.

Figure 7.2 – Pets

In the next section, let us learn how to navigate to a details screen when we click on a pet item in the list.

Navigating to Compose destinations

In this section, we will learn how to navigate to a details screen when we click on a pet item in the list. First, we need to create a new composable for `PetDetailsScreen`. Let us create a new file called `PetDetailsScreen.kt` and create the `PetDetailsScreenContent` composable as follows:

```
@OptIn(ExperimentalLayoutApi::class)
@Composable
fun PetDetailsScreenContent(modifier: Modifier) {
    Column(
        modifier = modifier
            .fillMaxSize()
            .padding(16.dp),
        verticalArrangement = Arrangement.Center,
        horizontalAlignment = Alignment.CenterHorizontally
    ) {
        AsyncImage(
            model = "https://cataas.com/cat/rV1MVEh0Af2Bm4O0",
            contentDescription = "Cute cat",
            modifier = Modifier
                .fillMaxWidth()
                .height(200.dp),
            contentScale = ContentScale.FillWidth
        )
        FlowRow(
            modifier = Modifier
                .padding(start = 6.dp, end = 6.dp)
        ) {
            repeat(2) {
                SuggestionChip(
                    modifier = Modifier
                        .padding(start = 3.dp, end = 3.dp),
                    onClick = { },
                    label = {
                        Text(text = "Tag $it")
                    }
                )
            }
        }
    }
}
```

Here, we created a composable that has `Column` as the root element. Inside the `Column` element, we added an `AsyncImage` composable that displays a cat image. We also added a `FlowRow` composable to flow items to the next line when space runs out, which cannot be achieved with rows. `FlowRow` displays two `SuggestionChip` composables. We will use this composable to display the details of a pet. Notice we are using hardcoded cat IDs and tags for now. We will pass this data from the `PetList` composable in the next section. Next, let us create the `PetDetailsScreen` composable as follows:

```
@OptIn(ExperimentalMaterial3Api::class)
@Composable
fun PetDetailsScreen(onBackPressed: () -> Unit) {
    Scaffold(
        topBar = {
            TopAppBar(
                title = {
                    Text(text = "Pet Details")
                },
                colors = TopAppBarDefaults.smallTopAppBarColors(
                    containerColor = MaterialTheme.colorScheme.
primary,
                ),
                navigationIcon = {
                    IconButton(
                        onClick = onBackPressed,
                        content = {
                            Icon(
                                imageVector = Icons.Default.ArrowBack,
                                contentDescription = "Back"
                            )
                        }
                    )
                }
            )
        },
        content = { paddingValues ->
            PetDetailsScreenContent(
                modifier = Modifier
                    .padding(paddingValues)
            )
        }
    )
}
```

The `PetDetailsScreen` composable displays the details of a pet. We have added a `Scaffold` composable as the root element. Inside the `Scaffold` composable, we have added a `TopAppBar` composable. We have also used the `PetDetailsScreenContent` composable we created earlier as the content of the `Scaffold` composable. We have added a new `onBackPressed` callback to the `PetDetailsScreen` composable. We will be using this callback to navigate back to the previous screen when we click on the back button in `TopAppBar`.

Our next step is to add a composable for `PetDetailsScreen` to our `AppNavigation.kt` file. Let us add the following code to our `NavHost` below the composable for `PetsScreen`:

```
composable(Screens.PetDetailsScreen.route) {
    PetDetailsScreen(
        onBackPressed = {
            navController.popBackStack()
        }
    )
}
```

Here, we have added a composable for `PetDetailsScreen`. We passed in the route for the screen and the `PetDetailsScreen` composable as the content. `PetDetailsScreen` has the `onBackPressed` argument. The argument handles the situation where a user taps the back arrow icon, which is normally at the top left. We use `navController.popBackStack()` inside the `onBackPressed` argument. This method attempts to pop the current destination off the back stack and navigates to the previous destination.

Now we need to do the actual navigation to `PetDetailsScreen` when we click on a pet item in the list. Let us head over to the `PetListItem` composable. We will add a new `onPetClicked` callback to the `PetListItem` composable. The modified composable should look like this:

```
@OptIn(ExperimentalLayoutApi::class)
@Composable
fun PetListItem(cat: Cat, onPetClicked: (Cat) -> Unit) {
    ElevatedCard(
        modifier = Modifier
            .fillMaxWidth()
            .padding(6.dp)
    ) {
        Column(
            modifier = Modifier
                .fillMaxWidth()
                .padding(bottom = 10.dp)
                .clickable {
                    onPetClicked(cat)
                }
        ) {
```

```
AsyncImage(
    model = "https://cataas.com/cat/${cat.id}",
    contentDescription = "Cute cat",
    modifier = Modifier
        .fillMaxWidth()
        .height(200.dp),
    contentScale = ContentScale.FillWidth
)
FlowRow(
    modifier = Modifier
        .padding(start = 6.dp, end = 6.dp)
) {
    repeat(cat.tags.size) {
        SuggestionChip(
            modifier = Modifier
                .padding(start = 3.dp, end = 3.dp),
            onClick = { },
            label = {
                Text(text = cat.tags[it])
            }
        )
    }
}
}
}
}
}
```

In the preceding code, we have added a new onPetClicked callback to the composable. We have added the clickable modifier to Column and called the onPetClicked callback inside the modifier. We pass in the cat object to the callback. Next, we need to add the onPetClicked callback to the PetList composable, as follows:

```
@Composable
fun PetList(modifier: Modifier, onPetClicked: (Cat) -> Unit) {
    // other code
}
```

Next, we need to pass this callback where we use our PetListItem composable. The modified PetListItem composable at the call site inside the items block should look like this:

```
PetListItem(
    cat = pet,
    onPetClicked = onPetClicked
)
```

Lastly, we need to modify the `AppNavigation` composable to pass the `onPetClicked` callback to the `PetsScreen` composable. The modified `AppNavigation` composable should look like this:

```
PetsScreen(
    onPetClicked = {
        navController.navigate(Screens.PetDetailsScreen.route)
    }
)
```

Here, we pass the `onPetClicked` callback to the `PetsScreen` composable. Inside the callback, we call the `navigate()` function on `navController` and pass in the route for `PetDetailsScreen`. This will navigate to `PetDetailsScreen` when we click on a pet item in the list.

Build and run the app. Click on a pet item in the list. You will see that the app navigates to `PetDetailsScreen`.

Figure 7.3 – Pet Details screen

We can see a cute cat image and some tags. Additionally, if we press the back button in `TopAppBar`, we will be able to navigate back to `PetsScreen`.

So far, we have been able to navigate from `PetsScreen` to `PetDetailsScreen`. However, we are not passing any data to `PetDetailsScreen`. In the next section, we will learn how to pass data to `PetDetailsScreen`.

Passing arguments to destinations

In our `PetDetailsScreen`, we need to remove the hardcoded cat IDs and tags and pass them from the `PetList` composable. Follow these steps:

1. Let us head over to the `PetDetailsScreenContent` composable inside the `PetDetailsScreen.kt` file and modify it as follows:

```
@OptIn(ExperimentalLayoutApi::class)
@Composable
fun PetDetailsScreenContent(modifier: Modifier, cat: Cat) {
    Column(
        modifier = modifier
            .fillMaxSize()
            .padding(16.dp),
        verticalArrangement = Arrangement.Center,
        horizontalAlignment = Alignment.CenterHorizontally
    ) {
        AsyncImage(
            model = "https://cataas.com/cat/${cat.id}",
            contentDescription = "Cute cat",
            modifier = Modifier
                .fillMaxWidth()
                .height(200.dp),
            contentScale = ContentScale.FillWidth
        )
        FlowRow(
            modifier = Modifier
                .padding(start = 6.dp, end = 6.dp)
        ) {
            repeat(cat.tags.size) {
                SuggestionChip(
                    modifier = Modifier
                        .padding(start = 3.dp, end = 3.dp),
                    onClick = { },
                    label = {
                        Text(text = cat.tags[it])
```

```
                    }
                )
            }
        }
    }
}
```

We have added a new `cat` parameter to the composable. We have used the `cat` object to display the cat image and tags.

2. Next, let us head over to the `PetDetailsScreen` composable and modify it as follows:

```
@OptIn(ExperimentalMaterial3Api::class)
@Composable
fun PetDetailsScreen(onBackPressed: () -> Unit, cat: Cat) {
    Scaffold(
        topBar = {
            TopAppBar(
                title = {
                    Text(text = "Pet Details")
                },
                colors =  TopAppBarDefaults.
smallTopAppBarColors(
                    containerColor = MaterialTheme.colorScheme.
primary,
                ),
                navigationIcon = {
                    IconButton(
                        onClick = onBackPressed,
                        content = {
                            Icon(
                                imageVector = Icons.Default.
ArrowBack,
                                contentDescription = "Back"
                            )
                        }
                    )
                }
            )
        },
        content = { paddingValues ->
            PetDetailsScreenContent(
                modifier = Modifier
                    .padding(paddingValues),
                cat = cat
```

```
                )
            }
        )
    }
```

Here, we have added a new `cat` parameter to the composable. We have passed the `cat` object to the `PetDetailsScreenContent` composable.

3. Next, let us head over to the `AppNavigation` composable and add the logic for passing the `cat` object to `PetDetailsScreen`. We need to first modify the composable for `PetDetailsScreen`, as follows:

```
composable(
    route = "${Screens.PetDetailsScreen.route}/{cat}",
    arguments = listOf(
        navArgument("cat") {
            type = NavType.StringType
        }
    )
){
    PetDetailsScreen(
        onBackPressed = {
            navController.popBackStack()
        },
        cat = Json.decodeFromString(it.arguments?.
getString("cat") ?: "")
    )
}
```

Let's explain the changes:

*   On the route, we have added a new parameter called `cat`. This is the parameter we will use to pass the `cat` object to `PetDetailsScreen`.

*   We have added a new `arguments` parameter. This parameter is used to pass arguments to the destination screen. We have added `navArgument` for the `cat` parameter. We have set the type to be `String`. This is because we will be passing a string representation of the `cat` object.

*   We pass the `cat` object to the `PetDetailsScreen` composable. We have used `Json.decodeFromString()` from the Kotlinx Serialization library that we learned about in *Chapter 6* to convert the string value of the `cat` object into a `Cat` object. We have used the `arguments` property of `NavBackStackEntry` to get the string value of the `cat` object. We have used the Elvis operator to return an empty string if the `arguments` property is null.

4. Lastly, we need to modify the `onPetClicked` callback of `PetsScreen` in the `AppNavigation` composable, as follows:

```
composable(Screens.PetsScreen.route) {
    PetsScreen(
        onPetClicked = { cat ->
            navController.navigate(
                "${Screens.PetDetailsScreen.route}/${Json.
encodeToString(cat)}"
            )
        }
    )
}
```

We have modified the `navigate()` function to pass the `Cat` object as a string. We also used `Json.encodeToString()` from the Kotlinx Serialization library to convert the `Cat` object into a string. This will be passed as an argument to `PetDetailsScreen` when we click on a pet item in the list.

5. Build and run the app. Click on any cute cat picture from the list and now the details screen will display the cat image and tag of the cute cat that we selected:

Figure 7.4 – Pet Details

We have now been able to pass data to `PetDetailsScreen`. We have learned how to navigate to a compose destination and pass data to the details screen. In the next section, we will learn how to handle navigation in foldables and large screens.

Navigation in foldables and large screens

In the *Designing UIs for large screens and foldables* section of *Chapter 4*, we learned about the `WindowSize` class and how we can make our apps responsive in foldable devices and large screens. In this section, we are going to make our Pets app responsive in foldable devices and large screens. We are going to make several changes, as follows:

- Add a bottom bar to `PetsScreen`, which will have several options.

- Add `NavigationRail` and `NavigationDrawer`, which will be used depending on the screen size.

- Observe the device's foldable state and change the layout of the app depending on the foldable state.

- Depending on the screen size, we will also change the content type. On large screens, we will display the list of cats and the details of the selected cat side by side. On small screens, we will display the list of cats and the details of the selected cat on different screens.

Quite a lot of changes are required. The good thing is that I have already made the changes and you can find the final version in the `chapterseven` folder in the project's repository. Let us go through the changes one by one:

1. We will start by creating a `sealed interface` named `NavigationType` that represents the different types of navigation we will be using in our app. Let us create a new file inside the `navigation` package called `NavigationType.kt` and add the following code:

    ```
    sealed interface NavigationType {
        object BottomNavigation : NavigationType
        object NavigationDrawer : NavigationType
        object NavigationRail : NavigationType
    }
    ```

    We are using a sealed interface instead of a sealed class here. This is because we do not need to hold any state in our `NavigationType`. We also do not need to pass properties to any of the `NavigationTypes`. We have three options: `BottomNavigation`, `NavigationDrawer`, and `NavigationRail`. We will be using these options to change the navigation type depending on the screen size.

2. Next, let us create yet another sealed interface called `ContentType`. This interface will be used to change the content display type depending on the screen size. Let us create a new file called `ContentType.kt` still inside the `navigation` package and add the following code:

```
sealed interface ContentType {
    object List : ContentType
    object ListAndDetail : ContentType
}
```

This represents the two modes in which we can display our content depending on the screen size. We have the `List` mode, which displays the list of cats only. We also have the `ListAndDetail` mode, which displays the list of cats and the details of the selected cat side by side.

3. Next, in our `Screens.kt` file, we have to add a new destination screen called `FavoritesScreen`. The final code for the file should look like this:

```
sealed class Screens(val route: String) {
    object PetsScreen : Screens("pets")
    object PetDetailsScreen : Screens("petDetails")
    object FavoritePetsScreen : Screens("favoritePets")
}
```

We now have three destinations for our app.

4. Next, let us add the `WindowSize` dependencies to the libraries section in the `libs.versions.toml` file:

```
compose-window-size = "androidx.compose.material3:material3-
window-size-class:1.2.0-alpha07"
androidx-window = "androidx.window:window:1.1.0"
```

5. We also need to add the dependencies to our app module's `build.gradle.kts` file:

```
implementation(libs.compose.window.size)
implementation(libs.androidx.window)
```

Do a Gradle sync to be able to add the dependencies to our project.

6. Next, we need to create the composables for `NavigationRail`, `NavigationDrawer`, and `BottomNavigation`. Let us create a new file called `PetsNavigationRail.kt` inside the `view` package and add the following code:

```
@Composable
fun PetsNavigationRail(
    onFavoriteClicked: () -> Unit,
    onHomeClicked: () -> Unit,
    onDrawerClicked: () -> Unit
) {
```

```kotlin
    val items = listOf(Screens.PetsScreen, Screens.
FavoritePetsScreen)
    val selectedItem = remember { mutableStateOf(items[0]) }

    NavigationRail(
        modifier = Modifier
            .fillMaxHeight()
    ) {
        NavigationRailItem(
            selected = false,
            onClick = onDrawerClicked,
            icon = {
                Icon(
                    imageVector = Icons.Default.Menu,
                    contentDescription = "Menu Icon"
                )
            }
        )

        NavigationRailItem(
            selected = selectedItem.value == Screens.PetsScreen,
            onClick = {
                onHomeClicked()
                selectedItem.value = Screens.PetsScreen
            },
            icon = {
                Icon(
                    imageVector = Icons.Default.Home,
                    contentDescription = "Home Icon"
                )
            }
        )

        NavigationRailItem(
            selected = selectedItem.value == Screens.
FavoritePetsScreen,
            onClick = {
                onFavoriteClicked()
                selectedItem.value = Screens.FavoritePetsScreen
            },
            icon = {
                Icon(
                    imageVector = Icons.Default.Favorite,
                    contentDescription = "Favorite Icon"
```

```
                )
            }
        )
    }
}
```

In the preceding code, we created the `PetsNavigationRail()` composable, which has three parameters: `onFavoriteClicked`, `onHomeClicked`, and `onDrawerClicked`. The first two are callbacks that will be used to navigate to the different screens. We use the `onDrawerClicked` callback to close or open the drawer when the user interacts with it. At the top, we have the `items` variable, which holds a list of all our screens, and the `selectedItem` variable, which holds the currently selected screen. We use the `NavigationRail` composable from the Material 3 library to display the navigation rail. To add items to `NavigationRail`, we use the `NavigationRailItem` composable. We pass in the selected state of the item, the `onClick` callback, and the icon to display.

7. Next, let us create the `PetsBottomNavigationBar` composable. Let us create a new file called `PetsBottomNavigationBar.kt` inside the `view` package and add the following code:

```
@Composable
fun PetsBottomNavigationBar(
    onFavoriteClicked: () -> Unit,
    onHomeClicked: () -> Unit
) {
    val items = listOf(Screens.PetsScreen, Screens.
FavoritePetsScreen)
    val selectedItem = remember { mutableStateOf(items[0]) }
    NavigationBar(
        modifier = Modifier
            .fillMaxWidth(),
        containerColor = MaterialTheme.colorScheme.background
    ) {
        NavigationBarItem(
            selected = selectedItem.value == Screens.PetsScreen,
            onClick = {
                onHomeClicked()
                selectedItem.value = Screens.PetsScreen
            },
            icon = {
                Icon(
                    imageVector = Icons.Default.Home,
                    contentDescription = "Home Icon"
                )
            }
        )
```

```
            NavigationBarItem(
                selected = selectedItem.value == Screens.
    FavoritePetsScreen,
                onClick = {
                    onFavoriteClicked()
                    selectedItem.value = Screens.FavoritePetsScreen
                },
                icon = {
                    Icon(
                        imageVector = Icons.Default.Favorite,
                        contentDescription = "Favorite Icon"
                    )
                }
            )
        }
    }
```

The PetsBottomNavigationBar composable is similar to the PetsNavigationRail composable. The only difference is that we are using the NavigationBar composable instead of the NavigationRail composable. We have the home and favorite items. We use the NavigationBarItem composable to add items to NavigationBar. We pass in the selected state of the item, the onClick callback, and the icon to display.

8. Next, let us create the PetsNavigationDrawer composable. Let us create a new file called PetsNavigationDrawer.kt inside the view package and add the following code:

```
@Composable
fun PetsNavigationDrawer(
    onFavoriteClicked: () -> Unit,
    onHomeClicked: () -> Unit,
    onDrawerClicked: () -> Unit = {}
) {
    val items = listOf(Screens.PetsScreen, Screens.
FavoritePetsScreen)
    val selectedItem = remember { mutableStateOf(items[0]) }
    Column(
        modifier = Modifier
            .wrapContentWidth()
            .fillMaxHeight()
            .background(MaterialTheme.colorScheme.
inverseOnSurface)
            .padding(16.dp)
    ) {
        Row(
```

```
            modifier = Modifier
                .fillMaxWidth()
                .padding(16.dp),
            horizontalArrangement = Arrangement.SpaceBetween,
            verticalAlignment = Alignment.CenterVertically
        ) {
            Text(
                text = "Chapter Seven",
                style = MaterialTheme.typography.titleMedium,
                color = MaterialTheme.colorScheme.primary
            )
            IconButton(
                onClick = onDrawerClicked
            ) {
                Icon(
                    imageVector = Icons.Default.Menu,
                    contentDescription = "Navigation Drawer
Icon"
                )
            }
        }
        NavigationDrawerItem(
            label = { Text(text = "Pets") },
            selected = selectedItem.value == Screens.PetsScreen,
            onClick = {
                onHomeClicked()
                selectedItem.value = Screens.PetsScreen
            },
            icon = {
                Icon(
                    imageVector = Icons.Default.Home,
                    contentDescription = "Home Icon"
                )
            }
        )

        NavigationDrawerItem(
            label = { Text(text = "Favorites") },
            selected = selectedItem.value == Screens.
FavoritePetsScreen,
            onClick = {
                onFavoriteClicked()
                selectedItem.value = Screens.FavoritePetsScreen
            },
```

```
            icon = {
                Icon(
                    imageVector = Icons.Default.Favorite,
                    contentDescription = "Favorite Icon"
                )
            }
        )


    }
}
```

We used the `NavigationDrawer` composable from the Material 3 library to display the navigation drawer. We used the `NavigationDrawerItem` composable to add items to `NavigationDrawer`. We passed in the label, the selected state of the item, the `onClick` callback, and the icon to display.

9. Since our `PetsNavigationDrawer`, `PetsNavigationRail`, and `PetsBottom-NavigationBar` composables have `FavoritesScreen`, let us create a new file called `FavoritePetsScreen.kt` inside the view package and add the following code:

```
@Composable
fun FavoritePetsScreen() {
    Column(
        modifier = Modifier
            .fillMaxSize(),
        verticalArrangement = Arrangement.Center,
        horizontalAlignment = Alignment.CenterHorizontally
    ) {
        Text(text = "Favorite Pets")
    }
}
```

This is a simple composable that displays the text `"Favorite Pets"`. We will use this composable as the content of `FavoritesScreen`. We also need to refactor our `AppNavigation()` composable to make it ready to handle the different navigation and content types. The final modified composable should look like this:

```
@Composable
fun AppNavigation(
    contentType: ContentType,
    navHostController: NavHostController =
rememberNavController()
) {
    NavHost(
        navController = navHostController,
        startDestination = Screens.PetsScreen.route
```

```
    ) {
        composable(Screens.PetsScreen.route) {
            PetsScreen(
                onPetClicked = { cat ->
                    navHostController.navigate(
                        "${Screens.PetDetailsScreen.
route}/${Json.encodeToString(cat)}"
                    )
                },
                contentType = contentType
            )
        }
        composable(
            route = "${Screens.PetDetailsScreen.route}/{cat}",
            arguments = listOf(
                navArgument("cat") {
                    type = NavType.StringType
                }
            )
        ) {
            PetDetailsScreen(
                onBackPressed = {
                    navHostController.popBackStack()
                },
                cat = Json.decodeFromString(it.arguments?.
getString("cat") ?: "")
            )
        }
        composable(Screens.FavoritePetsScreen.route) {
            FavoritePetsScreen()
        }
    }
}
```

Let's highlight the changes:

- Our `AppNavigation()` composable now takes in a `contentType` parameter of type `ContentType`. This is the parameter we will use to change the content type depending on the screen size. We also pass in a `navHostController` parameter of type `NavHostController`. This is the parameter we will use to navigate to different screens in our app. Previously, `navHostController` was created inside the `AppNavigation()` composable. We have moved it to the call site so that we can be able to use the same `navHostController` in different composables.

- We have used the new `PetsScreen()` composable, which takes in the `contentType` parameter. Same as before, we still pass `onPetClicked`, which navigates to `PetDetailsScreen`. Previously, we were using the `PetList` composable.

- Lastly, we have added our new `FavoritePetsScreen` destination to the `NavHost` composable.

10. Let us see what the new update `PetsScreen` composable looks like. Let us head over to the `PetsScreen.kt` file and modify the composable as follows:

```
@Composable
fun PetsScreen(
    onPetClicked: (Cat) -> Unit,
    contentType: ContentType,
) {
    val petsViewModel: PetsViewModel = koinViewModel()
    val petsUIState by petsViewModel.petsUIState.
collectAsStateWithLifecycle()
    PetsScreenContent(
        modifier = Modifier
            .fillMaxSize(),
        onPetClicked = onPetClicked,
        contentType = contentType,
        petsUIState = petsUIState
    )
}
```

We have added a new `contentType` parameter to the composable. We have also added a new `petsUIState` parameter. This is the UI state of `PetsScreen`. We will use this state to display the list of cats.

11. Next, create a new file called `PetsScreenContent.kt` and add the following code:

```
@Composable
fun PetsScreenContent(
    modifier: Modifier,
    onPetClicked: (Cat) -> Unit,
    contentType: ContentType,
    petsUIState: PetsUIState
) {
    Column(
        modifier = modifier
            .padding(16.dp),
        verticalArrangement = Arrangement.Center,
        horizontalAlignment = Alignment.CenterHorizontally
    ) {
        AnimatedVisibility(
```

```
                    visible = petsUIState.isLoading
            ) {
                CircularProgressIndicator()
            }

            AnimatedVisibility(
                visible = petsUIState.pets.isNotEmpty()
            ) {
                if (contentType == ContentType.List) {
                    PetList(
                        onPetClicked = onPetClicked,
                        pets = petsUIState.pets,
                        modifier = Modifier
                            .fillMaxWidth()
                    )
                } else {
                    PetListAndDetails(
                        pets = petsUIState.pets
                    )
                }

            }
            AnimatedVisibility(
                visible = petsUIState.error != null
            ) {
                Text(text = petsUIState.error ?: "")
            }
        }
    }
```

Let's explain the preceding code:

- `PetsScreenContent` has a parent `Column` composable. Inside the `Column` composable, we have added three `AnimatedVisibility` composables. The first one is used to display `CircularProgressIndicator` when `petsUIState` is loading. The second one is used to display the list of cats when the `pets` variable from `petsUIState` is not empty. The third one is used to display an error message when `petsUIState` has an error.

- When displaying the list of cats, we check `contentType`. If `contentType` is `List`, we display the `PetList` composable. If `contentType` is `ListAndDetail`, we display the `PetListAndDetails` composable. We will create the `PetListAndDetails` composable shortly. Note the `PetList` composable is also modified to take in the `pets` parameter. We will use this parameter to display the list of cats. We will see the changes shortly.

- Lastly, we show the error message if `petsUIState` has an error.

Our updated `PetList` composable should look like this:

```
@Composable
fun PetList(
    onPetClicked: (Cat) -> Unit,
    pets: List<Cat>,
    modifier: Modifier
) {
    LazyColumn(
        modifier = modifier
    ) {
        items(pets) { pet ->
            PetListItem(
                cat = pet,
                onPetClicked = onPetClicked
            )
        }
    }
}
```

No major changes here: we have just added the `pets` parameter. We use this parameter to display the list of cats in our `LazyColumn`. With this update, it is time to create the `PetListAndDetails` composable.

12. Let us create a new file called `PetListAndDetails.kt` inside the view package and add the following code:

```
@Composable
fun PetListAndDetails(pets: List<Cat>) {
    var currentPet by remember {
        mutableStateOf(pets.first())
    }
    Row(
        modifier = Modifier
            .fillMaxWidth(),
        horizontalArrangement = Arrangement.SpaceEvenly
    ) {
        PetList(
            onPetClicked = {
                currentPet = it
            },
            pets = pets,
            modifier = Modifier
                .fillMaxWidth()
                .weight(1f)
        )
```

```
            PetDetailsScreenContent(
                modifier = Modifier
                    .fillMaxWidth()
                    .padding(16.dp)
                    .weight(1f),
                cat = currentPet
            )
        }
    }
```

This composable has a Row, which has two items each with a weight of 1f. We have used the updated PetListComposable and PetDetailsScreenContent that we created earlier. We have also added a currentPet variable, which holds the currently selected cat. We use this variable to display the details of the selected cat. We also use this variable to update currentPet when we click on a pet item in the list. Make sure you also update PetDetailsScreenContent to take in the new modifier parameter.

With the modifications we have made, let us now create a new composable called AppNavigationContent, which has logic for displaying NavigationRail or BottomNavigation depending on NavigationType.

13. Let us create a new file called AppNavigationContent.kt inside the navigation package and add the following code:

```
@Composable
fun AppNavigationContent(
    contentType: ContentType,
    navigationType: NavigationType,
    onFavoriteClicked: () -> Unit,
    onHomeClicked: () -> Unit,
    navHostController: NavHostController,
    onDrawerClicked: () -> Unit = {}
) {
    Row(
        modifier = Modifier
            .fillMaxSize(),
    ) {
        AnimatedVisibility(
            visible = navigationType == NavigationType.
NavigationRail
        ) {
            PetsNavigationRail(
                onFavoriteClicked = onFavoriteClicked,
                onHomeClicked = onHomeClicked,
                onDrawerClicked = onDrawerClicked
            )
        }
```

```
Scaffold(
    content = { paddingValues ->
        Column(
            modifier = Modifier
                .fillMaxSize()
                .padding(paddingValues)
        ) {
            AppNavigation(
                contentType = contentType,
                navHostController = navHostController
            )
        }
    },
    bottomBar = {
        AnimatedVisibility(
            visible = navigationType == NavigationType.
BottomNavigation
        ) {
            PetsBottomNavigationBar(
                onFavoriteClicked = onFavoriteClicked,
                onHomeClicked = onHomeClicked
            )
        }
    }
)
    }
}
```

Let's explain the preceding code:

- The AppNavigationContent composable takes a number of parameters. The contentType parameter is used to display the content type. The navigationType parameter is used to toggle the navigation options. onFavoriteClicked and onHomeClicked are callbacks that will be used to navigate to the different screens. navHostController is an object that manages navigation within the NavHost onDrawerClicked is used to close or open the drawer when the user interacts with it.

- We have Row as the root element. Inside Row, we have an AnimatedVisibility composable that displays the PetsNavigationRail composable when navigationType is NavigationType.NavigationRail. We have also added a Scaffold composable. We have used the AppNavigation composable as the content of Scaffold, passing in contentType and navHostController. We have also used the PetsBottomNavigationBar composable as the bottom bar of Scaffold. We have used the AnimatedVisibility composable to display the PetsBottomNavigationBar composable when navigationType is NavigationType.BottomNavigation.

14. The last step is to refactor the `MainActivity.kt` file to use the new `AppNavigationContent` composable. We will walk through the changes step by step. There are several changes:

I.   To begin with, we need to observe the device's foldable state. This will enable us to change the content type and navigation type. Let us create a new file called `DeviceFoldPosture.kt` inside the `navigation` package and add the following code:

```
sealed interface DeviceFoldPosture {
    data class BookPosture(val hingePosition: Rect) :
DeviceFoldPosture
    data class SeparatingPosture(
        val hingePosition: Rect,
        val orientation: FoldingFeature.Orientation
    ) : DeviceFoldPosture

    object NormalPosture : DeviceFoldPosture
}


@OptIn(ExperimentalContracts::class)
fun isBookPosture(foldFeature: FoldingFeature?): Boolean {
    contract { returns(true) implies (foldFeature != null) }
    return foldFeature?.state == FoldingFeature.State.HALF_
OPENED &&
            foldFeature.orientation == FoldingFeature.
Orientation.VERTICAL
}


@OptIn(ExperimentalContracts::class)
fun isSeparating(foldFeature: FoldingFeature?): Boolean {
    contract { returns(true) implies (foldFeature != null) }
    return foldFeature?.state == FoldingFeature.State.FLAT &&
foldFeature.isSeparating
}
```

In the preceding code, we have a sealed interface that represents the different postures a foldable device can be in. We have `BookPosture`, which represents the posture when the device is in portrait orientation and its fold state is half opened. We have `SeparatingPosture`, which represents the posture when the fold or hinge device creates two logical display areas. We also have `NormalPosture`, which represents the posture when the device is not folded. We have two utility functions, `isBookPosture()` and `isSeparating()`, which are used to check the posture of the device. We will use these functions to check the posture of the device and change the layout of the app depending on the posture.

II.   Let us head over to the `MainActivity.kt` file and add the following code before the `setContent` block:

```
val deviceFoldingPostureFlow = WindowInfoTracker.
getOrCreate(this).windowLayoutInfo(this)
    .flowWithLifecycle(this.lifecycle)
    .map { layoutInfo ->
        val foldingFeature =
            layoutInfo.displayFeatures
                .filterIsInstance<FoldingFeature>()
                .firstOrNull()
        when {
            isBookPosture(foldingFeature) ->
                DeviceFoldPosture.BookPosture(foldingFeature.
bounds)
            isSeparating(foldingFeature) ->
                DeviceFoldPosture.SeparatingPosture(
                    foldingFeature.bounds,
                    foldingFeature.orientation
                )
            else -> DeviceFoldPosture.NormalPosture
        }
    }
    .stateIn(
        scope = lifecycleScope,
        started = SharingStarted.Eagerly,
        initialValue = DeviceFoldPosture.NormalPosture
    )
```

Here, we use `WindowInfoTracker` to get the window layout info. We use `flowWithLifecycle()` to make sure we only get the layout info when the activity is in the correct life cycle state. We then use the map operator to map the layout info to the different postures. We use the `stateIn()` operator, which converts a cold `Flow` into a hot `StateFlow` that is started in the given coroutine scope, sharing the most recently emitted value of device posture. We use `SharingStarted.Eagerly` to make sure we get the latest value of the posture when the activity is in the started state. We use the `initialValue` parameter to set the initial value of the posture to `DeviceFoldPosture.NormalPosture`. We will use this flow to observe the device's posture and change the app's layout depending on the posture.

III.   Next, inside our `setcontent` block, we need to add the variables before the theme block:

```
val devicePosture = deviceFoldingPostureFlow.
collectAsStateWithLifecycle().value
val windowSizeClass = calculateWindowSizeClass(activity = this)
val scope = rememberCoroutineScope()
val drawerState = rememberDrawerState(initialValue =
```

```
DrawerValue.Closed)
val navController = rememberNavController()
```

We have added the `devicePosture` variable, which holds the posture of the device. We have also added the `windowSizeClass` variable, which holds the window size class of the device; the `scope` variable, which holds `CoroutineScope`; the `drawerState` variable, which holds the state of the drawer; and the `navController` variable, which holds `NavHostController`. We will use this variable to navigate to different screens in our app.

IV.   Inside our `ChapterSevenTheme`, we need to add the following code:

```
val navigationType: NavigationType
val contentType: ContentType
when (windowSizeClass.widthSizeClass) {
    WindowWidthSizeClass.Compact -> {
        navigationType = NavigationType.BottomNavigation
        contentType = ContentType.List
    }
    WindowWidthSizeClass.Medium -> {
        navigationType = NavigationType.NavigationRail
        contentType = if (devicePosture is DeviceFoldPosture.
BookPosture
            || devicePosture is DeviceFoldPosture.
SeparatingPosture
        ) {
            ContentType.ListAndDetail
        } else {
            ContentType.List
        }
    }
    WindowWidthSizeClass.Expanded -> {
        navigationType = if (devicePosture is DeviceFoldPosture.
BookPosture) {
            NavigationType.NavigationRail
        } else {
            NavigationType.NavigationDrawer
        }
        contentType = ContentType.ListAndDetail
    }
    else -> {
        navigationType = NavigationType.BottomNavigation
        contentType = ContentType.List
    }
}
```

Here, we have two variables: `navigationType` and `contentType`. We use `windowSizeClass` to get the width of our device and, depending on the width size, we assign the values for our `navigationType` and `contentType` variables:

- If the width size is `Compact`, we use `BottomNavigation` for `navigationType` and `List` for `contentType`.

- If the width size is `Medium`, we use `NavigationRail` for `navigationType`. For `contentType`, we check `devicePosture`. If `devicePosture` is `DeviceFoldPosture.BookPosture` or `DeviceFoldPosture.SeparatingPosture`, we use `ListAndDetail` for `contentType`. If `devicePosture` is not `DeviceFoldPosture.BookPosture` or `DeviceFoldPosture.SeparatingPosture`, we use `List` for `contentType`.

- If the width size is `Expanded`, we check `devicePosture`. If `devicePosture` is `DeviceFoldPosture.BookPosture`, we use `NavigationRail` for `navigationType`. If `devicePosture` is not `DeviceFoldPosture.BookPosture`, we use `NavigationDrawer` for `navigationType`. We use `ListAndDetail` for `contentType`.

- Lastly, if the width size is anything else, we use `BottomNavigation` for `navigationType` and `List` for `contentType`.

V. Below the preceding code, add this `if` statement:

```
if (navigationType == NavigationType.NavigationDrawer) {
    PermanentNavigationDrawer(
        drawerContent = {
            PermanentDrawerSheet {
                PetsNavigationDrawer(
                    onFavoriteClicked = {
                        navController.navigate(Screens.
FavoritePetsScreen.route)
                    },
                    onHomeClicked = {
                        navController.navigate(Screens.
PetsScreen.route)
                    }
                )
            }
        }
    ) {
        AppNavigationContent(
            navigationType = navigationType,
            contentType = contentType,
            onFavoriteClicked = {
```

```
            navController.navigate(Screens.
FavoritePetsScreen.route)
            },
            onHomeClicked = {
                navController.navigate(Screens.PetsScreen.route)
            },
            navHostController = navController
        )
    }
}
```

The condition checks whether `navigationType` is `NavigationType.NavigationDrawer`. If it is, we use the `PermanentNavigationDrawer` composable from the Material 3 library. We use the `PetsNavigationDrawer` composable that we created for `drawerContent`. We use the `AppNavigationContent` composable as the content of `PermanentNavigationDrawer`. We pass in the `navigationType`, `contentType`, `onFavoriteClicked`, `onHomeClicked`, and `navHostController` parameters.

VI.   Next, let us add the `else` condition for our `if` statement:

```
else {
  ModalNavigationDrawer(
      drawerContent = {
          ModalDrawerSheet {
              PetsNavigationDrawer(
                  onFavoriteClicked = {
                      navController.navigate(Screens.
FavoritePetsScreen.route)
                  },
                  onHomeClicked = {
                      navController.navigate(Screens.PetsScreen.
route)
                  },
                  onDrawerClicked = {
                      scope.launch {
                          drawerState.close()
                      }
                  }
              )
          }
      },
```

```
                drawerState = drawerState
        ) {
            AppNavigationContent(
                navigationType = navigationType,
                contentType = contentType,
                onFavoriteClicked = {
                    navController.navigate(Screens.FavoritePetsScreen.
    route)
                },
                onHomeClicked = {
                    navController.navigate(Screens.PetsScreen.route)
                },
                navHostController = navController,
                onDrawerClicked = {
                    scope.launch {
                        drawerState.open()
                    }
                }
            )
        }
    }
```

Here, when `navigationType` is not `NavigationType.NavigationDrawer`, we use the `ModalNavigationDrawer` composable from the Material 3 library. We use the `PetsNavigationDrawer` composable for `drawerContent`. We use the `AppNavigationContent` composable as the content of `ModalNavigationDrawer`. We pass in the `navigationType`, `contentType`, `onFavoriteClicked`, `onHomeClicked`, and `navHostController` parameters. We also pass in the `drawerState` parameter. We use the `onDrawerClicked` callback to open or close the drawer when the user interacts with it.

Those were a lot of changes; great work on adding them! We now need to run these changes and see them into action. Luckily, we have a **resizable emulator** to help test these changes. We will be creating one and testing the app in the next subsection.

Creating and using the resizable emulator

To create and use the resizable emulator, follow these steps:

1. Open the **Device Manager** window from the right sidebar in Android Studio. If you cannot find it there, use the **View** menu option at the top and select **Tool Windows**; then, you will see the **Device Manager** option.

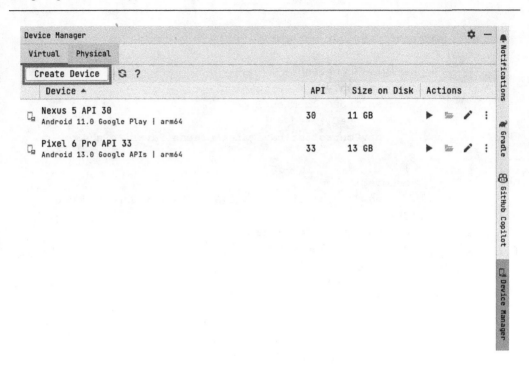

Figure 7.5 – Device Manager

2. Select the **Virtual** devices tab and click on **Create Device**, which brings you this pop-up window:

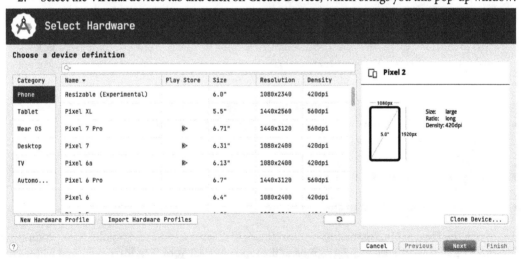

Figure 7.6 – New device configurations

The window enables you to customize the properties of the device you want to create. You can change the device category and you also select the device you want to create.

3. Let us select the **Resizable (Experimental)** option under the **Phone** category. This will enable us to create a resizable device. Click **Next** and you will see the following window:

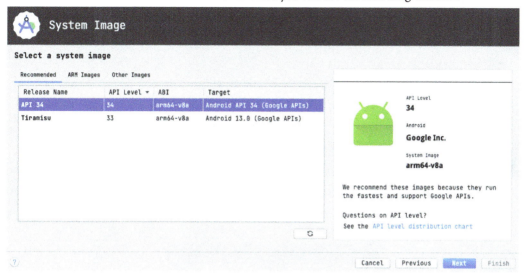

Figure 7.7 – System Image

4. Here, you select the system image you want to use. Let us select the **API 34** system image. Click **Next** and you will see the following window:

Figure 7.8 – Device information

This is the last step where you confirm the device name and the device orientation. We will maintain the name generated and use portrait as the default orientation.

5.   Click **Finish** and you will see the device has been added to your list of devices:

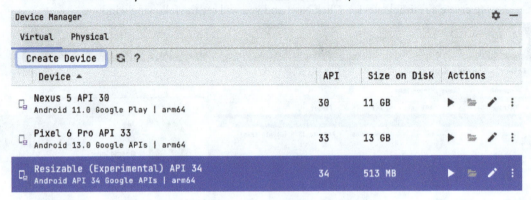

Figure 7.9 – Devices list

6.   Start the emulator and run the app.

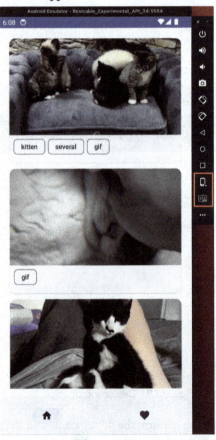

Figure 7.10 – Resizable emulator

From the emulator, we can see we have two options highlighted. The first one allows us to change the device from a small/normal device to a foldable or tablet device. The second one allows us to change the options when we change to a foldable device. Let us change the device to a foldable device. The app now changes the navigation option to navigation rail and the screen has a list and details of the first cat opened too.

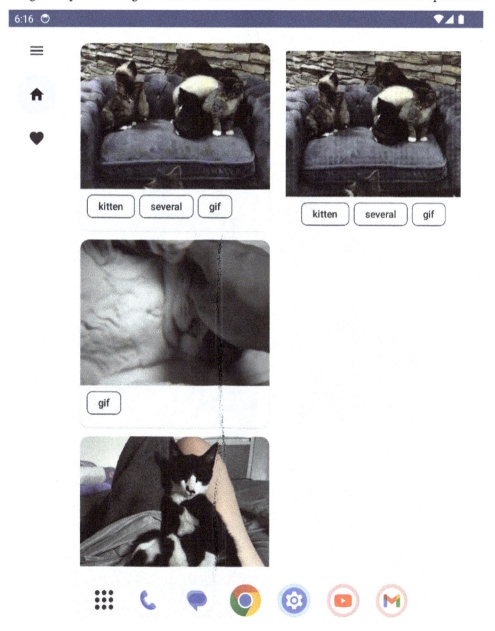

Figure 7.11 – Foldable device navigation rail

On tapping the **Foldable** options, we can see the following options:

Figure 7.12 – Foldable options

Selecting the second option in the foldables section brings us to the following screen:

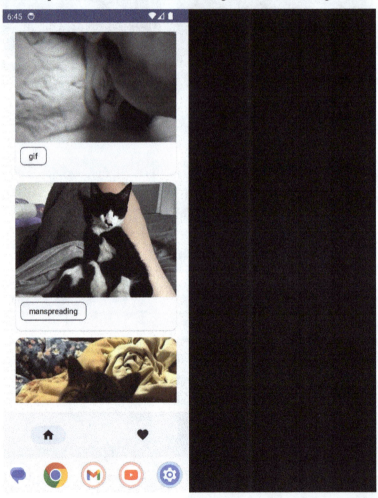

Figure 7.13 – Foldable device

From the device size option, we can also switch to tablet view:

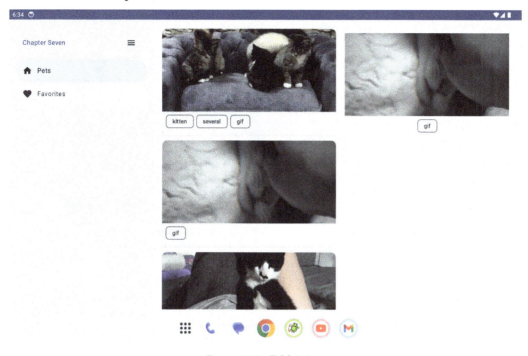

Figure 7.14 – Tablet view

You can see the app now has a permanent navigation drawer and the screen has a list and details of the first cat opened too. Tap a different cat and you will see the details of the cat displayed on the right side of the screen. We can also navigate to the **Favorites** screen and back to the **Pets** screen.

Figure 7.15 – Favorite Pets screen

We can also see the modal navigation drawer:

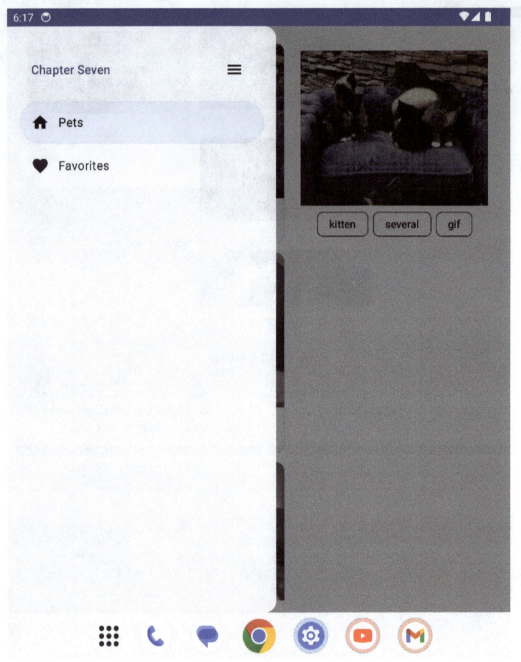

Figure 7.16 – Modal navigation drawer

The resizable emulator is a great way for us to test our app across different device sizes, but it has its own limitations. The following are the limitations of resizable emulators:

- **Hinge simulation**: While resizable emulators offer multi-window support and simulate various orientations, they might not accurately replicate the behavior of a physical hinge on foldable devices. The hinge's physical characteristics and behavior may affect app layouts and interactions differently.

- **Hardware specifics**: Emulators lack physical hardware components present in foldable devices, such as the actual hinge mechanism, flexible displays, sensors, and proprietary features, impacting the true emulation of foldable device behavior.

- **Performance variation**: Emulators may not accurately represent the performance capabilities of real foldable devices, especially in terms of hardware-specific optimizations and performance characteristics.

- **Real-world testing environment**: Foldable devices may have unique environmental factors that impact user experience, such as external lighting conditions affecting the flexible display. Emulators may not replicate these real-world scenarios accurately.

- **Software emulation versus hardware interaction**: Certain foldable device behaviors, such as drag-and-drop interactions across screens or unique gestures, might not be fully emulated in software due to hardware-specific interactions.

We have learned how to handle navigation in foldable devices and large screens and how to provide a great user experience as the user is switching between the different screen sizes. This ensures that our app is responsive to different devices and that we satisfactorily use the available screen sizes. The team at Google has published stories of companies that support large screens and foldables; you can have a look here: `https://developer.android.com/large-screens/stories`.

Summary

In this chapter, we have learned how to use the Jetpack Compose Navigation library to navigate to different Jetpack Compose screens within our app. We have also learned tips and best practices for using this library. Additionally, we have covered how to pass arguments as we navigate to screens. Lastly, we have built on what we learned in *Chapter 4*, by handling navigation in large screens and foldables in detail.

We have created `FavoritePetsScreen`, but as of now it only has a `Text` label. In the next chapter, we will be adding functionality to persist data locally and retrieve that data locally too without any internet access. We will learn how to save our cute cat photos to Room, another Jetpack library for offline storage, and also add pets to our favorites list.

8

Persisting Data Locally and Doing Background Work

To provide better user experiences, we must ensure that apps don't fetch data every time the user opens the app. At times, the user can be in areas that do not have internet access, and this can be very frustrating when the user can't use your app in such situations. For such scenarios, we have to store data locally. We also have to store and update the data in an efficient way that doesn't drain the device's battery or block the user from doing other things on the app. In this chapter, we will be exploring how to do so for our apps.

In this chapter, we will learn how to save data to a local database, **Room**, which is part of the Jetpack libraries. We will be able to save items and read from the Room database. Additionally, we will learn how to do long-running operations using **WorkManager** and some of the best practices.

In this chapter, we're going to cover the following main topics:

- Saving and reading data from a local database
- Handling updates and migrations in the Room database
- Using WorkManager to schedule background tasks
- Testing your workers

Technical requirements

To follow the instructions in this chapter, you will need to have Android Studio Hedgehog or later (`https://developer.android.com/studio`) downloaded.

You can use the previous chapter's code to follow the instructions in this chapter. You can find the code for this chapter at `https://github.com/PacktPublishing/Mastering-Kotlin-for-Android/tree/main/chaptereight`.

Saving and reading data from a local database

We are going to build up on the Pets app, which displays a list of cute cats. We will save our cute cats in a local database, Room, which is a part of the Android Jetpack libraries and provides a wrapper and abstraction layer over SQLite. We will also use the **repository pattern** to abstract away the data source from `ViewModel`. The Room database provides an abstraction layer over SQLite to allow fluent database access while harnessing the full power of SQLite. It also has inbuilt support for Kotlin coroutines and flows to allow for asynchronous database access. Room is also compile-time safe and hence any errors in SQL queries are caught at compile time. It allows us to do all this with concise code.

To use Room in our project, we need to add its dependency to our `libs.versions.toml` file. Let us start by defining the Room version in the `versions` section as the following:

```
room = "2.5.2"
```

Next, let us add the dependencies in our `libraries` section:

```
room-runtime = { module = "androidx.room:room-runtime" , version.ref = "room" }
room-compiler = { module = "androidx.room:room-compiler", version.ref = "room" }
room-ktx = { module = "androidx.room:room-ktx", version.ref = "room" }
```

Sync the project for the changes to be added. Before we add these dependencies to the app level `build.gradle.kts` file, we need to set up an annotation processor for the room compiler. Room uses the **annotation processor** to generate the code that will be used to read, write, update, and delete data from the database. To do this, we need to add the following to the plugins section of the project level `build.gradle.kts` file:

```
id("com.google.devtools.ksp") version "1.9.0-1.0.13" apply false
```

We have added the **Kotlin Symbol Processing (KSP)** plugin to our project. This is a new annotation processing tool that is faster than the **Kotlin Annotation Processing Tool (KAPT)**. KSP analyses the Kotlin code directly and has a better understanding of the Kotlin language constructs. KSP is now the recommended annotation processing tool for Kotlin. Next, we need to add KSP to our app level `build.gradle.kts` file:

```
id("com.google.devtools.ksp")
```

This allows us to use KSP in our app module. To finalize setting up Room, now let us add the dependencies we declared earlier to the app level `build.gradle.kts` file:

```
implementation(libs.room.runtime)
implementation(libs.room.ktx)
ksp(libs.room.compiler)
```

We have added our Room dependencies and the Room KTX library with the `implementation` configuration and the Room compiler with the `ksp` configuration. We are now ready to start using Room in our project. Let us start by creating an entity class for our `Cat` object. This will be the data class that will be used to store our pets in the database. Inside the `data` package, create a new file called `CatEntity.kt` and add the following code:

```
@Entity(tableName = "Cat")
data class CatEntity(
    @PrimaryKey
    val id: String,
    val owner: String,
    val tags: List<String>,
    val createdAt: String,
    val updatedAt: String
)
```

This data class represents the Room table for our cats. The `@Entity` annotation is used to define the table for our cats. We have passed the `tableName` value to specify the name of our table. The `@PrimaryKey` annotation is used to define the **primary key** for our table. The other properties are the columns in our table. One thing to keep in mind is that Room needs type converters to save fields such as `tags`, which is a list of strings. Room provides functionality to save non-primitive types using the `@TypeConverter` annotation. Let us create a new file named `PetsTypeConverters.kt` and add the following code:

```
class PetsTypeConverters {
    @TypeConverter
    fun convertTagsToString(tags: List<String>): String {
        return Json.encodeToString(tags)
    }

    @TypeConverter
    fun convertStringToTags(tags: String): List<String> {
        return Json.decodeFromString(tags)
    }
}
```

This class has two functions annotated with the `@TypeConverter` annotation. The first function converts a list of strings to a string. The second function converts a string to a list of strings. We have used the Kotlinx serialization library to convert the list of strings to a string and vice versa. This class will be referenced in our database class that we will create shortly.

We are now ready to create our database. We need to create a **Data Access Object (DAO)** to access our database. A DAO is an interface that defines the methods to create, read, update, and delete values from our database. Inside the data package, create a new file called CatDao.kt and add the following code:

```
@Dao
interface CatDao {
    @Insert(onConflict = OnConflictStrategy.REPLACE)
    suspend fun insert(catEntity: CatEntity)

    @Query("SELECT * FROM Cat")
    fun getCats(): Flow<List<CatEntity>>
}
```

The interface is annotated with the @Dao annotation to tell Room that we will use this class as our DAO. We have defined two functions in our DAO. The insert function is used to insert a cat into our database. Notice that this is a suspend function. This is because we will be using coroutines to insert the cats into our database. Inserting items into the database needs to happen on a background thread since it is a resource-intensive operation. We also use the @Insert annotation with the onConflict parameter set to OnConflictStrategy.REPLACE. This tells Room to replace the cat if it already exists in the database. The getCats function is used to get all the cats from our database. It has the @Query annotation, which is used to define a query to get the cats from our database. We are using Flow to return the cats from our database. Flow is a stream of data that can be observed. This means that every time we update the database, the changes will be emitted to the view layers immediately without us doing any extra work. Cool, right?

We now need to create our database class. Inside the data package, create a new file called CatDatabase.kt and add the following code:

```
@Database(
    entities = [CatEntity::class],
    version = 1
)
@TypeConverters(PetsTypeConverters::class)
abstract class CatDatabase: RoomDatabase() {
    abstract fun catDao(): CatDao
}
```

We have defined an abstract class that extends the `RoomDatabase` class. We passed the `entities` parameter to specify the entities or tables stored in our database. We have also passed the `version` parameter to specify the version of our database. We have used the `@TypeConverters` annotation to specify the type converters that we will be using in our database. We have also defined an abstract method that returns our `CatDao`. We need to provide an instance of the database to classes that need it. We will do this by using the dependency injection pattern we have been using in our project. Let us head over to the `di` package and in the `Module.kt` file, add the Room dependency just below the Retrofit dependency:

```
single {
    Room.databaseBuilder(
        androidContext(),
        CatDatabase::class.java,
        "cat-database"
    ).build()
}
single { get<CatDatabase>().carDao() }
```

First, we have created a single instance of our database. We have used the `databaseBuilder` method to create our database. We have passed the `androidContext()` method from Koin to get the context of our application. We have also passed `CatDatabase::class.java` to specify the class of our database. We have also passed the `name` of our database. We have then created a single instance of our `CatDao`. We are using the `get` method to get the instance of our database and then calling the `catDao` function to get our `CatDao`.

Our database is now ready to be used in our repository. We are going to modify `PetRepository` and its implementation to be able to do the following:

- Save items to our database

- Read items from our database

- Change our `getPets()` function to return a `Flow` of pets

The modified `PetRepository.kt` file should look like the following:

```
interface PetsRepository {
    suspend fun getPets(): Flow<List<Cat>>
    suspend fun fetchRemotePets()
}
```

We have modified the getPets function to return a Flow of pets. Room does not allow database access on the main thread, therefore, our queries have to be asynchronous. Room provides support for observable queries that read data from our database every time data in our database changes and emits new values to reflect the changes. This is the reason we return a Flow instance type from the getPets function. We have also added the fetchRemotePets function to fetch the pets from the remote data source. Let us now modify PetRepositoryImpl.kt with a few changes:

```kotlin
class PetsRepositoryImpl(
    private  val catsAPI: CatsAPI,
    private val dispatcher: CoroutineDispatcher,
    private val catDao: CatDao
): PetsRepository {
    override suspend fun getPets(): Flow<List<Cat>> {
        return withContext(dispatcher) {
            catDao.getCats()
                .map { petsCached ->
                    petsCached.map { catEntity ->
                        Cat(
                            id = catEntity.id,
                            owner = catEntity.owner,
                            tags = catEntity.tags,
                            createdAt = catEntity.createdAt,
                            updatedAt = catEntity.updatedAt
                        ) }
                }
                .onEach {
                    if (it.isEmpty()) {
                        fetchRemotePets()
                    }
                }
        }
    }

    override suspend fun fetchRemotePets() {
        withContext(dispatcher) {
            val response = catsAPI.fetchCats("cute")
            if (response.isSuccessful) {
                response.body()!!.map {
                    catDao.insert(CatEntity(
                        id = it.id,
                        owner = it.owner,
                        tags = it.tags,
                        createdAt = it.createdAt,
                        updatedAt = it.updatedAt
```

```
                    ))
                }
            }
        }
    }
}
```

We have made the following changes:

- We have added the `catDao` property to the constructor of the class.

- We have modified the `getPets` function to return a `Flow` of pets. Additionally, we have added a `map` operator to map `CatEntity` to a `Cat` object. We have also added an `onEach` operator to check if the list of pets is empty. If it is empty, we call the `fetchRemotePets` function to fetch the pets from the remote data source. This provides an **offline first experience** to our users; that is, we first check if we have the data in our database and if we don't, we fetch it from the remote data source.

- Lastly, we have modified the `fetchRemotePets` function that fetches the pets from the remote data source. When the response is successful, we map the response to a `CatEntity` instance type and insert it into our database.

We need to update the `PetsRepository` dependency in our `Module.kt` file to add the `CatDao` dependency:

```
single<PetsRepository> { PetsRepositoryImpl(get(), get(), get()) }
```

In our `PetsRepositoryImpl` class, we have been able to read and fetch data from the Room database. Next, we are going to modify the `getPets()` function in `PetsViewModel` to accommodate these new changes. Head over to the `PetsViewModel.kt` file and modify the `getPets()` function to look like the following:

```
private fun getPets() {
    petsUIState.value = PetsUIState(isLoading = true)
    viewModelScope.launch {
        petsRepository.getPets().asResult().collect { result ->
            when (result ) {
                is NetworkResult.Success -> {
                    petsUIState.update {
                        it.copy(isLoading = false, pets = result.data)
                    }
                }
                is NetworkResult.Error -> {
                    petsUIState.update {
                        it.copy(isLoading = false, error = result.
error)
```

```
                        }
                    }
                }
            }
        }
    }
```

We have made a few minor changes. We have used the `asResult()` extension function to convert the `Flow` of pets to a `Flow` of `NetworkResult`. This is because we are now returning a `Flow` of pets from our repository. The rest of the code remains the same as before. We will get an error since we have not created the `asResult()` extension function. Let us create it in our `NetworkResult.kt` file:

```
fun <T> Flow<T>.asResult(): Flow<NetworkResult<T>> {
    return this
        .map<T, NetworkResult<T>> {
            NetworkResult.Success(it)
        }
        .catch { emit(NetworkResult.Error(it.message.toString())) }
}
```

This is an extension function on the `Flow` class. It maps a `Flow` of items to the `NetworkResult` class. We can now head back to our `PetsViewModel` class and add the extension function imports to resolve the error.

The last change we need to make is to provide the application context to our Koin instance in the `Application` class. Head over to the `ChapterEightApplication.kt` file and modify the `startKoin` block to the following:

```
startKoin {
    androidContext(applicationContext)
    modules(appModules)
}
```

We have provided the application context to our Koin instance. Now, we can run the app. You should see the list of cute cats.

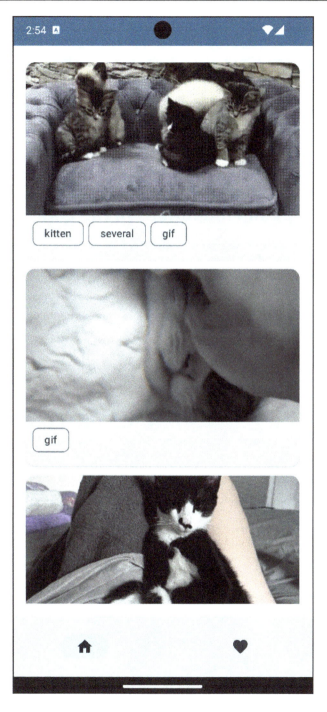

Figure 8.1 – Cute cats

The app still works as before, but now we are reading items from the Room database. If you turn off your data and Wi-Fi, the app still shows the list of cute cats! Amazing, isn't it? We have been able to make the app work offline. One of the benefits of having an architecture in place for our app is that we can change the different layers without necessarily affecting the other layers. We have been able to change the data source from the remote data source to the local data source without affecting the view layer. This is the power of having a good architecture in place.

We know how to insert and read data from our Room database, but what about updating it? In the next section, we will learn how to update the data that is in our Room database. In the process, we will also learn how to migrate from one database version to the other using the Room **automated migration** feature.

Handling updates and migrations in the Room database

`FavoritePetsScreen` doesn't have any functionality yet. We are going to add the functionality to favorite pets and update this information in the Room database. To achieve this, we need to do the following:

- Set up a Room schema directory.

- Add a new column to our `CatEntity` class to store the favorite status of the cat.

- Add a new function to `CatDao` to update the favorite status of the cat.

- Update our UIs with a favorite icon and, once clicked, update the favorite status of the cat. This means the ViewModel and repository classes will also be updated in the process.

Let's get started with the steps:

1. Let us start by setting up the schema directory. In our app level `build.gradle.kts` file, add the following code:

```
ksp {
    arg("room.schemaLocation", "$projectDir/schemas")
}
```

Do a Gradle sync and then build the project. This generates a `schema json` file with the name of the current database version as shown in the following figure:

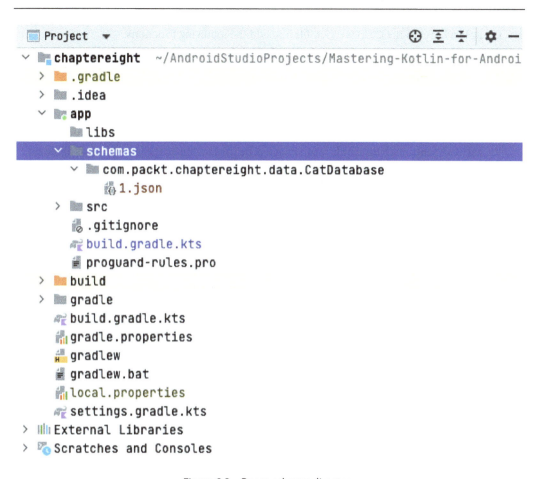

Figure 8.2 – Room schema directory

As shown in the preceding image, you have to switch to the **Project** view to see the schema directory. The contents of the file are the table name and the columns in our table. We are now ready to add a new column to our `CatEntity` interface to store the favorite status of the cat.

2. We will add this field to the `CatEntity` and the `Cat` data classes. Head over to the `CatEntity.kt` file and add a new field called `isFavorite`:

    ```
    @ColumnInfo(defaultValue = "0")
    val isFavorite: Boolean = false
    ```

This is a Boolean whose default value is `false`. We have used the `@ColumnInfo` annotation to specify the default value of the column in our database, too. We will use this field to store the favorite status of the cat. Ensure you add the `val isFavorite: Boolean = false` field to the `Cat` data class, too. We now need to update our `CatDao` class to be able to update the favorite status of the cat.

3. Let us head over to the `CatDao.kt` file and add the following functions:

```
@Update
suspend fun update(catEntity: CatEntity)

@Query("SELECT * FROM Cat WHERE isFavorite = 1")
fun getFavoriteCats(): Flow<List<CatEntity>>
```

We have two functions here. The first function will be used to update the favorite status of the cat. We have used the `@Update` annotation to tell Room that this function will be used to update the `CatEntity` class in our database. The second function will be used to get the favorite cats from our database. We have used the `@Query` annotation to define the query to get the favorite cats from our database. We have used `Flow` to return the favorite cats from our database. Now, we need to add a migration to our database to add the new column to our database. This ensures that we don't lose any data when we update our database. **Room version 2.4.0-alpha01** introduced a new way of handling migrations – automated migrations. This means that we don't have to write any SQL queries to handle migrations; Room will automatically handle the migrations for us.

4. Let us modify `CatDatabase` to add `autoMigration` as follows:

```
@Database(
    entities = [CatEntity::class],
    version = 2,
    autoMigrations = [
        AutoMigration(from = 1, to = 2)
    ]
)
```

We have added the `autoMigrations` parameter to our database. We have passed a list of `AutoMigration` objects to the parameter. We have passed the `from` and `to` parameters to specify the version of our database. Ensure you add the imports for the `AutoMigration` class. Notice that we have also increased the `version` of our database. This is because we have added a new column to our database. Build the project to be able to generate the `schema` `json` file. You should see a new schema JSON file with the name of the new database version. Our schema directory should look like the following:

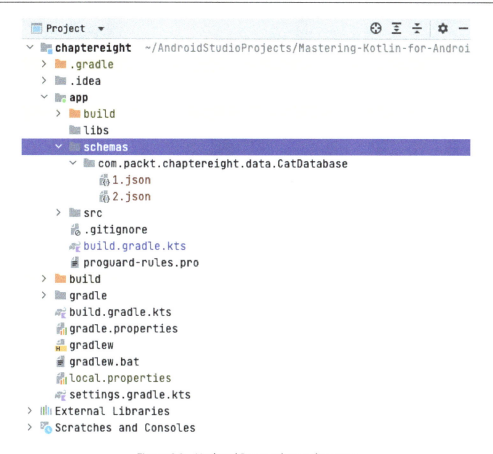

Figure 8.3 – Updated Room schema directory

If we open the 2.json file, we will notice that the new isFavorite column has been added to our table. That it's for automated migration. We are now ready to update our repository to be able to update the favorite status of the cat.

5. Let us head over to the PetsRepository.kt file and add the following functions:

    ```
    suspend fun updatePet(cat: Cat)
    suspend fun getFavoritePets(): Flow<List<Cat>>
    ```

The updatePet(cat: Cat) and getFavoritePets() functions will be used to update the favorite status of the cat and get favorite cats.

1. Let us add the implementation of the two functions in our PetsRepositoryImpl.kt class:

    ```
    override suspend fun updatePet(cat: Cat) {
        withContext(dispatcher) {
            catDao.update(CatEntity(
    ```

```
                    id = cat.id,
                    owner = cat.owner,
                    tags = cat.tags,
                    createdAt = cat.createdAt,
                    updatedAt = cat.updatedAt,
                    isFavorite = cat.isFavorite
            ))
        }
    }
    override suspend fun getFavoritePets(): Flow<List<Cat>> {
        return withContext(dispatcher) {
            catDao.getFavoriteCats()
                .map { petsCached ->
                    petsCached.map { catEntity ->
                        Cat(
                            id = catEntity.id,
                            owner = catEntity.owner,
                            tags = catEntity.tags,
                            createdAt = catEntity.createdAt,
                            updatedAt = catEntity.updatedAt,
                            isFavorite = catEntity.isFavorite
                        )
                    }
                }
        }
    }
```

Here is an explanation of the functions:

- In the updatePet function, we have used the update method of our CatDao interface to update the favorite status of the cat. We have also used withContext to ensure that the update runs on a background thread. We have created a new CatEntity class from the Cat object that we have passed to the function.

- In the getFavoritePets function, we have used the getFavoriteCats function from our CatDao interface to get the favorite cats from our database. We have also mapped the list of CatEntity to a list of Cat. We then returned a Flow instance type of favorite cats.

2. In the PetsRepositoryImpl.kt file, we need to update the fetchRemotePets and getPets functions to update the favorite status of the cat as follows:

```
override suspend fun getPets(): Flow<List<Cat>> {
    return withContext(dispatcher) {
        catDao.getCats()
            .map { petsCached ->
                petsCached.map { catEntity ->
```

```
                        Cat (
                            id = catEntity.id,
                            owner = catEntity.owner,
                            tags = catEntity.tags,
                            createdAt = catEntity.createdAt,
                            updatedAt = catEntity.updatedAt,
                            isFavorite = catEntity.isFavorite
                        )
                    }
                }
                .onEach {
                    if (it.isEmpty()) {
                        fetchRemotePets()
                    }
                }
            }
        }
        override suspend fun fetchRemotePets() {
            withContext(dispatcher) {
                val response = catsAPI.fetchCats("cute")
                if (response.isSuccessful) {
                    response.body()!!.map {
                        catDao.insert(CatEntity(
                            id = it.id,
                            owner = it.owner,
                            tags = it.tags,
                            createdAt = it.createdAt,
                            updatedAt = it.updatedAt,
                            isFavorite = it.isFavorite
                        ))
                    }
                }
            }
        }
    }
```

We add the `isFavorite` parameter to the `Cat` object when we are mapping the `CatEntity` class to a `Cat`. This will ensure that we have the favorite status of the cat when we are fetching the cats from the remote and local data sources.

3. Let us head over to the `PetsViewModel` class and add the following variables below the `petsUIState` variable:

```
private val _favoritePets =
MutableStateFlow<List<Cat>>(emptyList())
val favoritePets: StateFlow<List<Cat>> get() = _favoritePets
```

Here, we have created a private `MutableStateFlow` of favorite cats and a public `StateFlow` of favorite cats. We will use the `_favoritePets` variable to update the favorite cats and the `favoritePets` variable to observe the favorite cats. This pattern is normally recommended to prevent exposing mutable states to the view layer.

4. Next, let us add these two functions below the `getPets()` function in the `PetsViewModel`:

```
fun updatePet(cat: Cat) {
    viewModelScope.launch {
        petsRepository.updatePet(cat)
    }
}
fun getFavoritePets() {
    viewModelScope.launch {
        petsRepository.getFavoritePets().collect {
            _favoritePets.value = it
        }
    }
}
```

The `updatePet` function will be called from the UI to update the favorite status of the cat. The `getFavoritePets` function will be called from the UI to fetch the favorite cats from our database. We collect the favorite cats from our database and update the `_favoritePets` variable. With these changes, we are now ready to make changes to our views to be able to favorite a cat and see a list of favorite pets.

5. We will start by adding our favorite icon to the `PetListItem` composable. Let us head over to the `PetList.kt` file and update the `PetListItem` composable to be the following:

```
@OptIn(ExperimentalLayoutApi::class)
@Composable
fun PetListItem(
    cat: Cat,
    onPetClicked: (Cat) -> Unit,
    onFavoriteClicked: (Cat) -> Unit
) {
    ElevatedCard(
        modifier = Modifier
            .fillMaxWidth()
            .padding(6.dp)
    ) {
        Column(
            modifier = Modifier
                .fillMaxWidth()
                .padding(bottom = 10.dp)
                .clickable {
```

```
                            onPetClicked(cat)
                        }
            ) {
            AsyncImage(
                model = "https://cataas.com/cat/${cat.id}",
                contentDescription = "Cute cat",
                modifier = Modifier
                    .fillMaxWidth()
                    .height(200.dp),
                contentScale = ContentScale.FillWidth
            )

            Row(
                modifier = Modifier
                    .padding(start = 6.dp, end = 6.dp)
                    .fillMaxWidth(),
                verticalAlignment = Alignment.CenterVertically,
                horizontalArrangement = Arrangement.SpaceBetween
            ) {
                FlowRow(
                    modifier = Modifier
                        .padding(start = 6.dp, end = 6.dp)
                ) {
                    repeat(cat.tags.size) {
                        SuggestionChip(
                            modifier = Modifier
                                .padding(start = 3.dp, end =
3.dp),
                            onClick = { },
                            label = {
                                Text(text = cat.tags[it])
                            }
                        )
                    }
                }
                Icon(
                    modifier = Modifier
                        .clickable {
                            onFavoriteClicked(cat.
copy(isFavorite = !cat.isFavorite))
                        },
                    imageVector = if (cat.isFavorite) {
                        Icons.Default.Favorite
                    } else {
```

```
                              Icons.Default.FavoriteBorder
                  },
                  contentDescription = "Favorite",
                  tint = if (cat.isFavorite) {
                      Color.Red
                  } else {
                      Color.Gray
                  },
              )

          }
      }
  }
}
```

We have added the `Icon` composable to the `PetListItem` composable. We have used the `Icons.Default.Favorite` icon if the cat is favorited and the `Icons.Default.FavoriteBorder` icon if the cat is not favorited. We have also used the `tint` parameter to change the color of the icon depending on the favorite status of the cat. `Icon` is now inside a Row together with `FlowRow`, which displays a list of tags. We have also added the `onFavoriteClicked` parameter to the `PetListItem` composable. We have used this parameter to update the favorite status of the cat.

6.   Let us update the `PetList` composable to add a new callback parameter called `onFavoriteClicked` and pass the parameter to the `PetListItem` composable:

```
@Composable
fun PetList(
    onPetClicked: (Cat) -> Unit,
    pets: List<Cat>,
    modifier: Modifier,
    onFavoriteClicked: (Cat) -> Unit
) {
    LazyColumn(
        modifier = modifier
    ) {
        items(pets) { pet ->
            PetListItem(
                cat = pet,
                onPetClicked = onPetClicked,
                onFavoriteClicked = onFavoriteClicked
            )
        }
    }
}
```

7. Next, we will add the onFavoriteClicked callback as a parameter to the PetsScreen-Content:

```
@Composable
fun PetsScreenContent(
    modifier: Modifier,
    onPetClicked: (Cat) -> Unit,
    contentType: ContentType,
    petsUIState: PetsUIState,
    onFavoriteClicked: (Cat) -> Unit
) {
    // code
    }
```

8. We can now pass the parameter to the PetList composable:

```
PetList(
    onPetClicked = onPetClicked,
    pets = petsUIState.pets,
    modifier = Modifier
    .fillMaxWidth(),
    onFavoriteClicked = onFavoriteClicked
)
```

9. Let us update the PetAndDetails composable to add the onFavoriteClicked parameter:

```
@Composable
fun PetListAndDetails(
    pets: List<Cat>,
    onFavoriteClicked: (Cat) -> Unit
) {
    // code
    }
```

10. We can now pass the parameter to the PetList composable:

```
PetList(
    onPetClicked = {
    currentPet = it
    },
    pets = pets,
    modifier = Modifier
    .fillMaxWidth()
    .weight(1f),
    onFavoriteClicked = onFavoriteClicked
)
```

11. Back in the `PetsScreenContent.kt` file, we need to pass the `onFavoriteClicked` parameter to the `PetListAndDetails` composable:

```
PetListAndDetails(
    pets = petsUIState.pets,
    onFavoriteClicked = onFavoriteClicked
)
```

The final `PetScreenContent.kt` file with all the changes we have made so far should look like this:

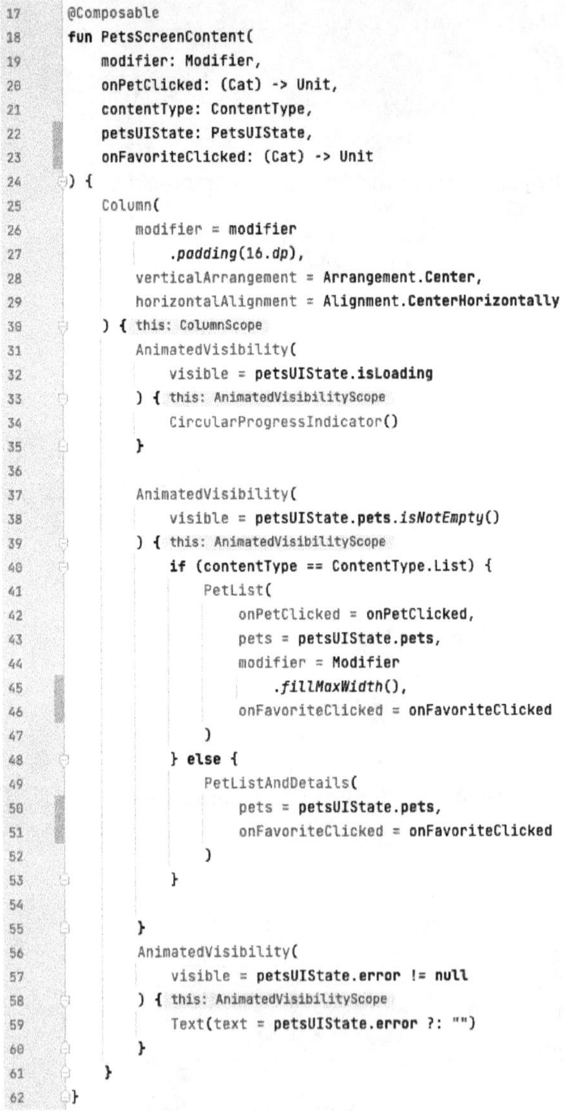

```
17   @Composable
18   fun PetsScreenContent(
19       modifier: Modifier,
20       onPetClicked: (Cat) -> Unit,
21       contentType: ContentType,
22       petsUIState: PetsUIState,
23       onFavoriteClicked: (Cat) -> Unit
24   ) {
25       Column(
26           modifier = modifier
27               .padding(16.dp),
28           verticalArrangement = Arrangement.Center,
29           horizontalAlignment = Alignment.CenterHorizontally
30       ) { this: ColumnScope
31           AnimatedVisibility(
32               visible = petsUIState.isLoading
33           ) { this: AnimatedVisibilityScope
34               CircularProgressIndicator()
35           }
36
37           AnimatedVisibility(
38               visible = petsUIState.pets.isNotEmpty()
39           ) { this: AnimatedVisibilityScope
40               if (contentType == ContentType.List) {
41                   PetList(
42                       onPetClicked = onPetClicked,
43                       pets = petsUIState.pets,
44                       modifier = Modifier
45                           .fillMaxWidth(),
46                       onFavoriteClicked = onFavoriteClicked
47                   )
48               } else {
49                   PetListAndDetails(
50                       pets = petsUIState.pets,
51                       onFavoriteClicked = onFavoriteClicked
52                   )
53               }
54
55           }
56           AnimatedVisibility(
57               visible = petsUIState.error != null
58           ) { this: AnimatedVisibilityScope
59               Text(text = petsUIState.error ?: "")
60           }
61       }
62   }
```

Figure 8.4 – Updated PetscreenContent

12. Next, in the `PetsScreen` composable, which is in the `PetsScreen.kt` file, we need to add the `onFavoriteClicked` parameter to the `PetsScreenContent` composable:

```
PetsScreenContent(
    modifier = Modifier
        .fillMaxSize(),
    onPetClicked = onPetClicked,
    contentType = contentType,
    petsUIState = petsUIState,
    onFavoriteClicked = {
        petsViewModel.updatePet(it)
    }
)
```

We have passed the `onFavoriteClicked` callback to the `PetsScreenContent` composable. We have called the `updatePet` method of our `PetsViewModel` class with the updated cat object. Let us run the app; it now has a new favorite icon. If we click on the icon, the icon changes to a filled heart icon with a red color:

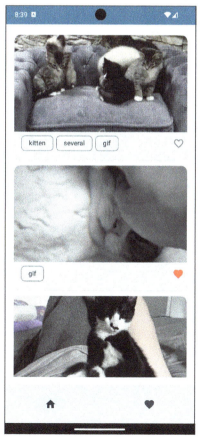

Figure 8.5 – Cute cats with favorite

13. Lastly, we are going to update `FavoritePetsScreen` to display a list of favorite cats. Let us head over to the `FavoritePetsScreen.kt` file and update the `FavoritePetsScreen` composable to be the following:

```
@Composable
fun FavoritePetsScreen(
    onPetClicked: (Cat) -> Unit
) {
    val petsViewModel: PetsViewModel = koinViewModel()
    LaunchedEffect(Unit) {
        petsViewModel.getFavoritePets()
    }
    val pets by petsViewModel.favoritePets.
collectAsStateWithLifecycle()

    if (pets.isEmpty()) {
        Column(
            modifier = Modifier
                .fillMaxSize(),
            verticalArrangement = Arrangement.Center,
            horizontalAlignment = Alignment.CenterHorizontally
        ) {
            Text(text = "No favorite pets")
        }
    } else {
        LazyColumn(
            modifier = Modifier
                .fillMaxSize()
        ) {
            items(pets) { pet ->
                PetListItem(
                    cat = pet,
                    onPetClicked = onPetClicked,
                    onFavoriteClicked = {
                        petsViewModel.updatePet(it)
                    }
                )
            }
        }
    }
}
```

Here is an explanation of the changes:

- We have added a new parameter, onPetClicked to the FavoritePetsScreen composable. We will use this parameter to navigate to the PetDetailsScreen composable.

- We have created a new instance of our PetsViewModel class using the koinViewModel() method.

- We have called the getFavoritePets function from our PetsViewModel class to get the favorite cats from our database. We used LaunchedEffect to call this method when the composable was first launched. This is to ensure that we do not call the function every time the composable recomposes.

- We have a new variable called pets, which is a StateFlow of favorite cats. We have used the collectAsStateWithLifecycle method to collect the favorite cats from our database. This method is lifecycle aware and hence it will only collect the favorite cats when the composable is active.

- We have added a check to see if the list of favorite cats is empty. If it is empty, we display a message to the user. If it is not empty, we display a list of favorite cats.

14. We need to update the AppNavigation.kt file to pass the onPetClicked callback to the FavoritePetsScreen composable:

```
FavoritePetsScreen(
    onPetClicked = { cat ->
        navHostController.navigate(
            "${Screens.PetDetailsScreen.route}/${Json.
encodeToString(cat)}"
        )
    }
)
```

This logic is like what we had in the PetsScreen and it handles navigation to PetDetailsScreen when we are in FavoritePetsScreen. Build and run the app. Tap the favorite icon on the bottom bar and you should see a list of your favorite cute cats. If you tap the favorite icon, the cat is immediately removed from the list of favorite cats. This is because the list of favorite cats is a Flow and every time Room updates the data, they are immediately emitted to the view layer.

Figure 8.6 – Favorite Pets Screen

We have been able to add the functionality to favorite cats and update this information in the Room database. We have also been able to handle updates and migrations in the Room database. In the next section, we will see how to use WorkManager to schedule background tasks. In this case, we will use WorkManager to fetch the cats from the remote data source and save them to our database. This improves our first offline experience since we will always have the latest data in our database.

Using WorkManager to schedule background tasks

WorkManager is a Jetpack library that is best suited for performing long-running tasks in the background. It ensures that background tasks are completed even when your app restarts or the phone restarts. With WorkManager, you can either schedule one-time jobs or recurring jobs.

We will start by adding the WorkManager dependency to our project. Follow these steps:

1. Let us head over to the `libs.versions.toml` file and define the work version in our `versions` section as follows:

    ```
    work = "2.8.1"
    ```

2. In the libraries section, add the following dependencies:

    ```
    work-runtime = { module = "androidx.work:work-runtime-ktx",
    version.ref = "work" }
    workmanager-koin = { module = "io.insert-koin:koin-androidx-
    workmanager", version.ref = "koin" }
    ```

    Here, we have two dependencies: the `work-runtime-ktx` dependency, which is the core dependency for WorkManager, and the `koin-androidx-workmanager` dependency, which is used to integrate WorkManager with Koin. Sync the project for the changes to be added.

3. Next, we need to add the dependencies to the app-level `build.gradle.kts` file:

    ```
    implementation(libs.work.runtime)
    implementation(libs.workmanager.koin)
    ```

4. Do a Gradle sync to add these dependencies to our project.

We are now ready to start using WorkManager in our project. We will use WorkManager to fetch the cats from the remote data source and save them to our database. We will use the `OneTimeWorkRequest` class to schedule a one-time job to fetch the cats from the remote data source and save them to our database. Let's get started with the steps:

1. Let us create a new package named `workers` and create a new file inside it called `PetsSyncWorker.kt` and add the following code:

    ```
    class PetsSyncWorker(
        appContext: Context,
        workerParams: WorkerParameters,
        private val  petsRepository: PetsRepository
    ): CoroutineWorker(appContext, workerParams) {

        override suspend fun doWork(): Result {
            return try {
                petsRepository.fetchRemotePets()
    ```

```
            Result.success()
        } catch (e: Exception) {
            Result.failure()
        }
    }
}
```

In the preceding code block, we have created a class that implements the `CoroutineWorker` class. We implement this class when we want to perform a long-running task in the background. It uses coroutines to perform long-running tasks. We have passed the `appContext` and `workerParams` parameters to the constructor of the class. We have also passed the `petsRepository` parameter to the constructor of the class. We have overridden the `doWork` method, which is a `suspend` function that will be called when the work is scheduled. We have called `fetchRemotePets` from `PetsRepository` to fetch the cats from the remote data source and save them to our database. We are also returning `Result.success()` if the work is successful and `Result.failure()` if the work fails.

2. Next, let us create an instance of `PetsSyncWorker` in our `Module.kt` file:

    ```
    worker { PetsSyncWorker(get(), get(), get()) }
    ```

    We are using the `worker` Koin DSL to create an instance of `PetsSyncWorker`. This is from the Koin WorkManager library that we just added. We have passed the `appContext`, `workerParams`, and `petsRepository` parameters to the constructor of `PetsSyncWorker`.

3. Next, let us add this function in our `MainActivity.kt` file:

    ```
    private fun startPetsSync() {
        val syncPetsWorkRequest =
    OneTimeWorkRequestBuilder<PetsSyncWorker>()
            .setConstraints(
                Constraints.Builder()
                    .setRequiredNetworkType(NetworkType.CONNECTED)
                    .setRequiresBatteryNotLow(true)
                    .build()
            )
            .build()
        WorkManager.getInstance(applicationContext).
    enqueueUniqueWork(
            "PetsSyncWorker",
            ExistingWorkPolicy.KEEP,
            syncPetsWorkRequest
        )
    }
    ```

In the preceding code, we created a new `OneTimeWorkRequest` using `PetSyncWorker`. We have also set some constraints on our work request. We have set the network type to `NetworkType.CONNECTED` to ensure that the work request is only executed when the device is connected to the internet. We also have other network types, which are as follows:

- NOT_REQUIRED: For this type, a network is not required. This is useful for tasks that do not need any internet connection to work.

- UNMETERED: An unmetered network connection such as Wi-Fi is required for this type of network. This is suitable for tasks that involve large data transfers.

- METERED: A metered network connection is required for this type of network. Tasks that require a significant amount of data might be deferred when the device is on a metered connection to avoid unnecessary costs.

- NOT_ROAMING: For this type of work, a non-roaming connection is required. This is relevant for tasks that might incur additional costs when executed when the device is roaming.

We have also set the `BatteryNotLow constraint` to `true` to ensure that the work request is only executed when the battery is not low. We then used `WorkManager.getInstance(applicationContext)` to get an instance of the WorkManager and then called the `enqueueUniqueWork` method to enqueue our work request. We have passed the name of our work request, `ExistingWorkPolicy`, and the work request to the `enqueueUniqueWork` method. `ExistingWorkPolicy` is used to specify what should happen if there is already a work request with the same name. We have used `ExistingWorkPolicy.KEEP` to ensure that the work request is not replaced if there is already a work request with the same name. The following are other available policies:

- REPLACE: This cancels existing work with the same unique name and enqueues the new work. This is suitable when we want only the latest version of the work to be executed, discarding previous instances.

- APPEND: Enqueues the new work even if there is existing work with the same unique name. Both new and existing work will be executed independently. This is appropriate when we want multiple instances of the same work to coexist.

We are now ready to start our work request. We will start the work request in the `onCreate` method of `MainActivity`.

4. In the `MainActivity.kt` file, add the following code in the `onCreate` method:

    ```
    startPetsSync()
    ```

    Since we are using Koin, we need to disable the default WorkManager initialization in our app manifest.

5. Let us head over to the `AndroidManifest.xml` file and add the following code inside the application tag:

    ```
    <provider
        android:name="androidx.startup.InitializationProvider"
        android:authorities="${applicationId}.androidx-startup"
        android:exported="false"
        tools:node="merge">
        <!-- Removing WorkManager Default Initializer-->
        <meta-data
            android:name="androidx.work.WorkManagerInitializer"
            android:value="androidx.startup"
            tools:node="remove" />
    </provider>
    ```

    Adding the preceding code prevents WorkManager from being initialized automatically. Not doing this causes an app to crash once you set up Koin initialization. The crash is caused by a conflict between Koin's dependency injection and WorkManager's default initialization. Lastly, we have also removed App Startup (https://developer.android.com/topic/libraries/app-startup), which is used internally within WorkManager from WorkManager 2.6.

6. To set up a custom WorkManager instance, head over to the `ChapterEightApplication.kt` file and add the following code inside the `startKoin` block:

    ```
    workManagerFactory()
    ```

7. Build and run the app, and nothing changes. However, we have scheduled a background task to fetch the cats from the remote data source and save them to our database.

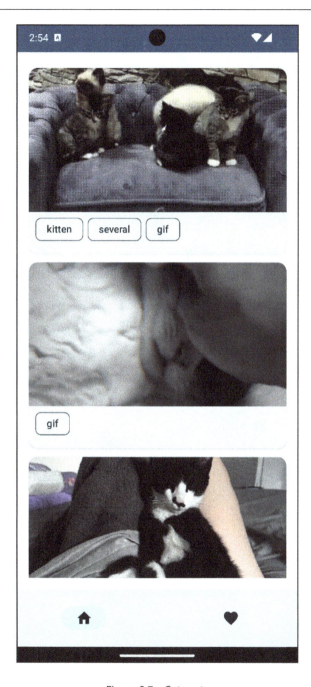

Figure 8.7 – Cute cats

We have created our `PetsSyncWorker` class and learned how to do work in the background. In the next section, we are going to write tests for our `PetsSyncWorker` class.

Testing your workers

Testing the code is very important. It ensures that our code works as expected and it also helps us to catch bugs early. We will be writing tests for our workers in this section. To test our workers, we first need to set up WorkManager testing dependencies with the following steps:

1. Let us head over to the `libs.versions.toml` file and add the following dependency to the `libraries` section:

    ```
    work-testing = { module = "androidx.work:work-testing", version.
    ref = "work" }
    ```

    Sync your project. This will add the `work-testing` artifact that helps in testing workers to our project.

2. Next, we need to add the dependency to our app level `build.gradle.kts` file:

    ```
    androidTestImplementation(libs.work.testing)
    ```

    We have used `androidTestImplementation` because we will be writing our tests in the `androidTest` folder. Do a Gradle sync to add the dependency to our project. We are now ready to start writing our tests.

Since our `PetsSyncWorker` class requires some dependencies, we will create a test rule that provides the Koin dependencies that we need. Let us head over to the `androidTest` folder, create a new file called `KoinTestRule.kt`, and add the following code:

```kotlin
class KoinTestRule: TestRule {
    override fun apply(base: Statement?, description: Description?):
Statement {
        return object : Statement() {
            override fun evaluate() {
                stopKoin()
                startKoin {
                    androidLogger(Level.ERROR)
                    androidContext(ApplicationProvider.
getApplicationContext())
                    modules(appModules)
                }
            }
        }
    }
}
```

KoinTestRule implements the TestRule interface. We have used this rule to provide the Koin dependencies that we need in our tests. We have used the startKoin method to provide the Koin dependencies that we need. We have used the androidContext(ApplicationProvider. getApplicationContext()) method to get the application context. We have also used the modules(appModules) method to provide the Koin modules that we need. Now, we are ready to start writing our tests. Let us create a new file called PetsSyncWorkerTest.kt and add the following code:

```
@RunWith(AndroidJUnit4::class)
class PetsSyncWorkerTest {

    @get:Rule
    val koinTestRule = KoinTestRule()

    @Before
    fun setUp() {
        val config = Configuration.Builder()
            .setMinimumLoggingLevel(Log.DEBUG)
            .setExecutor(SynchronousExecutor())
            .build()

        // Initialize WorkManager for instrumentation tests.
        WorkManagerTestInitHelper.initializeTestWorkManager(
            ApplicationProvider.getApplicationContext(),
            config
        )
    }
}
```

We have created a test class called PetsSyncWorkerTest. We have annotated the class with the @RunWith(AndroidJUnit4::class) annotation. We have also created a KoinTestRule instance and annotated it with the @get:Rule annotation to provide the KoinTestRule to our test class. We have also created a setup function and annotated it with the @Before annotation. This function will be executed before each test. We are using the WorkManagerTestInitHelper class to initialize WorkManager for instrumentation tests. We are using the SynchronousExecutor class to ensure that the work is executed synchronously. This is to ensure that our tests are deterministic. We are now ready to start writing our tests.

Follow these steps to create our test:

1. We will start by creating a test function that will test the functionality of our worker. Add the following code to the `PetsSyncWorkerTest.kt` file below the `setup` function:

    ```
    @Test
    fun testPetsSyncWorker() {


    }
    ```

    This is an empty function annotated with the `@Test` annotation.

2. Create a work request as follows:

    ```
    val syncPetsWorkRequest =
    OneTimeWorkRequestBuilder<PetsSyncWorker>()
        .setConstraints(
            Constraints.Builder()
                .setRequiredNetworkType(NetworkType.CONNECTED)
                .setRequiresBatteryNotLow(true)
                .build()
        )
        .build()
    ```

    In the preceding code, we have created a one-time request using our `PetsSyncWorker` class. We have also set the constraints to our work request. We have set the network type to `NetworkType.CONNECTED` to ensure that the work request is only executed when the device is connected to the internet. We have also set the `BatteryNotLow` constraint to `true` to ensure that the work request is only executed when the battery is not low.

3. Next, set up the test drivers:

    ```
    val workManager = WorkManager.getInstance(ApplicationProvider.
    getApplicationContext())
    val testDriver =
        WorkManagerTestInitHelper.getTestDriver(ApplicationProvider.
    getApplicationContext())!!
    ```

    Here, we have set up the test drivers that help us simulate conditions needed for our tests. For example, it simulates that constraints are met.

4. Enqueue the work request:

    ```
    workManager.enqueueUniqueWork(
        "PetsSyncWorker",
        ExistingWorkPolicy.KEEP,
        syncPetsWorkRequest).result.get()
    ```

We have used the `enqueueUniqueWork` method to enqueue our work request. We have passed the name of our work request, `ExistingWorkPolicy`, and the work request to the `enqueueUniqueWork` method. We have used `ExistingWorkPolicy.KEEP` to ensure that the work request is not replaced if there is already a work request with the same name. We have also used the `result.get()` method to get the result of our work request.

5. Get the information about our work request using the `WorkInfo` class:

```
val workInfo = workManager.getWorkInfoById(syncPetsWorkRequest.
id).get()
```

We are getting `WorkInfo` for our work request. We have used the `getWorkInfoById` method to get `WorkInfo` for our work request. We are using the `result.get()` method to get the result of our work request.

6. Next, let us get the worker state and assert that our work is enqueued:

```
assertEquals(WorkInfo.State.ENQUEUED, workInfo.state)
```

We have used the `assertEquals` method to assert that our work is enqueued. We have used the `WorkInfo.State.ENQUEUED` to check if our work is enqueued.

7. Next, let us simulate our constraints being met by using the `testDriver` instance that we created earlier:

```
testDriver.setAllConstraintsMet(syncPetsWorkRequest.id)
```

We use `testDriver` to simulate that the constraints are met. We have used the `setAllConstraintsMet function` to simulate that the constraints are met. We have passed the `id` of our work request to the `setAllConstraintsMet` method. The work request `id` has an instance type of `Universally Unique Identifier (UUID)`.

8. Lastly, let us get the output and state of our workers:

```
val postRequirementWorkInfo =
    workManager.getWorkInfoById(syncPetsWorkRequest.id).get()
assertEquals(WorkInfo.State.RUNNING, postRequirementWorkInfo.
state)
```

This is the final step of our test. We have used the `getWorkInfoById` method to get the `WorkInfo` of our work request. We have used the `result.get()` method to get the result of our work request. We have used `WorkInfo.State.RUNNING` to check if our work is running. Our final test function should look like the following:

```
@Test
fun testPetsSyncWorker() {
    // Create request
    val syncPetsWorkRequest : OneTimeWorkRequest = OneTimeWorkRequestBuilder<PetsSyncWorker>()
        .setConstraints(
            Constraints.Builder()
                .setRequiredNetworkType(NetworkType.CONNECTED)
                .setRequiresBatteryNotLow(true)
                .build()
        )
        .build()

    // Setting up Test Drivers
    val workManager : WorkManager = WorkManager.getInstance(ApplicationProvider.getApplicationContext())
    val testDriver : TestDriver =
        WorkManagerTestInitHelper.getTestDriver(ApplicationProvider.getApplicationContext())!!

    // Enqueue and wait for result.
    workManager.enqueueUniqueWork(
        uniqueWorkName: "PetsSyncWorker",
        ExistingWorkPolicy.KEEP,
        syncPetsWorkRequest).result.get()

    // Get WorkInfo and outputData
    val workInfo : WorkInfo! = workManager.getWorkInfoById(syncPetsWorkRequest.id).get()

    // Assert
    assertEquals(WorkInfo.State.ENQUEUED, workInfo.state)

    // Tells the testing framework that the constraints have been met
    testDriver.setAllConstraintsMet(syncPetsWorkRequest.id)

    // Get WorkInfo and outputData
    val postRequirementWorkInfo : WorkInfo! =
        workManager.getWorkInfoById(syncPetsWorkRequest.id).get()
    assertEquals(WorkInfo.State.RUNNING, postRequirementWorkInfo.state)
}
```

Figure 8.8 – PetsSyncWorker test

9.   Click the green run icon on the left of our test to run the test. The test runs and it's all green! Our test passes, as seen in the following screenshot:

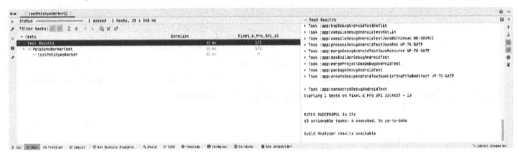

Figure 8.9 – Test results

Making all these tests work together is amazing work.

Summary

In this chapter, we learned how to save data to a local database, Room, which is part of the Jetpack libraries. We also saved items and read from the Room database. In the process, we also learned how to update items in the Room database and how to handle automated migrations in our database. Additionally, we learned how to do long-running operations using WorkManager, its best practices, and how to write tests for our workers.

In the next chapter, we will learn about runtime permissions and how to request them in our app.

9

Runtime Permissions

As we build our Android apps, there are some functionalities that require permissions to be granted for them to function properly. Due to privacy and data security policies, we as developers can not automatically grant permissions to the apps that we develop. We need to inform the users of the permissions that the apps need and why they need them.

In this chapter, we will understand runtime permissions and how to request them in our app.

In this chapter, we're going to cover the following main topics:

- Understanding runtime permissions
- Requesting permissions at runtime

Technical requirements

To follow the instructions in this chapter, you will need to have Android Studio Hedgehog or later (`https://developer.android.com/studio`) downloaded.

You can use the previous chapter's code to follow the instructions in this chapter. You can find the code for this chapter at `https://github.com/PacktPublishing/Mastering-Kotlin-for-Android/tree/main/chapternine`.

Understanding runtime permissions

Runtime permissions are permissions that are requested at runtime by an app. They are also called **dangerous permissions**. The user can grant or deny each permission, and the app can continue to run with limited capabilities even if the user denies a permission request. Android provides several methods you can use to request permission, such as `requestPermissions()` and `checkSelfPermission()`. The user only needs to grant permission once during the lifetime of the app.

Some of the features that need permission to be granted to work are camera, location, microphone and storage. Before using them, ensure that a user has permission to use them. If the user has not granted permission, you must request it from them. If the user has denied the permission, you must show a dialog explaining why you need it and ask the user to grant it from the settings. If the user has granted permission, you can use the feature. Failing to do these checks often results in an app crashing or a feature not working. If your app targets Android 6.0 and above, you must request these permissions at runtime, and the user must grant the permission for the app to work.

The flow for requesting permissions is shown in the following chart:

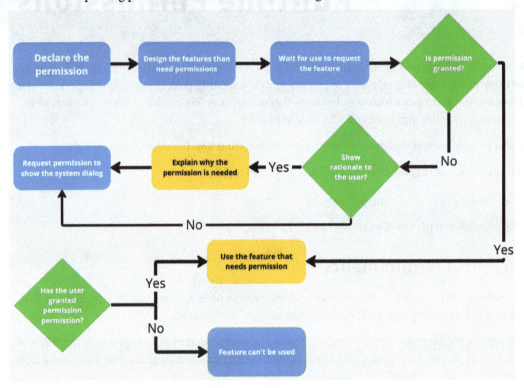

Figure 9.1 – The runtime permissions flow

As shown in the preceding diagram, this is the flow:

1. The initial step is to *declare* the permission in the manifest file. This is done by adding the permission to the manifest file.

2. After adding the permission to the manifest file, we must *design the UX* for the feature that needs the permission to be granted.

3. The next step is *waiting for the user to use* the feature that needs permission to be granted. At this point, we check whether the user has granted permission. If the user has granted permission, we proceed to use the feature.

4. If the user *has not granted permission*, we first check whether we need to *show a rationale* that explains why we need permission. If we need to show the rationale, we show it with explanations and then request permission from the user. If we do not need to show the rationale, we just request permission from the user.

5. Once the permission is requested, we wait for the *user to grant or deny* permission. If the user grants permission, we proceed to use the feature. If the user denies permission, we allow the app to work, but the user cannot use the feature that needs permission to work.

With this flow in mind, let us look at how to implement it in code. We are going to request permission to access a location.

Requesting permissions at runtime

We will follow the steps covered in *Figure 9.1* to request runtime permissions for our app:

1. Let us start by adding the permission to the manifest file. We will request permission to access the user's location. To do this, we add the following permission to the manifest file:

    ```
    <uses-permission android:name="android.permission.ACCESS_COARSE_
    LOCATION" />
    ```

    This specifies that our app will be using the `ACCESS_COARSE_LOCATION` permission. Declaring permissions in the manifests is crucial for enhancing security, user awareness, and overall app compatibility. By explicitly specifying the actions or resources apps require access to permissions informs users during installations, allowing them to make informed decisions about granting or denying access. This declaration ensures compatibility across different Android versions and devices, facilitates inter-app communication, and supports intent filtering to control component access. Permissions also play a role in runtime permission requests for dangerous permissions and help maintain platform compatibility. Additionally, Play Store reviews declare permissions as part of the submission process, contributing to adherence to policies and guidelines. In essence, manifest-based permission declarations are fundamental for creating secure, transparent, and user-controlled environments in our apps.

    The next thing is to create the UX for the feature that needs permission. We will create a dialog to request permissions from the user. It will also have the logic that shows the rationale to the user if permission was previously denied.

2. Let's create a new file in the `view` package named `PermissionDialog.kt` and add the utility functions to the file:

    ```
    fun checkIfPermissionGranted(context: Context, permission:
    String): Boolean {
        return (ContextCompat.checkSelfPermission(context,
    permission)
                == PackageManager.PERMISSION_GRANTED)
    ```

```
    }

    fun shouldShowPermissionRationale(context: Context, permission:
    String): Boolean {
        val activity = context as Activity?
        if (activity == null)
            Log.d("Permissions", "Activity is null")

        return ActivityCompat.shouldShowRequestPermissionRationale(
            activity!!,
            permission
        )
    }
}
```

The first function checks whether the permission has been granted using the `ContextCompat.checkSelfPermission()` function. The second function checks whether we need to show the rationale to the user. This is done using the `ActivityCompat.shouldShowRequestPermissionRationale()` function. This function returns `true` if the app has requested this permission previously and the user denied the request. If the user turned down the permission request in the past and chose the **Don't ask again** option in the permission request system dialog, this method returns `false`.

Next, let us create a sealed class that will be used to represent the state of the permission request.

3. Create a new file named `PermissionAction.kt` in the `data` package, and add the following code to the file:

```
sealed class PermissionAction {
    data object PermissionGranted : PermissionAction()
    data object PermissionDenied : PermissionAction()
}
```

The class has two states, `PermissionGranted` and `PermissionDenied`. A user can either grant or deny permission.

4. Next, let us create the dialog that will be used to request permission from the user. Head back to the `PermissionDialog.kt` file and add the following code to the file:

```
@Composable
fun PermissionDialog(
    context: Context,
    permission: String,
    permissionAction: (PermissionAction) -> Unit
) {

    val isPermissionGranted = checkIfPermissionGranted(context,
permission)
```

```
    if (isPermissionGranted) {
        permissionAction(PermissionAction.PermissionGranted)
        return
    }


    val permissionsLauncher = rememberLauncherForActivityResult(
        ActivityResultContracts.RequestPermission()
    ) { isGranted: Boolean ->
        if (isGranted) {
            permissionAction(PermissionAction.PermissionGranted)
        } else {
            permissionAction(PermissionAction.PermissionDenied)
        }
    }


    val showPermissionRationale =
shouldShowPermissionRationale(context, permission)
    var isDialogDismissed by remember { mutableStateOf(false) }
    var isPristine by remember { mutableStateOf(true) }


    if ((showPermissionRationale && !isDialogDismissed) ||
(!isDialogDismissed && !isPristine)) {
        isPristine = false
        AlertDialog(
            onDismissRequest = {
                isDialogDismissed = true
                permissionAction(PermissionAction.
PermissionDenied)
            },
            title = { Text(text = "Permission Required") },
            text = { Text(text = "This app requires the location
permission to be granted.") },
            confirmButton = {
                Button(
                    onClick = {
                        isDialogDismissed = true
                        permissionsLauncher.launch(permission)
                    }
                ) {
                    Text(text = "Grant Access")
                }
            },
            dismissButton = {
```

```
                    Button(
                        onClick = {
                            isDialogDismissed = true
                            permissionAction(PermissionAction.
PermissionDenied)
                        }
                    ) {
                        Text(text = "Cancel")
                    }
                }
            )
        } else {
            if (!isDialogDismissed) {
                SideEffect {
                    permissionsLauncher.launch(permission)
                }
            }
        }
    }
}
```

Let's break down the preceding code:

- We have created a composable, `PermissionDialog`, which takes three parameters, `context`, `permission` string, and a `permissionAction` callback, which passed the option the user selected to the call site.

- Inside the composable, the first thing we do is check whether permission has been granted. If permission has been granted, we call the `permissionAction` callback with the `PermissionGranted` state and return.

- Next, we also created `permissionsLauncher`, which is used to request permission from the user. We use the `rememberLauncherForActivityResult()` function to create a launcher for the contract. We then use the launcher to request permission from the user. If the user grants the permission, we call the `permissionAction` callback with the `PermissionGranted` state. If the user denies the permission, we call the `permissionAction` callback with the `PermissionDenied` state.

- If the permission has not been granted, we check whether we need to show the rationale to the user. If we need to, we show the rationale with explanations and then request permission from the user. If we do not need to show the rationale, we must request permission from the user. In our case, the rationale is `AlertDialog`, with two action items and a message explaining why we need the permission. The first action item is used to request permission from the user. The second action item is used to cancel the permission request. If we tap the

Grant Access option, we launch the permission request once again, and a dialog will pop up again, asking them to allow permission. If we tap **Cancel**, the `permissionAction` callback is called with the `PermissionDenied` state, and the dialog is dismissed. We also have two mutable states, `isDialogDismissed` and `isPristine`. The first is used to check whether the dialog has been dismissed. The second one let's know whether the dialog was shown before. We use these states combined to know whether to show the dialog or not.

- Lastly, if we do not need to show the rationale, we just request permission from the user. We use `SideEffect` to request permission from the user because we want to request permission from the user as soon as the dialog is shown.

Since we do not have an actual feature in our app currently that uses location, we are going to simulate permission flow with our `PetsScreen` composable.

5. Let's head to the `PetsScreen.kt` file and modify it to the following:

```
@Composable
fun PetsScreen(
    onPetClicked: (Cat) -> Unit,
    contentType: ContentType,
) {
    val petsViewModel: PetsViewModel = koinViewModel()
    val petsUIState by petsViewModel.petsUIState.
collectAsStateWithLifecycle()

    val context = LocalContext.current
    var showContent by rememberSaveable { mutableStateOf(false)
}

    PermissionDialog(
        context = context,
        permission = Manifest.permission.ACCESS_COARSE_LOCATION
    ) { permissionAction ->
        when (permissionAction) {
            is PermissionAction.PermissionDenied -> {
                showContent = false
            }

            is PermissionAction.PermissionGranted -> {
                showContent = true
                Toast.makeText(
                    context,
                    "Location permission granted!",
```

```
                        Toast.LENGTH_SHORT
                ).show()
            }
        }
    }
    if (showContent) {
        PetsScreenContent(
            modifier = Modifier
                .fillMaxSize(),
            onPetClicked = onPetClicked,
            contentType = contentType,
            petsUIState = petsUIState,
            onFavoriteClicked = {
                petsViewModel.updatePet(it)
            }
        )
    }
}
```

We have only made a few changes to this file:

- First, we have added a `showContent` mutable state that is used to check whether we should show the content of the screen. We have also set the initial value of the state to `false`. We will use this state to show the content of the screen if the user grants permission. We also have the `context` variable used to get the screen's context.

- We have also added the `PermissionDialog` composable to the `PetsScreen` composable. We have passed the context and the permission – in this case, the `ACCESS_COARSE_LOCATION` permission – to the composable. We have also passed a callback to the composable that is used to get the state of the permission request. If the user grants the permission, we set the `showContent` state to `true` and show a toast with the **Location permission granted** message. If the user denies the permission, we set the `showContent` state to `false`.

- Lastly, we have added a check to see whether the `showContent` state is `true`. If the state is `true`, we show the content of the screen. If the state is `false`, we do not show the content of the screen.

6. Build and run the app. At first, we will see the permission dialog, as shown in the following screenshot:

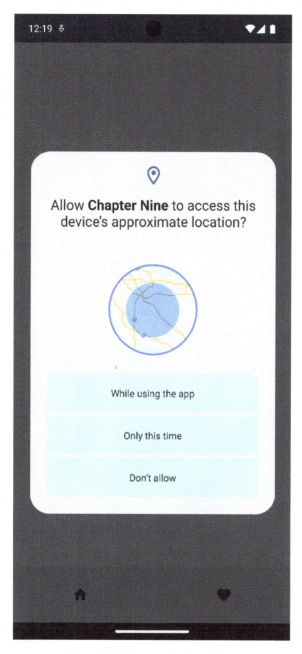

Figure 9.2 – The permission dialog

7. Tap the **Don't allow** option, which will show an empty white screen, since we don't show any content when the user has not granted the app permission.

Figure 9.3 – The no permission screen

The next time we run the app, we will see the rationale dialog showing why the app needs permission.

Figure 9.4 – The permission rationale

On this rationale dialog, we can either cancel the request or grant access. Tapping the **Grant Access** option should bring up the permission dialog shown in *Figure 9.2*, and by tapping the **While using the app** option, we grant the app the location permission, and now, we should be able to see the list of cute cats once again. Running the app again does not show the dialogs, since we have already granted the app the location permission.

Figure 9.5 – Cute cats

Summary

In this chapter, we explored what runtime permissions are and why we should declare and request permissions in our apps. Step by step, we learned how to request runtime permissions in our app and how to show permission rationale dialogs, explaining to users why we need access to runtime permissions in cases where they have denied apps access to permissions.

In the next chapter, we will learn debugging tips and tricks, how to detect leaks using LeakCanary, how to inspect HTTPS requests/responses fired by our app using Chucker, and how to inspect the Room database.

Part 3:
Code Analysis and Tests

In this part, you will gain proficiency in debugging through a series of valuable tips and tricks. Unveiling the intricacies, you will discover techniques for detecting memory leaks within your app and adeptly inspecting HTTP requests triggered by your application. Our exploration extends to inspecting your local database, offering insights into its inner workings. Diving into Kotlin best practices, you will delve into code analysis for your application, addressing code smells for enhanced code quality. This part also includes a comprehensive exploration of testing methodologies, empowering you to seamlessly integrate tests across various layers of your MVVM architecture.

This section contains the following chapters:

- *Chapter 10, Debugging Your App*
- *Chapter 11, Enhancing Code Quality*
- *Chapter 12, Testing Your App*

10

Debugging Your App

Debugging is a very important aspect of developing apps. It helps us identify and fix bugs in our code. It is a very important skill to have as a developer. It also helps us avoid bugs in the future. Many tools can help us debug our code. In this chapter, we will be looking at some of the tools that can help us debug our code.

In this chapter, we will learn debugging tips and tricks, how to detect leaks using LeakCanary, how to inspect network requests/responses fired by our app using Chucker, and how to inspect our Room database, network requests, and background tasks using App Inspection.

In this chapter, we're going to cover the following main topics:

- General debugging tips and tricks
- Detecting leaks with LeakCanary
- Inspecting network requests with Chucker
- Using App Inspection

Technical requirements

To follow the instructions in this chapter, you will need to have Android Studio Hedgehog or later (`https://developer.android.com/studio`) downloaded.

You can use the previous chapter's code to follow the instructions in this chapter. You can find the code for this chapter at `https://github.com/PacktPublishing/Mastering-Kotlin-for-Android/tree/main/chapterten`.

General debugging tips and tricks

Android Studio provides us with a variety of features that help us debug our code. Some of the features are listed in the following points:

- **Logcat**
- **Stack Traces**
- **Breakpoints**

Let us look at each of these closely.

Logcat

Logcat in Android Studio displays log messages in real-time from our apps. Each log message has a priority level attached to it. We add log messages in our app using the Log class. This class offers different priority levels that we can use to log messages. The different priority levels are as follows:

- **V**: Verbose (lowest priority)
- **D**: Debug
- **I**: Info
- **W**: Warning
- **E**: Error
- **F**: Fatal
- **S**: Silent (highest priority)

We use the preceding letters to specify the log level. For example, if we want to log a message with the debug level, we will use the following code:

```
Log.d("TAG", "Message")
```

The first parameter is the tag. The tag is used to identify the source of a log message. The second parameter is the message that we want to log. Each time we run our app, Logcat shows up at the bottom of the Android Studio window, as shown in the following figure:

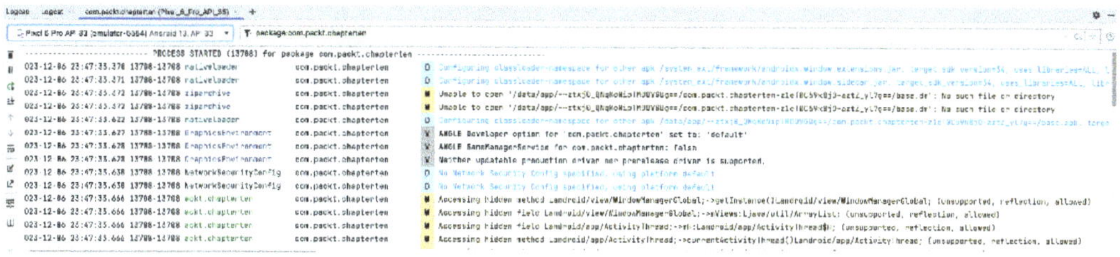

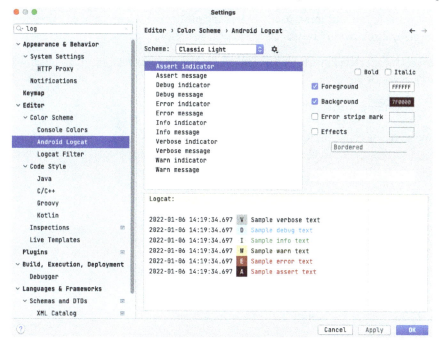

Figure 10.1 – Logcat

From the preceding figure, we can see at the top that the Logcat window shows the device we are running our app on. In this case, we are running our app on a **Pixel 6 Pro API 33** emulator; yours can be different depending on the emulator you have installed. Next to the device, we can see the **package** of the app we are running. This has a search bar that allows us to search for specific logs with their tags. Below the search are the actual logs. We can see that each log has a tag, the priority level, the package name of the app, the time the log was created, and the message. We can also see that the logs are color-coded. To see all the color settings for our Logcat, we go to **Settings** | **Editor** | **Color Scheme** | **Android Logcat**, which shows the color settings as shown in the following figure:

Figure 10.2 – Logcat color settings

This way, we can set a color scheme for our Logcat. In the preceding figure, the color scheme has been set to **Classic Light**. There is a list that shows the colors for each log level, and you can change the color for each log level. We can also change the font style and size for our Logcat.

With this, let us see how to create our first Logcat message. Let us head over to the `MainActivity.kt` file and add a log message in the `onCreate()` method as follows:

```
Log.d("First Log", "This is our first log message")
```

Run the app and add `First Log` as a search query in the search bar:

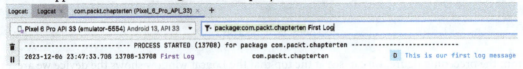

Figure 10.3 – Logcat search

This only shows the log message that has the tag **First Log**. This is particularly useful when we have a lot of logs, and we want to search for a specific log.

Stack traces

A **stack trace** is a list of method calls from the point where the app was started to the point where the exception was thrown. It is extremely useful in helping us identify the cause of an exception. Stack traces are normally displayed in Logcat.

To be able to see our first stack trace, let us head over to the `MainActivity.kt` file and add the following code in the `onCreate()` method:

```
throw RuntimeException("This is a crash")
```

The preceding code will cause the app to crash when you run it. The app crashes immediately after executing the preceding code, and by checking our Logcat, we should be able to see the stack trace:

```
E  FATAL EXCEPTION: main
   Process: com.packt.chapterten, PID: 7168
   java.lang.RuntimeException: Unable to start activity ComponentInfo{com.packt.chapterten/com.packt.chapterten.MainActivity}: java.lang.RuntimeException: This is a crash
       at android.app.ActivityThread.performLaunchActivity(ActivityThread.java:3645)
       at android.app.ActivityThread.handleLaunchActivity(ActivityThread.java:3782)
       at android.app.servertransaction.LaunchActivityItem.execute(LaunchActivityItem.java:101)
       at android.app.servertransaction.TransactionExecutor.executeCallbacks(TransactionExecutor.java:335)
       at android.app.servertransaction.TransactionExecutor.execute(TransactionExecutor.java:95)
       at android.app.ActivityThread$H.handleMessage(ActivityThread.java:2387)
       at android.os.Handler.dispatchMessage(Handler.java:106)
       at android.os.Looper.loopOnce(Looper.java:201)
       at android.os.Looper.loop(Looper.java:288)
       at android.app.ActivityThread.main(ActivityThread.java:7872) <1 internal line>
       at com.android.internal.os.RuntimeInit$MethodAndArgsCaller.run(RuntimeInit.java:548)
       at com.android.internal.os.ZygoteInit.main(ZygoteInit.java:936)
   Caused by: java.lang.RuntimeException: This is a crash
       at com.packt.chapterten.MainActivity.onCreate(MainActivity.kt:48)
       at android.app.Activity.performCreate(Activity.java:8505)
       at android.app.Activity.performCreate(Activity.java:8284)
       at android.app.Instrumentation.callActivityOnCreate(Instrumentation.java:1417)
       at android.app.ActivityThread.performLaunchActivity(ActivityThread.java:3626)<12 more...>
```

Figure 10.4 – Crash stack trace

As shown in the preceding figure, the stack trace shows the exception or reason for the crash. Additionally, it shows the class and method where the exception was thrown. It also shows the line number where the exception was thrown. This is particularly useful in helping us identify the cause of the exception. We can click on the line number directly and it will take us to the line of code where the exception was thrown.

The stack trace is a crucial tool in helping us debug our code and quickly detect crashes and the cause of crashes. Before moving on, remember to remove the code that throws the exception so that we can continue with the rest of the chapter.

Android Studio allows us to copy and paste stack traces from a different source and see them in our Logcat. Copy the following stack trace:

```
FATAL EXCEPTION: main
Process: com.packt.chapterten, PID: 7168
java.lang.RuntimeException: Unable to start activity
ComponentInfo{com.packt.chapterten/com.packt.chapterten.MainActivity}:
java.lang.RuntimeException: This is a crash
    at android.app.ActivityThread.performLaunchActivity(ActivityThread.
java:3645)
    at android.app.ActivityThread.handleLaunchActivity(ActivityThread.
java:3782)
    at android.app.servertransaction.LaunchActivityItem.
execute(LaunchActivityItem.java:101)
    at android.app.servertransaction.TransactionExecutor.
executeCallbacks(TransactionExecutor.java:135)
    at android.app.servertransaction.TransactionExecutor.
execute(TransactionExecutor.java:95)
    at android.app.ActivityThread$H.handleMessage(ActivityThread.
java:2307)
    at android.os.Handler.dispatchMessage(Handler.java:106)
    at android.os.Looper.loopOnce(Looper.java:201)
    at android.os.Looper.loop(Looper.java:288)
    at android.app.ActivityThread.main(ActivityThread.java:7872)
    at java.lang.reflect.Method.invoke(Native Method)
    at com.android.internal.os.RuntimeInit$MethodAndArgsCaller.
run(RuntimeInit.java:548)
    at com.android.internal.os.ZygoteInit.main(ZygoteInit.java:936)
Caused by: java.lang.RuntimeException: This is a crash
    at com.packt.chapterten.MainActivity.onCreate(MainActivity.kt:48)
    at android.app.Activity.performCreate(Activity.java:8305)
    at android.app.Activity.performCreate(Activity.java:8284)
    at android.app.Instrumentation.callActivityOnCreate(Instrumentation.
java:1417)
    at android.app.ActivityThread.performLaunchActivity(ActivityThread.
java:3626)
    at android.app.ActivityThread.handleLaunchActivity(ActivityThread.
```

```
java:3782)
at android.app.servertransaction.LaunchActivityItem.
execute(LaunchActivityItem.java:101)
at android.app.servertransaction.TransactionExecutor.
executeCallbacks(TransactionExecutor.java:135)
at android.app.servertransaction.TransactionExecutor.
execute(TransactionExecutor.java:95)
at android.app.ActivityThread$H.handleMessage(ActivityThread.
java:2307)
at android.os.Handler.dispatchMessage(Handler.java:106)
at android.os.Looper.loopOnce(Looper.java:201)
at android.os.Looper.loop(Looper.java:288)
at android.app.ActivityThread.main(ActivityThread.java:7872)
at java.lang.reflect.Method.invoke(Native Method)
at com.android.internal.os.RuntimeInit$MethodAndArgsCaller.
run(RuntimeInit.java:548)
at com.android.internal.os.ZygoteInit.main(ZygoteInit.java:936)
```

Once you are done copying the stack trace, head over to the **Code** tab at the top of Android Studio and select **Analyze Stack Trace or Thread Dump**, paste the stack trace, and you will see the following dialog with the stack trace:

Figure 10.5 – Analyze stack trace

This shows the preview of the stack trace we just pasted. Clicking on **OK** takes us to Logcat and shows us the stack trace as in *Figure 10.4*

Breakpoints

We use **breakpoints** to debug code for our apps. A breakpoint is a point in our code where we want the debugger to pause the execution of our code. This is useful when we are trying to find bugs that only appear under certain conditions. Android Studio allows us to add breakpoints to our code. We can add breakpoints to our code by clicking on the left side of the line number as shown in the following figure:

```
43    class MainActivity : ComponentActivity() {
          ± Harun Wangereka ★
44        @OptIn(ExperimentalMaterial3WindowSizeClassApi::class)
45        override fun onCreate(savedInstanceState: Bundle?) {
46            super.onCreate(savedInstanceState)
47            Log.d( tag: "First Log",  msg: "This is our first log message")
48            startPetsSync()
```

Figure 10.6 – Breakpoint

As shown in *Figure 10.6*, a red circle is displayed when we add a breakpoint. To be able to see how the breakpoint works, we need to run the app in **debug mode**. We can do this by clicking on the **Debug** button:

Figure 10.7 – Debug app

Since the breakpoint is on the `onCreate()` method, the debugger will pause the execution of our code at the breakpoint. Android Studio will highlight the line where the breakpoint is:

```
43    class MainActivity : ComponentActivity() {
          ± Harun Wangereka ★
44        @OptIn(ExperimentalMaterial3WindowSizeClassApi::class)
45        override fun onCreate(savedInstanceState: Bundle?) {    savedInstanceState: null
46            super.onCreate(savedInstanceState)    savedInstanceState: null
47            Log.d( tag: "First Log",  msg: "This is our first log message")
48            startPetsSync()
```

Figure 10.8 – Line breakpoint

It also shows a **Debug** window at the bottom:

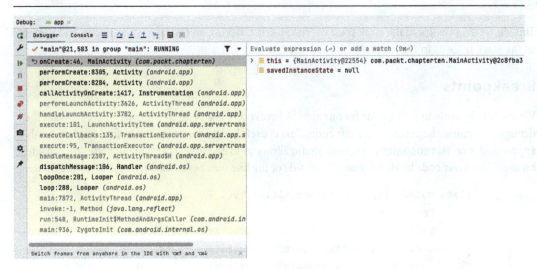

Figure 10.9 – Debug window

The **Debug** window shows us the variables that are in the scope of the breakpoint. We can also see the call stack, which shows us the methods that have been called before the breakpoint. We can also see the threads that are running in our app. We can also see the breakpoints that we have added to our code.

The **Debug** window has some buttons at the top that are immensely helpful in debugging our code:

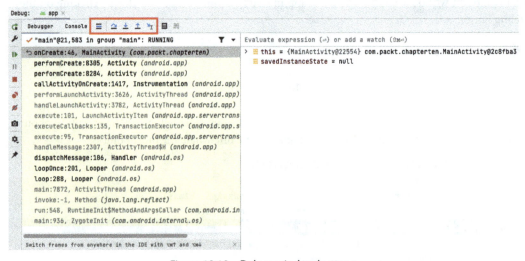

Figure 10.10 – Debug window buttons

The buttons are as highlighted in *Figure 10.10*. Starting from the left to right, the buttons are:

- **Show execution point**: This button shows the line of code where the debugger is paused

- **Step Over**: This button allows us to execute the current line of code and move to the next line of code

- **Step Into**: This button allows us to step into a method call

- **Step Out**: This button allows us to step out of a method call

- **Run to Cursor**: This button allows us to run the code until the cursor reaches the line of code where the cursor is

On the left of the **Debug** window, we can also see the **Play** and **Stop** buttons. The **Play** button allows us to resume the execution of our code and continue the debugging session until the next breakpoint or until the program completes execution. To learn more about breakpoints, visit the official documentation at `https://developer.android.com/studio/debug`.

In this section, we have learned about the different debugging options available in Android Studio. We learned about Logcat, stack traces, and breakpoints. We have also learned how to use these tools to debug our code. In the next section, we will learn about a different debugging tool, LeakCanary, and how to use it to detect memory leaks in our apps.

Detecting memory leaks with LeakCanary

LeakCanary is an open-source library developed by Square that helps us detect memory leaks in our apps. The library has knowledge of the internals of the Android Framework that allows it to narrow down the cause of the memory leak. It helps reduce the **Application Not Responding** (**ANR**) errors and **out-of-memory crashes** in our apps. Here are some of the most common causes of memory leaks:

- Storing instances of `Activity` as `Context` filed in an object that survives activity recreation due to configuration changes

- Forgetting to unregister broadcast receivers, listeners, callbacks, or RxJava subscriptions when they are no longer needed

- Storing references to `Context` in a background thread

LeakCanary is quite easy to set up and no code implementation is needed to use it. We just need to add the `leakcanary-android` dependency in our `libs.version.toml` file:

```
leakcanary-android = "com.squareup.leakcanary:leakcanary-android:2.12"
```

Tap the **Sync Now** button to sync the project. Next, let us now add the dependency in our app's `build.gradle.kts` file:

```
debugImplementation(libs.leakcanary.android)
```

We have added the dependency using the `debugImplementation` configuration so that it is only added to debug builds. This is because LeakCanary is only used for debugging purposes. We can now run our app and see how LeakCanary works. A separate app will be installed on our device or emulator as shown in the following figure:

Figure 10.11 – Leaks app

Opening the app brings up the following screen:

Figure 10.12 – LeakCanary screen

The screen shows the **Leaks**, **Heap Dumps**, and **About** tabs. The **Leaks** tab shows us the memory leaks that have been detected in our app. The **Heap Dumps** tab shows us the heap dumps that have been taken. The **About** tab shows us the version of LeakCanary we are using as well as general information. For now, there is no memory leak detected. When a memory leak is detected, LeakCanary will generate a notification or log output with detailed information about the memory leak. This information helps us identify the cause of the memory leak and fix it.

Let us now create a memory leak in our app and see how LeakCanary works:

1. Create a new file inside the `com.packt.chapterten` package and call it `LeakCanaryTest.kt`. Add the following code to the file:

    ```
    class LeakCanaryTest
    class LeakTestUtils {
        companion object {
            val leakCanaryTest = LeakCanaryTest()
        }
    }
    ```

    In the preceding code, we have created a class called `LeakCanaryTest` and another class called `LeakTestUtils`, with a companion object that stores the `LeakCanaryTest` singleton in a static field.

2. Let us now head over to the `MainActivity.kt` file and add the following code in the `onCreate()` code:

    ```
    AppWatcher.objectWatcher.expectWeaklyReachable(
        LeakTestUtils.leakCanaryTest,
        "Static reference to LeakCanaryTest"
    )
    ```

    In the preceding code, we are telling LeakCanary that the singleton instance of `LeakCanaryTest` will be garbage collected.

3. Let us run the app. We can see that LeakCanary has detected a memory leak and shows a notification as seen in the following figure:

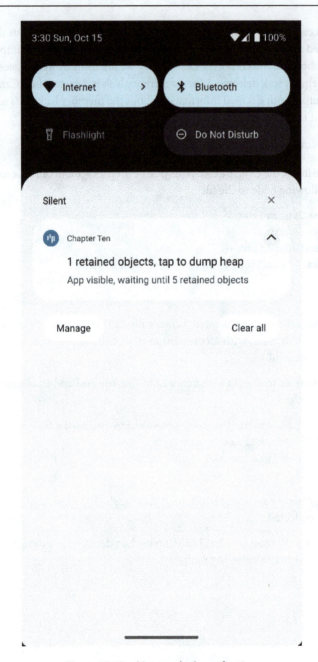

Figure 10.13 – Memory leak notification

4.   Click on the notification and it will take us to the LeakCanary app where we can see the details
      of the memory leak:

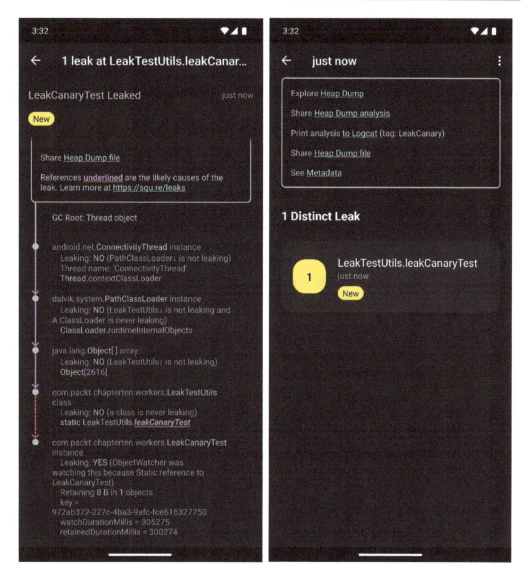

Figure 10.14 – Memory leak details

As shown in the preceding figure, LeakCanary shows the location of the memory leak and underlines the objects causing the leak. In this case, it is the `leakCanaryTest` object that is causing the memory leak. Every time we get a memory leak, we will receive such detailed information.

Remember to remove the code that causes the memory leak in the `MainActivity onCreate()` method so that we can continue with the rest of the chapter.

We have learned about LeakCanary and how to use it to detect memory leaks in our apps. You can learn more about LeakCanary at `https://square.github.io/leakcanary/`.

In the next section, we will learn about Chucker, another debugging tool that helps us inspect network requests in our apps.

Inspecting network requests with Chucker

This is from the Chucker GitHub (`https://github.com/ChuckerTeam/chucker`) page:

> *Chucker simplifies the inspection of HTTP(S) requests/responses fired by our Android apps. Chucker works as an OkHttp Interceptor persisting all those events inside our application, and providing a UI for inspecting and sharing their content. Chucker displays a notification showing a summary of the ongoing network request.*

Tapping the Chucker notification mentioned previously launches the Chucker UI. Chucker UI shows a list of all the network requests that have been made by our app. We can tap on a request to see the details of the request.

To use Chucker, follow these steps:

1. Add the `chucker` dependency in the `libs.versions.toml` file:

    ```
    chucker = "com.github.chuckerteam.chucker:library:4.0.0"
    chucker-no-op = "com.github.chuckerteam.chucker:library-
    no-op:4.0.0"
    ```

    In the preceding code, we have added two dependencies: the first one is the Chucker library, and the second one is a no-op library variant to isolate Chucker from release builds since we only want to see the requests on debug builds.

2. Tap the **Sync Now** button at the top to sync the project.

3. Next, we need to add the dependency in our app's `build.gradle.kts` file:

    ```
    debugImplementation(libs.chucker)
    releaseImplementation(libs.chucker.no.op)
    ```

4. Tap **Sync Now** at the top. This will add the Chucker dependency in debug builds only.

5. Next, we need to create a new `OkHttp` client and add the Chucker interceptor to it. Let us head over to the `Modules.kt` file and add the following module to the `appModules` module block:

    ```
    single {
        val chuckerCollector = ChuckerCollector(
            context = androidContext(),
            showNotification = true,
    ```

```
                retentionPeriod = RetentionManager.Period.ONE_HOUR
        )
        val chuckerInterceptor = ChuckerInterceptor.
    Builder(androidContext())
            .collector(chuckerCollector)
            .maxContentLength(250000L)
            .redactHeaders(emptySet())
            .alwaysReadResponseBody(false)
            .build()
        OkHttpClient.Builder()
            .addInterceptor(chuckerInterceptor)
            .build()
    }
```

The following explains the preceding code:

- We have created a `ChuckerCollector` instance and passed in the `context`, `showNotification`, and `retentionPeriod` parameters. The `context` is the Android context, `showNotification` is a boolean that determines whether to show a notification when a request is made, and `retentionPeriod` is the period for which the data is kept. In this case, we keep the data for one hour.

- We have created a `ChuckerInterceptor` instance and passed in the `context`, `collector`, `maxContentLength`, `redactHeaders`, and `alwaysReadResponseBody` parameters. The `context` is the Android context, `collector` is the `ChuckerCollector` instance we created previously, `maxContentLength` is the maximum length of the response body, `redactHeaders` is a set of headers to replace with `**` and `alwaysReadResponseBody` is a boolean that determines whether to always read the response body.

- We have created an `OkHttpClient` instance and added the `ChuckerInterceptor` to it.

We can now use the `OkHttpClient` instance to make network requests.

6. Let us modify our `Retrofit` instance to use the `OkHttpClient` instance we just created. Still in the `Modules.kt` file, modify the Retrofit instance as follows:

```
single {
    Retrofit.Builder()
        .addConverterFactory(
            Json.asConverterFactory(contentType = "application/
json".toMediaType())
        )
        .client(get())
        .baseUrl("https://cataas.com/api/")
        .build()
}
```

We have added the `client` parameter and passed it in the `OkHttpClient` instance we created previously using Koin's `get()` call.

With that, our Chucker setup is now complete.

7. Build and run the app. We can see that Chucker has detected the network request and shows a notification, as seen in the following figure:

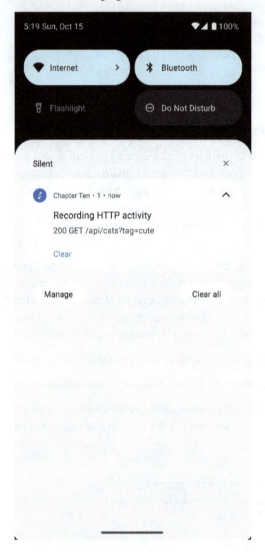

Figure 10.15 – Chucker notification

From the preceding figure, we can see that Chucker has detected the network request and shows the status code, the method, and the URL of the request.

8.   We can tap on the notification and it will take us to the Chucker UI:

Figure 10.16 – Chucker list of requests

This shows the list of the network requests that have been made by our app.

9. Tap on a request to see the details of the request:

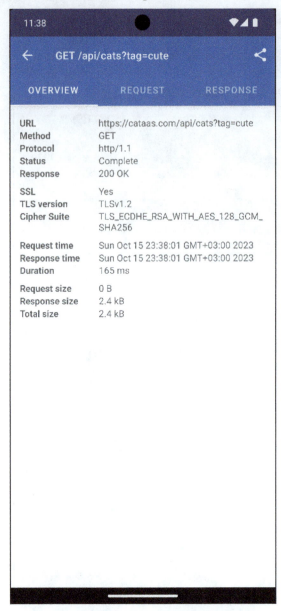

Figure 10.17 – Chucker overview tab

The details screen has three tabs as shown in the preceding figure. The first tab is the **Overview** tab, which is shown in *Figure 10.17*. The **Overview** tab shows the overview of the request. It shows the request details such as URL, method, response, duration, response size, and so on. The second tab is the **Request** tab, which shows the request headers and body:

Figure 10.18 – Chucker request tab

For this request, the body is empty since it was a get request. The third tab is the **Response** tab, which shows the response headers and body:

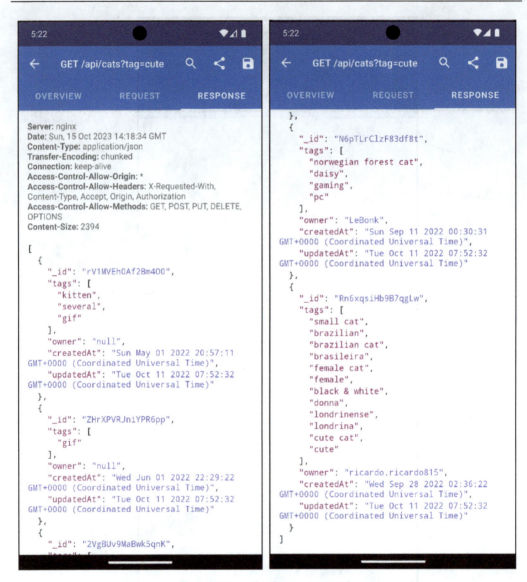

Figure 10.19 – Chucker response tab

From the preceding figure, we can see the response headers and body in JSON format.

The toolbar of the details screen has **Search**, **Share**, and **Save** buttons. The **Search** button allows us to search in either the request or the response. The **Share** button allows us to share the request or response details in JSON format. The **Save** button allows us to save the request or response details to a file.

Chucker is very helpful in debugging network requests in our apps. When non-technical teams test the debuggable version of our app, we can always tell them to share these requests, especially when they're facing issues with their network requests.

That's it for Chucker. Every time our app makes a network request, Chucker will show a notification and we can tap on the notification to see the details of the request.

We have learned about Chucker and how to use it to inspect network requests in our apps. In the next section, we will learn how to use App Inspection to inspect our app's room database and explore the features App Inspection offers.

Using App Inspection

App Inspection allows us to debug our database, inspect network traffic, and debug our background tasks. It is a very important tool in helping us debug our apps. To use App Inspection, let us run our app and then navigate to **View** | **Tool Windows** | **App Inspection** in Android Studio:

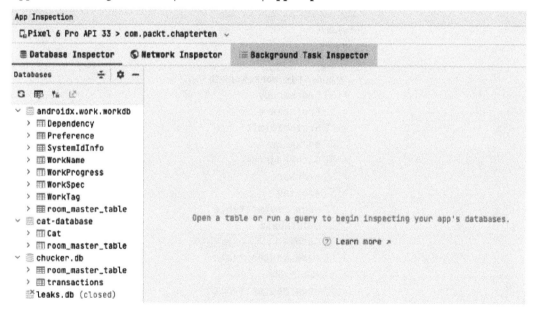

Figure 10.20 – App Inspection

App Inspection automatically connects to our app. The first tab is **Database Inspector**. On the left, we can see the different databases created by our app. We have the WorkManager, Chucker, LeakCanary, and Cat databases that we created earlier on. Let us click on the **Cat** database, and we can see the columns of the table that we created in the database:

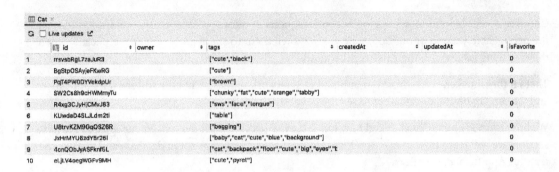

Figure 10.21 – Cat database

This shows the columns and the values that have been saved in the database. We can also run queries in the database. The query option is highlighted in the following figure:

Figure 10.22 – Execute query button

We want to run a query that shows the cats with a specific id. We can do this by running the following query:

```
SELECT * FROM CAT WHERE id == "rrsvsbRgL7zaJuR3"
```

You can use a different `id` per the data you have. The query results will be as follows:

Figure 10.23 – Query results

The data has all the cats that have the ID we specified. One thing to note is to ensure that you execute the queries on the correct database, as shown in *Figure 10.23*. The database inspector helps us debug and write queries to our database and is very useful when working on apps that use a database.

Let us now head over to the **Network Inspector** tab. This tab shows us the network requests that have been made by our app. We can see the request method, the URL, the status code, and the duration of the request:

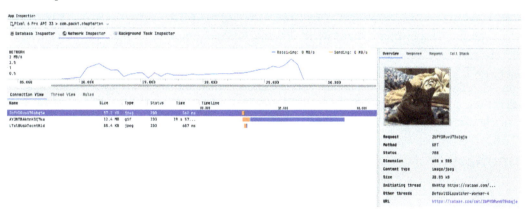

Figure 10.24 – Network Inspector

From the preceding figure, we can see that the requests are for loading the cute cat images and all the details of the request. Similar to Chucker, it also has the request and response tabs that provide more information on the request. However, unlike Chucker, **Network Inspector** captures the network requests made by the app without any additional setup in the code. The **Network Inspector** tab is very useful in helping us debug network requests in our apps, especially when working on apps that make a lot of network requests.

Lastly, let us head over to the **Background Task Inspector** tab. This tab shows us the background task requests that have been made by our app. Our app should show the following:

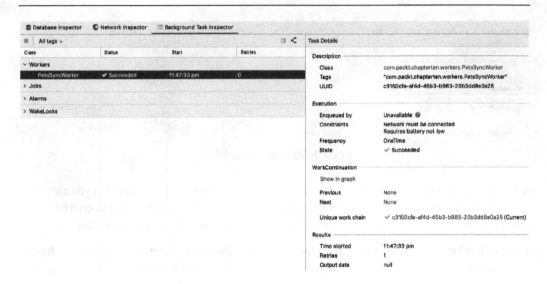

Figure 10.25 – Background Task Inspector

The Background Task Inspector shows us the details of our background tasks. It has information for WorkManager **Workers**, **Jobs**, **Alarms**, and **WakeLocks**. Since our app only has the workers, we can see that the `PetsSyncWorker` worker has succeeded. On the right are more details of the worker, as shown in *Figure 10.25*. The details show the UUID, constraints, state, and results of the worker, such as the output data, number of retries, and the time it started. This information is very helpful to check whether our background tasks are running as expected.

Summary

In this chapter, we learned some debugging tips and tricks, how to detect leaks using LeakCanary, how to inspect network requests/responses fired by our app using Chucker, and how to use App Inspection to debug our database, inspect our network requests, and inspect background tasks, too.

In the next chapter, we will learn Kotlin style and the best practices for writing Kotlin code. We will also learn how to use plugins such as Ktlint and Detekt to format, lint, and detect the code smells early.

11

Enhancing Code Quality

As we develop our Android apps, we must ensure that the code we write complies with the set rules and follows the best practices. This not only helps us to write good code but also makes it easier to maintain and easily onboard others to the code base.

In this chapter, we will learn about the Kotlin style and the best practices for writing Kotlin code. We will also learn how to use plugins such as Ktlint and Detekt to format, lint, and detect the code smells early.

In this chapter, we're going to cover the following main topics:

- Mastering Kotlin style and best practices
- Using Ktlint for static analysis
- Detecting code smells with Detekt

Technical requirements

To follow the instructions in this chapter, you will need to have Android Studio Hedgehog or later (https://developer.android.com/studio) downloaded.

You can use the previous chapter's code to follow the instructions in this chapter. You can find the code for this chapter at https://github.com/PacktPublishing/Mastering-Kotlin-for-Android/tree/main/chaptereleven

Mastering Kotlin style and best practices

As we learned in *Chapter 1*, Kotlin is a very concise and static language. As such, it is easier for us as developers to not follow some of the recommended practices. This leads to a lot of code smells and technical debt. A **code smell** is a pattern or practice that might indicate a deeper problem within the code. It indicates that the code might lead to potential problems or hinder maintainability. On the other hand, **technical debt** refers to the cost or consequences of choosing quick and suboptimal solutions in development to meet immediate needs rather than developing robust and maintainable solutions. We always have to come back later to such solutions to refactor them to be more scalable and maintainable. Let us start by learning about some of the best practices and how to avoid them.

Coding conventions

Kotlin has a wide variety of coding conventions that cover everything from naming conventions to formatting. Following these conventions makes it easier to read our code and makes it maintainable. Examples of these are the following:

- Variable names should be in **camelCase**

- Class names should be in **PascalCase**

- Constants should be in **UPPERCASE**

- Functions should be in **camelCase**

- Functions with multiple words should be separated by **underscores**

- Functions with a single expression should be **inlined**

Kotlin offers a lot of coding conventions. You can find them at `https://kotlinlang.org/docs/coding-conventions.html`.

Null safety

As discussed extensively in *Chapter 1*, Kotlin has a very strong **null safety** system. This is one of the most important features of Kotlin. It is important that we use this feature to its fullest extent. This will help us avoid a lot of null pointer exceptions. We have to use nullable types when variables can be `null`. When working with nullable types, it is recommended that we use the safe call operator (`?.`) and the Elvis operator (`?:`) to avoid null pointer exceptions. We should also use the `let` function to perform operations on nullable types. We should also use the safe cast operator (`as?`) to avoid class cast exceptions. An example is shown in the following snippet:

```
val name: String? = null
name?.let {
   println(it)
}
```

In the preceding example, we declared a `name` variable of the `String` type and assigned it `null`. Then, we used the `let` function to check whether the variable is `null` or not. If the variable is not `null`, then the `println(it)` function will print the value of the variable.

Data classes

Kotlin makes it easy for us to create **data classes**. Data classes are classes that are used to hold data. The classes also automatically generate the `equals`, `hashCode`, `toString`, and `copy` functions. We should use data classes when we need to hold data:

```
data class Person(val name: String, val age: Int)
```

In the preceding example, we created a `Person` data class with two properties: `name` (which is a `String` type) and `age` (which is an `Int` type).

Extensions functions

Kotlin provides **extension functions**, which allow us to add new functions to new classes without having to inherit from them. This will help us avoid creating utility classes. While extension functions are powerful, overuse or inappropriate use can lead to code that is hard to read and maintain. An example is shown in the following code block:

```
fun String.removeFirstAndLastChar(): String {
  return when {
  this.length <= 1 -> ""
  else -> this.substring(1, this.length - 1)
  }
}
// Example usage
fun main(args: Array<String>) {
  val myString = "Hello Everyone"
  val result = myString.removeFirstAndLastChar ()
  println(result)
}
```

In the preceding example, we created an extension function on the `String` class. The function removes the first and last character of the string and returns the remaining string. Additionally, we used the `when` expression to check whether the length of the string is less than or equal to 1. If the length is less than or equal to 1, then the function returns an empty string. Otherwise, it returns the substring of the string from index 1 to the length of the string – 1. We used the extension function in the `main` function to remove the first and last character of the `"Hello Everyone"` string. The result is then printed to the console as follows:

```
ello Everyon
```

Type inference

Kotlin has a very strong type system. As such, we can omit specifying the type of a variable and let the compiler infer the type. This will help us avoid a lot of boilerplate code. Here is an example:

```
val name = "John Doe" // Compiler infers that name is of type String
val age = 25 // Compiler infers that age is of type Int
```

Collections

Kotlin has a rich **collections** library. We use collections to store and manipulate groups of data. We have `List`, `Set`, `Map`, `Array`, and `Sequence` as collection types available in Kotlin. Collections can either be `mutable` or `immutable`. A `mutable` collection can be modified after creation, while an `immutable` collection cannot be modified after creation. An example of a `mutable` list is as follows:

```
val mutableList = mutableListOf("Kotlin", "Java", "Python")
mutableList.add("Swift")
```

In the preceding example, we created a `mutable` list of strings. We used the `mutableListOf` function to create the list. We then added a new string to the list using the `add` function. An example of an `immutable` list is as follows:

```
val immutableList = listOf("Kotlin", "Java", "Python")
```

In the preceding example, we created an `immutable` list of strings. We used the `listOf` function to create the list. We cannot add or remove items from the list after creation. We can only read items from the list. Kotlin collections also have a wide variety of functions that can be used to perform operations on collections. We should use these functions instead of writing our own functions. This helps us make our code concise and readable. Let us see the following example of creating a list and filtering odd and even numbers:

```
val numbers = listOf(1, 2, 3, 4, 5, 6, 7, 8, 9, 10)
val evenNumbers = numbers.filter { it % 2 == 0 }
val oddNumbers = numbers.filter { it % 2 != 0 }
```

In the preceding example, we created a list of numbers. We then used the `filter` function to filter even and odd numbers. The `filter` function takes a lambda as an argument. The lambda is used to filter the numbers. The `filter` function returns a new list with the filtered numbers. We used the `it` keyword to refer to the current item in the list. We then used the `%` operator to check whether the number is even or odd. If the number is even, then the `filter` function returns `true` and the number is added to the `evenNumbers` variable. For odd numbers, the `filter` function returns `false` and the number is added to the `oddNumbers` variable. Kotlin collections also have functions such as `map`, `reduce`, `fold`, `flatMap`, and so on. We should use these functions instead of writing our own functions. This helps us make our code concise and readable.

Sealed classes and interfaces

Kotlin provides **sealed classes**, which are used to represent restricted class and interface hierarchies. This improves code readability and ensures that we know all the possible subclasses of a class. Here's an example of a sealed class:

```
sealed class Shape {
  class Circle(val radius: Double) : Shape()
```

```
    class Square(val length: Double) : Shape()
    class Rectangle(val length: Double, val breadth: Double) : Shape()
}
```

In the preceding example, we created a sealed class called Shape. We then created three classes (Circle, Square, and Rectangle), which are subclasses of the Shape class. The Shape class can only be extended in the same file where it is declared. We cannot extend the Shape class in another file.

Formatting

We use four spaces for indentation in Kotlin. However, note that this is a convention and not a strict rule. We should always ensure that our code is properly formatted as per the conventions agreed upon by the team or company

Functional programming

We should take advantage of Kotlin **functional programming** features such as **lambdas, higher-order functions**, and **inline functions**. This will help us make our code more concise and readable. An example is shown in the following code block:

```
val total = numbers.reduce { sum, element -> sum + element }
```

Coroutines

Kotlin provides **coroutines**, which are used to perform asynchronous operations. They are very lightweight and easy to use and help us avoid callback hell. We should use coroutines when we need to perform asynchronous operations. An example of a coroutine in Kotlin is as shown here:

```
fun makeNetworkCall() {
    viewModelScope.launch {
        val result = async {
        // perform network call
        }
        // update UI
    }
}
```

In the preceding example, we used viewModelScope to launch a coroutine. This is to ensure that the coroutine is canceled when the view model is destroyed. We used the launch coroutine builder to create a new coroutine. Inside the launch lambda, we performed our network call, which is supposed to happen in the background. We used the async coroutine builder, which allows us to await the result of the network call. The async coroutine builder returns a Deferred object. Lastly, we updated the UI with the result of the network call.

The when statements

Kotlin provides when statements, which are used to replace switch statements. We should use when statements when we need to perform conditional operations. If we have blocks with more than one if else statement, we should consider using when statements. An example is shown in the following code:

```
val number = when {
  x % 2 == 0 -> "Even"
  x % 2 != 0 -> "Odd"
  else -> "Invalid"
}
```

Classes and functions

- Kotlin allows us to declare multiple classes in a single file. We should use this feature to avoid creating a lot of files, especially for classes that are closely related. We should, however, be keen not to have bloated files with a lot of classes, so we should use this feature with caution.

- We have to ensure that we define only one **primary constructor** per class. Instead of overloading the constructor with a second one, we can always consider using default values for the constructor parameters.

- We can use **companion objects** to create static members. Both Kotlin's companion objects and Java's **static members** facilitate the creation of class-level members that can be accessed without creating an instance of the class. However, Kotlin's companion objects provide additional flexibility by allowing access to non-static members and offer a more expressive syntax.

- We should always avoid returning null from functions. Instead, we should use nullable types.

- We can always use **scope functions** to perform operations on objects. This will help us avoid creating a lot of temporary variables.

This is just a small list of best practices. As the code base grows, it's hard at times to keep track of all the best practices. This is where static code analysis tools come in handy. They help us identify code smells and technical debt. They also help us identify bugs and security vulnerabilities. In the next section, we will learn about some of the static code analysis tools that we can use to improve the quality of our code.

Using Ktlint for static analysis

According to the official documentation, ktlint is "*an anti-bikeshedding Kotlin linter with a built-in formatter.*" It helps us do **static analysis** of our Kotlin code and has a built-in rule set and formatter. It has several integrations. For Android projects, we normally use the Gradle integration. We have Ktlint Gradle (https://github.com/jlleitschuh/ktlint-gradle), which provides a wrapper plugin over the ktlint project. After adding the project to our project, it creates gradle tasks that allow us to run ktlint on our project. We are also able to do auto-formatting.

To set up Ktlint in our project, we need to add the Ktlint plugin to our project's `build.gradle.kts` file in the plugins block, as follows:

```
id("org.jlleitschuh.gradle.ktlint") version "11.6.1"
```

Tap the **Sync Now** button at the top to add the changes to the project. This adds the Ktlint plugin to our project. We also need to set the plugin to be applied to all project modules. To do this, we add the following code to the project-level `build.gradle.kts` file below the plugins block:

```
subprojects {
    apply(plugin = "org.jlleitschuh.gradle.ktlint")
    ktlint {
        verbose.set(true)
        android.set(true)
        filter {
            exclude("**/generated/**")
        }
    }
}
```

This will apply the plugin to all the project modules. Tap the **Sync Now** button at the top to add the changes to the project. In the preceding code, we apply the plugin and do some additional configuration in the `ktlint` block. In our case, we are setting the `verbose` and `android` properties to `true`. We are also excluding the `generated` folder from the analysis.

With that, we are ready to use Ktlint. First, though, let's disable some formatting options. To do this, we need to create an `.editorconfig` file in the root of our project. In the file, we add the following code:

```
root = true

[*]
charset = utf-8
insert_final_newline = false
trim_trailing_whitespace = true

[*.{kt,kts}]
indent_size = 4
ij_kotlin_packages_to_use_import_on_demand = unset
ij_kotlin_name_count_to_use_star_import = 999
ij_kotlin_name_count_to_use_star_import_for_members = 999
```

This disables some formatting options, the key one being `insert_final_newline` at the end of each file. This is especially useful for existing projects as it prevents us from having to reformat the whole project. If you need to customize Ktlint behavior, this is the file you use to enable or disable some options.

Let us now run the `ktlintCheck` task. To do this, let us open the **Terminal** tab in our IDE and run the following command:

```
./gradlew ktlintCheck
```

After the task completes, we will see the following output:

Figure 11.1 – Ktlint check failure

Figure 11.2 – Ktlint check failure continued

From the preceding figures, we can see that the task was completed with failures, which means our project is not correctly formatted. The output also shows the specific formatting error and the file. We can see indentation, formatting, and new lines issues. We can opt to fix the issues by ourselves but, first, we should always check whether the Ktlint formatter can fix the issues for us. To do this, we can run the following command:

```
./gradlew ktlintFormat
```

This will run the `ktlintFormat` task. After the task is completed, we will see the following output:

```
harun@wangerekaharun chaptereleven % ./gradlew ktlintFormat

BUILD SUCCESSFUL in 2s
12 actionable tasks: 10 executed, 2 up-to-date
harun@wangerekaharun chaptereleven %
```

Figure 11.3 – ktlintFormat successful

As seen in the preceding figure, the task was completed successfully. This means the Ktlint formatter was able to fix the issues for us. If the Ktlint formatter is not able to fix the issues, it normally highlights the issues that the plugin is not able to fix and shows the file and line number. We can then fix the issues manually. For now, we don't have such issues. We can now run the `ktlintCheck` task again to confirm that the issues have been fixed. After the task completes, we will see the following output:

```
harun@wangerekaharun chaptereleven % ./gradlew ktlintFormat


BUILD SUCCESSFUL in 2s
12 actionable tasks: 10 executed, 2 up-to-date
harun@wangerekaharun chaptereleven %
```

Figure 11.4 – ktlintFormat successful

As seen in the preceding figure, the build was successful. This means our project is correctly formatted. By using the Git tool in our IDE by pressing *Command + K* on macOS and *Ctrl + K* on Windows, we can see the files that have changes and see the changes made by the Ktlint formatter. From our project, this is what the commit modal looks like:

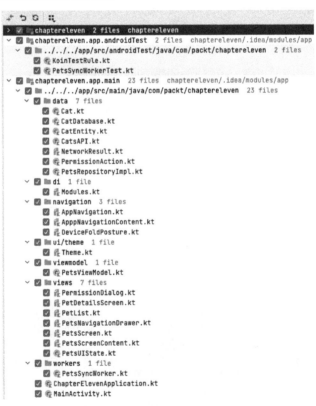

Figure 11.5 – Git commit modal

As shown in *Figure 11.5*, the `ktlintFormat` command has made a bunch of changes to our files. We can check each file for changes too. The formatter is a good tool to help us quickly format our code according to the Kotlin style and conventions. The `ktlintFormat` and `ktlintCheck` commands are the ones to run after you complete your changes before you commit your code. This will help you avoid committing code that is not formatted correctly.

We have done a basic setup, which is sufficient for most projects. For more information, you can learn more about the plugin, the rules available, and how to customize it here: `https://github.com/jlleitschuh/ktlint-gradle`.

We have seen how to use the Ktlint plugin to format and perform static analysis of our code. In the next section, we will learn how to use the detekt plugin to check for code smells and technical debt in our code.

Detecting code smells with detekt

detekt is another static code analysis tool for Kotlin. It helps us identify problems early and keep the technical debt low throughout the development process. It enforces a set of rules that help us avoid code smells and technical debt. It also gives us the flexibility to create our own custom rule sets. Detekt offers the following features:

- It identifies code smell for Kotlin projects
- It's easily configurable and customizable to suit our needs
- We can always suppress the warnings if we feel they are not applicable
- We can specify the code smell thresholds that we want to enforce

We will be using these features in our project. But before that, let us understand the rule sets. detekt has several rule sets that check the compliance of your code with the Kotlin style guide. The available rule sets are as follows:

- **Comments**: This rule set provides rules that address issues in comments and the documentation of the code. It checks header files, comments on private methods, and undocumented classes, properties, or methods.
- **Complexity**: This rule set contains rules that report complex code. It checks for complex conditions, methods, expressions, and classes, as well as long methods and long parameter lists.
- **Coroutines**: This rule set analyzes code for potential coroutine problems.
- **Empty-Blocks**: This rule set contains rules that report empty blocks of code. Examples include empty `catch` blocks, empty class blocks, and empty function and conditional function blocks.
- **Exceptions**: This rule set reports issues related to how code throws and handles exceptions. For example, it has rules for if you're catching generic exceptions, among other issues related to handling exceptions.

- **Formatting**: This rule set checks whether your code base follows a specific formatting rule set. It allows for checking indentation, spacing, semicolons, or even import ordering, among other things.

- **Naming**: This rule set contains rules that assert the naming of different parts of the code base. It checks how we name our classes, packages, functions, and variables. It reports the errors in case we're not following the set conventions.

- **Performance**: This rule set analyzes code for potential performance problems. Some of the issues it reports include the use of `ArrayPrimitives` or the misuse of `forEach` loops, for instance.

- **Potential-Bugs**: This rule set provides rules that detect potential bugs.

- **Ruleauthors**: This rule set provides rules that ensure good practices are followed when writing custom rules.

- **Style**: This rule set provides rules that assert the style of the code. This will help keep the code in line with the given code style guidelines.

With this understanding of detekt rule sets and features, let us now set up detekt in our project.

Setting up detekt

Similar to Ktlint, detekt is available as a Gradle plugin. To add the plugin to our project, we need to add the following code to our project's `build.gradle.kts` file in the plugins block:

```
id("io.gitlab.arturbosch.detekt") version "1.23.1"
```

Click on the **Sync Now** button at the top to add the changes to the project. This adds the detekt plugin to our project. We also need to set the plugin to be applied to all project modules. To do this, we add the following code to the project-level `build.gradle.kts` file below the plugins block:

```
apply(plugin = "io.gitlab.arturbosch.detekt")
detekt {
    parallel = true
}
```

This applies the detekt plugin to all the modules that will be in our project so we do not need to add the plugin to each module. We also set the `parallel` property to `true`. This will help us run the detekt tasks in parallel and save time when running the tasks. Click on the **Sync Now** button at the top to add the changes to the project. We are now set to use detekt. Open your terminal and run the following command:

```
./gradlew detekt
```

This will run the `detekt` task. After the task completes, we will see the following output:

Figure 11.6 – detekt errors

The first time we run the task, we will get a number of errors. As we can see from the preceding figure, detekt shows the file and line number with the error and the type of rule set that has not been complied with. In *Figure 11.6*, we can see the common ones being the function is too long, and magic numbers are included, among others. At the end of the list of errors, detekt normally shows the total number of weighted issues, as shown in the following figure:

```
FAILURE: Build failed with an exception.

* What went wrong:
Execution failed for task ':app:detekt'.
> Analysis failed with 121 weighted issues.

* Try:
> Run with --stacktrace option to get the stack trace.
> Run with --info or --debug option to get more log output.
> Run with --scan to get full insights.

* Get more help at https://help.gradle.org

BUILD FAILED in 6s
1 actionable task: 1 executed
```

Figure 11.7 – detekt errors summary

We have a total of 121 weighted issues. We are going to see how to suppress some as well as increase thresholds for others and fix the ones that we can shortly. First, we need to change the default behavior of detekt. To do this, we need to create a `detekt-config.yml` file in the root of our project. detekt has a task that does this. Let us open the **Terminal** tab in our IDE and run the following command:

```
./gradlew detektGenerateConfig
```

This will generate a `config` file if we don't have it already. After the task completes, we will see the following output:

Figure 11.8 – detekt config file

We need to reference this file to our detekt setup. Let us head over to the project-level `build.gradle.kts` file and modify our `detekt` block to look like this:

```
detekt {
    parallel = true
    config.setFrom(files("${project.rootDir}/config/detekt/detekt.yml"))
}
```

Here, we are using our newly created file as the `config` file. Click on the **Sync Now** button at the top to add the changes to the project. Next, let us now do some configuration to our detekt `config` file.

Customizing detekt

At times, `detekt` might be reporting issues that we do not want to fix or we might want to change the severity or thresholds of the issue. Here is where customizing detekt comes in handy. We can customize `detekt` in the `detekt.yml` file and customize the rules that we are interested in. The first issue we are going to disable is the **magic number** issue. This is the issue that is raised when we use numbers directly in our code. Let us open the `detekt.yml` file and press *Command + F* on macOS or *Ctrl + F* on Windows to search for the `MagicNumber` issue and modify it as follows:

```
MagicNumber:
  active: false
```

We are setting the `active` property to `false`. This will disable the issue. By running the `./gradlew detekt` command again, we can see that we have reduced the error from 121 to 60 now! That's a significant drop. We can also see that the `MagicNumber` issue is no longer present.

```
FAILURE: Build failed with an exception.

* What went wrong:
Execution failed for task ':app:detekt'.
> Analysis failed with 60 weighted issues.

* Try:
> Run with --stacktrace option to get the stack trace.
> Run with --info or --debug option to get more log
> Run with --scan to get full insights.

* Get more help at https://help.gradle.org

BUILD FAILED in 965ms
1 actionable task: 1 executed
```

Figure 11.9 – detekt with no magic numbers

Next, let us ensure that detekt doesn't complain about Jetpack Compose function naming. Search for the `FunctionNaming` issue and modify it to be as follows:

```
FunctionNaming:
  active: true
  excludes: ['**/test/**', '**/androidTest/**', '**/
commonTest/**', '**/jvmTest/**', '**/androidUnitTest/**', '**/
androidInstrumentedTest/**', '**/jsTest/**', '**/iosTest/**']
  functionPattern: '[a-z][a-zA-Z0-9]*'
  excludeClassPattern: '$^'
  ignoreAnnotated: ['Composable']
```

We have added `ignoreAnnotated: ['Composable']`. This will not report issues for all functions annotated with the `@Composable` annotation. Composable functions use the Pascal case naming convention. Next, we want to disable the new line at the end of the file rule on detekt since we disabled it on Ktlint. Search for the `FinalNewline` issue and modify it to be as follows:

```
NewLineAtEndOfFile:
  active: false
```

This will disable the issue. By running the `./gradlew detekt` command again, we can see that we have reduced the errors to only eight now:

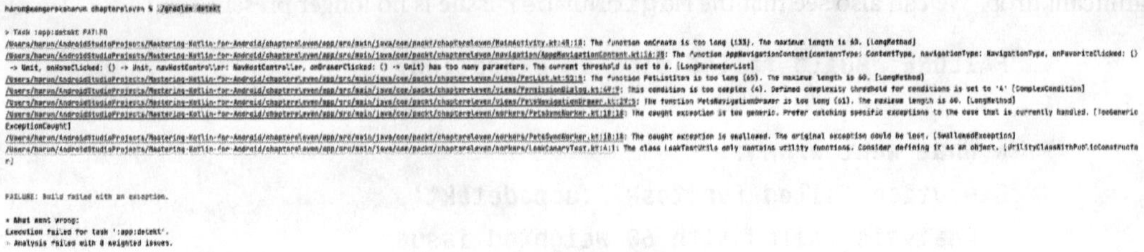

Figure 11.10 – detekt errors reduced

Now, let us see how to increase the thresholds to resolve the *function too long* issue. Search for the `FunctionTooLong` issue and modify it to be as follows:

```
LongMethod:
  active: true
  threshold: 140
```

This will solve all the issues related to the function being too long. Search for the `LongParameterList` issue and modify it to be as follows:

```
LongParameterList:
  active: true
  functionThreshold: 8
```

We have increased the threshold from 6 to 8. Lastly, search for the `ComplexCondition` issue and modify it to be as follows:

```
ComplexCondition:
  active: true
  threshold: 6
```

We have also increased the threshold from 4 to 6. By running the `./gradlew detekt` command again, we can see that we have reduced the errors to only three now:

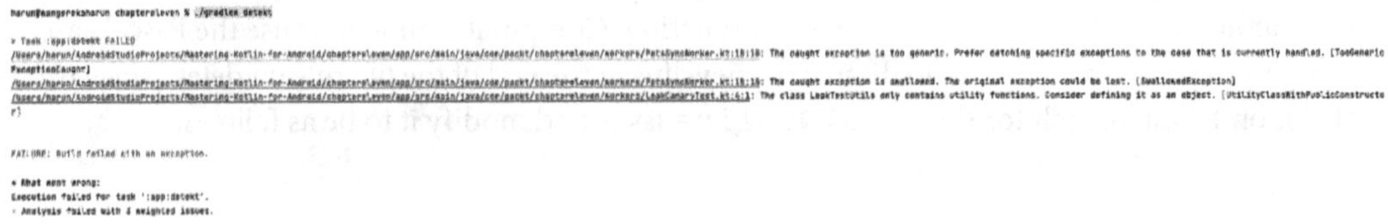

Figure 11.11 – More errors removed

Increasing thresholds is a good way of reducing errors. It's also great since it reduces the amount of refactoring that we have to do. However, we should be careful not to increase the thresholds too much. Let us now try to fix the remaining issues. Let us start with the `TooGenericExceptionCaught` and `SwallowedException` issues. This is in our `PetsSyncWorker doWork` function:

```
override suspend fun doWork(): Result {
    return try {
        petsRepository.fetchRemotePets()
        Result.success()
    } catch (e: Exception) {
        Result.failure()
    }
}
```

To resolve the issues, we need to add a `log` statement to the `catch` block and catch only the exceptions that we expect. Let us modify the code to be as follows:

```
override suspend fun doWork(): Result {
    return try {
        petsRepository.fetchRemotePets()
        Result.success()
    } catch (e: IOException) {
        Log.d("PetsSyncWorker", "Error fetching pets", e)
        Result.failure()
    }
}
```

We have added a `log` statement and we are only catching `IOException`. Lastly, let us fix the `UtilityClassWithPublicConstructor` issue. This is in our `LeakTestUtils` class:

```
class LeakTestUtils {
    companion object {
        val leakCanaryTest = LeakCanaryTest()
    }
}
```

This class only has a companion object, which returns an instance of the `LeakCanaryTest` class. We can use an object instead of a class. Let us modify the class to be as follows:

```
object LeakTestUtils {
    val leakCanaryTest = LeakCanaryTest()
}
```

All the issues should be fixed now. By running the `./gradlew detekt` command again, we can see that we have no errors now:

```
harun@wangerekaharun chaptereleven % ./gradlew detekt
Starting a Gradle Daemon, 1 stopped Daemon could not be reused, use --status for details

BUILD SUCCESSFUL in 4s
1 actionable task: 1 up-to-date
```

Figure 11.12 – detekt successful run

Our build successfully passes. Our project now has a plugin that helps us do static analysis of our code. We can now identify code smells and technical debt early in the development process. We can also use these plugins on **Continuous Integration/ Continuous Delivery (CI/CD)** pipelines to ensure that we don't merge code that has code smells and technical debt. This will help us keep our code base clean and maintainable, especially when we are working in teams. We will learn about this extensively in *Chapter 14*.

Summary

In this chapter, we have learned about the Kotlin style and the best practices for writing Kotlin code. We have also learned how to use plugins such as Ktlint and Detekt to format, lint, and detect code smells early.

In the next chapter, we will learn how to add tests for the different layers in the MVVM architecture. We will learn about the importance of adding tests to our apps and how to add unit tests, integration tests, and instrumentation tests.

12

Testing Your App

Testing Android apps is a crucial aspect of the development process, ensuring that our application functions as intended and meets user expectations. It helps us identify and fix bugs before they reach production and ensure that our app is stable and performs well. This chapter will equip you with the skills to write tests for the different layers of our app that we've created so far.

In this chapter, we will learn how to add tests for the different layers in our **MVVM** (**Model-View-ViewModel**) architecture. We will learn the importance of adding tests to our apps and how to add unit tests, integration tests, and instrumentation tests.

In this chapter, we're going to cover the following main topics:

- Importance of testing
- Testing the network and database layers
- Testing our `ViewModels`
- Adding UI tests to our composables

Technical requirements

To follow the instructions in this chapter, you will need to have Android Studio Hedgehog or later (`https://developer.android.com/studio`) downloaded.

You can use the previous chapter's code to follow the instructions in this chapter. You can find the code for this chapter at `https://github.com/PacktPublishing/Mastering-Kotlin-for-Android/tree/main/chaptertwelve`.

Importance of testing

Writing tests is a crucial aspect of app development. It has the following benefits:

- It helps us to **identify and fix bugs** before they reach production. When we write tests for our code, we can see issues at an early stage and quickly fix them before they reach our users, which is normally very costly.

- **Ensures code quality**. When we write tests, we are forced to write code that can be tested. This means that we write code that is modular and loosely coupled. This makes our code base more maintainable and easier to work with. When we find a piece of code that is hard to test, it is a sign that the code is not well written and needs to be refactored.

- Writing tests results in **improved documentation and code understanding**. When we write tests, we are forced to think about how our code works and how it should be used. This makes it easier for other developers to understand our code. While tests can serve as a form of documentation, they should not replace proper code documentation.

- Tests help us to **refactor our code with confidence**. When we have tests in place, we can refactor our code and be sure that we have not broken the existing features in our app that were working well before the refactoring. This is because we can run our tests and see whether they pass or fail.

- Tests help us **test regression**, especially adding new features or modifying existing ones. Tests ensure that the existing functionality still works as before, and nothing has been broken.

These are just to mention a few. There are many more benefits of writing tests, and the best way to realize them is to start writing tests for your code. One important thing to note is that we can also add tests to our **Continuous Integration/Continuous Delivery** (**CI/CD**) pipelines to ensure that our tests run automatically when we push our code to our repositories. This also ensures that as we collaborate with other people on our projects, we can be sure that our code is always in a good state and we can always deploy our code to production with confidence.

In Android, we have a concept called the **testing pyramid** that helps us to understand the several types of tests that we can write for our applications and how they relate to each other. The testing pyramid is divided into three layers, as shown in the following figure:

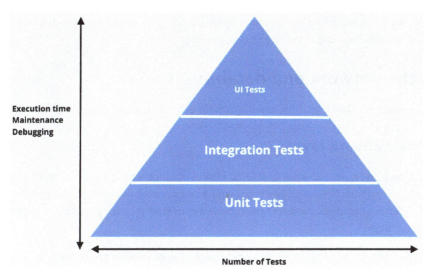

Figure 12.1 – Testing pyramid

As shown in the preceding diagram, we have three layers of tests:

- **Unit tests**: These tests sit at the bottom of the pyramid. These are tests that test a single unit of code in isolation. Unit tests are intended to test the smallest testable parts of an application – typically, methods and functions. They are the fastest to run and are the most reliable. They are also the easiest to write and maintain. Unit tests run on your local machine only. These tests are compiled to run locally on the **Java Virtual Machine** (**JVM**) to minimize execution time. For tests that depend on your own dependencies, we use mock objects to provide the external dependencies. **MockK** and **Mockito** are popular frameworks for mocking dependencies.

- **Integration tests**: These tests sit in the middle of the pyramid. They test how different units of code work together. They are slower to run than unit tests. They are also hard to write as they require multiple components and dependencies to work and maintain. **Roboletric** is a popular framework for writing integration tests.

- **UI tests**: These tests sit at the top of the pyramid. They test how the different components of our app work together. They are the slowest to run since they run on a real device or emulator and are the least reliable. They are also the most expensive to write and maintain. There are several frameworks for writing UI tests, including **Espresso**, **UI Automator**, and **Appium**.

The testing pyramid presents a way to distribute the tests that we write on our code base. The ideal distribution percentages are **70% for unit tests**, **20% for integration tests**, and **10% for UI tests**. Notice as we go up the pyramid that the number of tests reduces. This is because as we go up the pyramid, the tests become more expensive to write and maintain. This is why we should strive to write more unit tests than integration tests and more integration tests than UI tests.

Over the next few sections, we will write the tests for the different layers we have discussed. Let us start by testing our database and network layers in our app.

Testing the network and database layers

In this section, we are going to learn how to write tests for our network and database layers step by step.

Testing the network layer

To test our network layer, we will write unit tests. However, since we are using Retrofit to make our network requests, we will use MockWebServer to mock our network requests. The MockWebServer is a library that allows us to mock our network requests. Let us start by setting up the test dependencies in our version catalog:

1. Open the libs.version.toml file and add the following versions in the versions section:

    ```
    mockWebServer = "5.0.0-alpha.2"
    coroutinesTest = "1.7.3"
    truth = "1.1.5"
    ```

    We are setting up the versions for mockWebServer, coroutinesTest, and truth.

2. Next, in the libraries section, add the following:

    ```
    test-mock-webserver = { module = "com.squareup.
    okhttp3:mockwebserver", version.ref = "mockWebServer" }
    test-coroutines = { module = "org.jetbrains.kotlinx:kotlinx-
    coroutines-test", version.ref = "coroutinesTest" }
    test-truth = { module = "com.google.truth:truth", version.ref =
    "truth" }
    ```

    Here, we are adding the dependencies for these libraries.

3. Next, we will create a bundle so that it is easy to add all test dependencies at once. In the bundle section, add the following:

    ```
    test = ["test-mock-webserver", "test-coroutines", "test-truth"]
    ```

4. Click on the **Sync Now** button at the top to add the dependencies.

5. Lastly, let us head over to the app-level build.gradle.kts file and add the following:

    ```
    testImplementation(libs.bundles.test)
    ```

    This will add the test bundle to our test directory.

6. Click on the **Sync Now** button to add the dependencies to our app.

Before we start writing our tests, we need to do several setup tasks. First, we need to create a JSON response for the request that our test will use:

1. To do this, right-click on the `app` directory, select **New**, and at the bottom of the pop-up dialog, select **Folder**.

2. From the options presented, select **Java Resources Folder**. This should create a new folder named `resources`, as shown in the following figure:

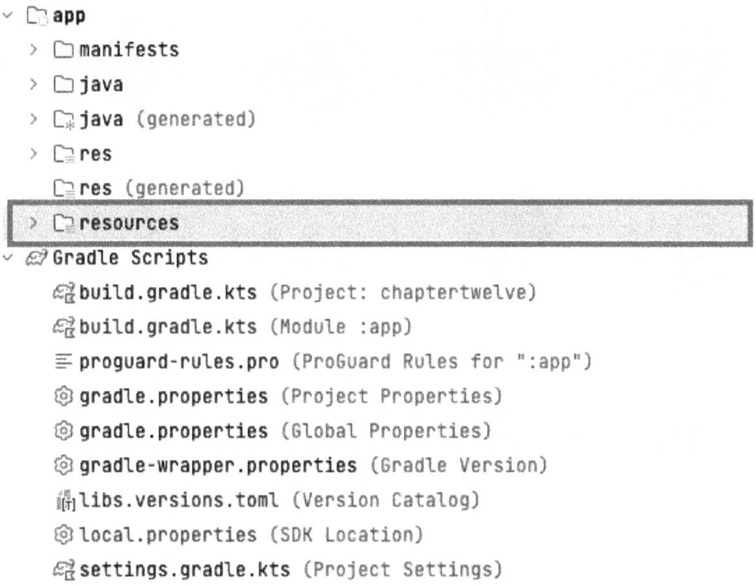

```
∨ ☐ app
   > ☐ manifests
   > ☐ java
   > ☐ java (generated)
   > ☐ res
     ☐ res (generated)
   > ☐ resources
∨ ☐ Gradle Scripts
     ☐ build.gradle.kts (Project: chaptertwelve)
     ☐ build.gradle.kts (Module :app)
     ≡ proguard-rules.pro (ProGuard Rules for ":app")
     ⊚ gradle.properties (Project Properties)
     ⊚ gradle.properties (Global Properties)
     ⊚ gradle-wrapper.properties (Gradle Version)
     ₥ libs.versions.toml (Version Catalog)
     ⊚ local.properties (SDK Location)
     ☐ settings.gradle.kts (Project Settings)
```

Figure 12.2 – The resources folder

3. Inside this folder, let us create a new JSON file called `catsresponse.json` and add the following JSON:

```
[
  {
    "_id": "eLjLV4oegWGFv9MH",
    "mimetype": "image/png",
    "size": 39927,
    "tags": [
      "cute",
      "pyret"
    ]
  },
  {
    "_id": "PA2gYEbMCzaiDrWv",
    "mimetype": "image/jpeg",
```

```
      "size": 59064,
      "tags": [
        "cute",
        "best",
        "siberian",
        "fluffy"
      ]
    },
    {
      "_id": "8PKU6iXscrogXrHm",
      "mimetype": "image/jpeg",
      "size": 60129,
      "tags": [
        "cute",
        "fat",
        "ragdoll",
        "beautiful",
        "sleeping"
      ]
    }
  ]
```

Our app uses the Cat as a Service API, which returns a list of cats per the filter you have applied. The API returns this list of cats in a JSON response, as shown previously. When testing, especially with mocked data, the structure and data types of the JSON response should match those of the real API to ensure our tests are correct.

4. Now that we have our response ready, we have to create a class that utilizes this response along with our test class in the com.packt.chaptertwelve (test) directory shown in the following figure:

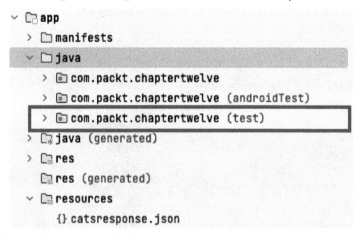

Figure 12.3 – Test directory

5. Inside the `com.packt.chaptertwelve (test)` directory, let us create a new Kotlin file called `MockRequestDispatcher.kt` and add the following code:

```kotlin
import com.google.common.io.Resources
import okhttp3.mockwebserver.Dispatcher
import okhttp3.mockwebserver.MockResponse
import okhttp3.mockwebserver.RecordedRequest
import java.io.File
import java.net.HttpURLConnection

class MockRequestDispatcher : Dispatcher() {

    override fun dispatch(request: RecordedRequest):
MockResponse {
        return when (request.path) {
            "/cats?tag=cute" -> {
                MockResponse()
                    .setResponseCode(HttpURLConnection.HTTP_OK)
                    .setBody(getJson("catsresponse.json"))
            }

            else -> throw IllegalArgumentException("Unknown
Request Path ${request.path}")
        }
    }

    private fun getJson(path: String): String {
        val uri = Resources.getResource(path)
        val file = File(uri.path)
        return String(file.readBytes())
    }
}
```

Here is a breakdown of the preceding code:

*   We have created a class called `MockRequestDispatcher` that extends `Dispatcher`. This class will be used to mock our network requests.

*   We override the `dispatch` function, which takes `RecordedRequest` and returns `MockResponse`. This function is called when a request is made to the server.

*   We check the path of the request, and if it matches the path of our request, we return `MockResponse` with a response code of `200` and a body of the `Json` response that we created earlier. For now, we have only mocked a successful response, but it's important to handle all the different HTTP response codes and error cases to properly mimic real-world scenarios.

- If the path does not match, we throw `IllegalArgumentException`.

- Lastly, we create a `getJson` function that takes a path and returns a `String` instance type. This function is used to read the `Json` response from the file that we created earlier.

We can add as many paths as we want to this class. Since our project only has one path, this is all we need.

6. Next, let us create our test class. Let us create a new Kotlin file called `CatsAPITest.kt` and add the following code:

```kotlin
class CatsAPITest {
    private lateinit var mockWebServer: MockWebServer
    private lateinit var catsAPI: CatsAPI

    @Before
    fun setup() {
        // Setup MockWebServer
        mockWebServer = MockWebServer()
        mockWebServer.dispatcher = MockRequestDispatcher()
        mockWebServer.start()

        // Setup Retrofit
        val json = Json {
            ignoreUnknownKeys = true
            isLenient = true
        }
        val retrofit = Retrofit.Builder()
            .baseUrl(mockWebServer.url("/"))
            .addConverterFactory(
                json.asConverterFactory(
                    contentType = "application/json".
toMediaType()
                )
            )
            .build()
        catsAPI = retrofit.create(CatsAPI::class.java)
    }


    @Test
    fun `fetchCats() returns a list of cats`() = runTest {
        val response = catsAPI.fetchCats("cute")
        assert(response.isSuccessful)
    }
}
```

```
    @After
    @Throws(IOException::class)
    fun tearDown() {
        mockWebServer.shutdown()
    }
}
```

Here is a breakdown of the preceding code:

- We have created a class called `CatsAPITest`. This class will be used to test our network layer.

- We have created two variables: `mockWebServer` and `catsAPI`. The `mockWebServer` variable will be used to mock our network requests. The `catsAPI` variable will be used to make our network requests.

- We have the `setup()` function, which is annotated with the `@Before` annotation. This means that this function will run before our tests run. In this function, we have done the following:

  - We have created a `MockWebServer` instance and assigned it to the `mockWebServer` variable. We then set the dispatcher of `mockWebServer` to an instance of `MockRequestDispatcher`. This is the class that we created earlier. We then start `mockWebServer`.

  - We have created a Retrofit instance and added the `kotlinx-serialization-converter` factory. We then assign the `catsAPI` variable to an instance of `CatsAPI`.

- We have our test function, which is annotated with the `@Test` annotation. This means that this function will be run as a test. In this function, we do the following:

  - We wrap the test in the `runTest()` function. This is because we want to test suspending functions. `runTest` is a coroutine test builder designed for testing coroutines. It is part of the `kotlinx-coroutines-test` library that we added earlier.

  - We make a network request to `mockWebServer` using the `catsAPI` instance that we created earlier. We then assert that the response is successful.

  - We have the `tearDown()` function, which is annotated with the `@After` annotation. This means that this function will run after our tests run. This function is used to shut down our `mockWebServer` instance.

7. Press the green *run* icon next to our test class to run our tests. We should see the following output in the **Run** window:

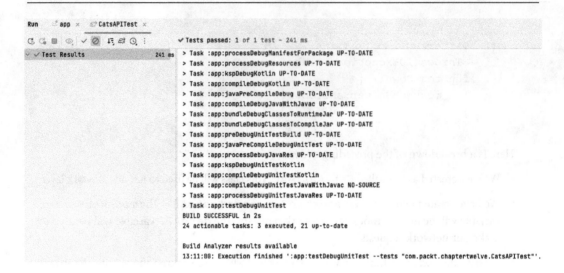

Figure 12.4 – Test passing

As seen in the preceding figure, our test runs successfully. This means that our network layer is working as expected. We can now move on to testing our database layer.

Testing the database layer

We are using **Room** for our database. To test our database layer, we will write JUnit tests that will run on an Android device. JUnit is a platform that serves as a foundation for launching testing frameworks. It also provides APIs for writing unit tests that run on the platform. The tests will execute faster than our UI tests since they do not require us to create an activity. This means our test will be in the androidTest directory shown in the following figure:

```
∨ ⌷ app
    > ⌷ manifests
    ∨ ⌷ java
        > ⌷ com.packt.chaptertwelve
        > ⌷ com.packt.chaptertwelve (androidTest)
        > ⌷ com.packt.chaptertwelve (test)
```

Figure 12.5 – Android test directory

Let us create a new file called CatsDaoTest.kt and add the following code:

```
@RunWith(AndroidJUnit4::class)
class CatDaoTest {
    private lateinit var database: CatDatabase
    private lateinit var catDao: CatDao
```

```kotlin
    @Before
    fun createDatabase() {
        database = Room.inMemoryDatabaseBuilder(
            ApplicationProvider.getApplicationContext(),
            CatDatabase::class.java
        ).allowMainThreadQueries().build()
        catDao = database.catDao()
    }

    @After
    fun closeDatabase() {
        database.close()
    }
}
```

Here is a breakdown of the preceding code:

- We have created two variables: `database` and `catDao`. The `database` variable will be used to create an instance of our database. The `catDao` variable will be used to create an instance of our `CatDao` interface.

- We have the `createDatabase()` function, which is annotated with the `@Before` annotation. This means that this function will run before our tests run. Inside the function, we create an instance of our database and assign it to the `database` variable. We are using the in-memory database.

- We have the `closeDatabase()` function, which is annotated with the `@After` annotation. This means that this function will run after our tests run. This function is used to close our database.

With this done, we can now start writing our tests:

1. In the `CatsDaoTest` class, add the following test function:

```kotlin
    @Test
    fun testInsertAndReadCat() = runTest {
        // Given a cat
        val cat = CatEntity(
            id = "1",
            owner = "John Doe",
            tags = listOf("cute", "fluffy"),
            createdAt = "2021-07-01T00:00:00.000Z",
            updatedAt = "2021-07-01T00:00:00.000Z",
            isFavorite = false
        )
```

```
        // Insert the cat to the database
        catDao.insert(cat)
        // Then the cat is in the database
        val cats = catDao.getCats()
        assert(cats.first().contains(cat))
    }
```

In this test, we have created a `CatEntity` object with the details of a cat. We then inserted the details of the cat into the database. Lastly, we assert that the details of the cat are in the database.

2. Click on the green *run* icon next to our test class to run our tests. You should see the following output in the **Run** window:

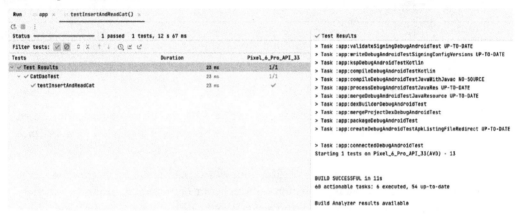

Figure 12.6 – Test to insert and read from the database

Our test runs successfully. This means that our database layer is working as expected. Let us add another test that tests adding a cat to the favorites.

3. Still inside the `CatsDaoTest` class, let us add the following test function:

```
@Test
fun testAddCatToFavorites() = runTest {
    // Given a cat
    val cat = CatEntity(
        id = "1",
        owner = "John Doe",
        tags = listOf("cute", "fluffy"),
        createdAt = "2021-07-01T00:00:00.000Z",
        updatedAt = "2021-07-01T00:00:00.000Z",
        isFavorite = false
    )

    // Insert the cat to the database
```

```
catDao.insert(cat)

// Favorite the cat
catDao.update(cat.copy(isFavorite = true))

// Assert that the cat is in the favorite list
val favoriteCats = catDao.getFavoriteCats()
assert(favoriteCats.first().contains(cat.copy(isFavorite =
true)))
}
```

In this test, we have created a `CatEntity` object with the details of a cat. We then insert the cat into the database. We then update the `CatEntity` object, passing `isFavorite` as `true`. Lastly, we assert that the cat is on the favorite list.

4. Click on the green *run* icon next to our test class to run our tests. You should see the following output in the **Run** window:

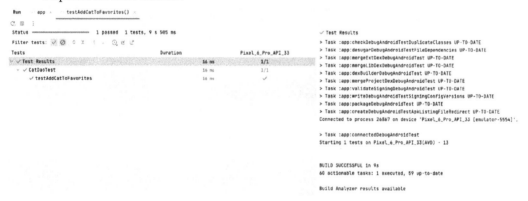

Figure 12.7 – Favoriting a cat test

Our tests run successfully. This means that our functionality for adding cats to favorites is working properly.

We have seen how to test our network and database layers. Next, let us test our ViewModel layer.

Testing our ViewModels

Our `ViewModel` class fetches data from the repository and exposes it to the UI. To test our `ViewModel`, we will write unit tests. Let us start by setting up the test dependencies in our version catalog:

1. Open the `libs.version.toml` file and add the following versions in the versions section:

```
mockk = "1.13.3"
```

2.   Next, in the libraries section, add the following:

```
test-mockk = { module = "io.mockk:mockk", version.ref = "mockk"
}
```

3.   Add the `test-mockk` dependency to the `test` bundle. Our updated `test` bundle should now look like this:

```
test = ["test-mock-webserver", "test-coroutines", "test-truth",
"test-mockk"]
```

4.   Click on the **Sync Now** button at the top to add the dependencies. Adding mockk allows us to mock our dependencies.

5.   We are now ready to create our test class. Create a new Kotlin file called `CatsViewModelTest.kt` inside the test directory and add the following code:

```
class PetsViewModelTest {
    private val petsRepository = mockk<PetsRepository>(relaxed =
true)
    private lateinit var petsViewModel: PetsViewModel

    @Before
    fun setup() {
        Dispatchers.setMain(Dispatchers.Unconfined)
        petsViewModel = PetsViewModel(petsRepository)
    }

    @After
    fun tearDown() {
        Dispatchers.resetMain()
    }
}
```

Here is a breakdown of the preceding code:

- We have created two variables: `petsRepository` and `petsViewModel`. The `petsRepository` variable will be used to mock our `PetsRepository` interface. We used `mockk<PetsRepository>` to provide a mock instance of `PetsRepository`. The `petsViewModel` variable will be used to create an instance of `PetsViewModel`.

- We have the `setup()` function, which is annotated with the `@Before` annotation. This means that this function will run before our tests run. We set the main dispatcher to `Dispatchers.Unconfined`. This is because we are using coroutines in our ViewModel. We then assign the `petsViewModel` property to an instance of `PetsViewModel`.

- We have the `tearDown()` function, which is annotated with the `@After` annotation. This means that this function will run after our tests run. This function is used to reset the main dispatcher.

With this, we are ready to write our test. Below the `tearDown()` function, add the following test function:

```
@Test
fun testGetPets() = runTest {
    val cats = listOf(
        Cat(
            id = "1",
            owner = "John Doe",
            tags = listOf("cute", "fluffy"),
            createdAt = "2021-07-01T00:00:00.000Z",
            updatedAt = "2021-07-01T00:00:00.000Z",
            isFavorite = false
        )
    )
    // Given
    coEvery { petsRepository.getPets() } returns flowOf(cats)
    // When
    petsViewModel.getPets()
    coVerify { petsRepository.getPets() }
    // Then
    val uiState = petsViewModel.petsUIState.value
    assertEquals(cats, uiState.pets)
}
```

In this test function, we have created a list of cats. We then mock the `getPets()` function of `PetsRepository` to return a flow of cats. It returns a flow of cats since our `getPets()` function in `PetsRepository` returns `Flow<List<Cat>>`; this way, we mock the correct behavior of this function. We then call the `getPets()` function of `PetsViewModel`. We then assert that the `getPets()` function of `PetsRepository` is called. Lastly, we assert that the list of cats that we created is the same as the list of cats that we get from `PetsViewModel`. Remember to remove the private marker in our `PetsViewModel` class in case you get an error when trying to access the `getPets()` function. Click on the green *run* icon next to our test class to run our tests. You should see the following output in the **Run** window:

Figure 12.8 – PetsViewModelTest

Our test runs successfully. This means that our `ViewModel` layer is working as expected. We can now move on to testing our UI layer. In the next section, we will learn how to write UI tests in Jetpack Compose.

Adding UI tests to our composables

Writing UI tests has been made easier for us. Jetpack Compose provides a set of testing APIs to find elements, verify their attributes, and perform actions on these elements. Jetpack Compose uses **semantics** to identify elements in our composables. Semantics are a way to describe the UI elements in our composables. Semantics are used by accessibility services to make our apps accessible. Testing dependencies are already set up as we created our new project in *Chapter 2* so no need to add any dependencies. We have a number of composables on our project. For this chapter, we will write tests for the `PetListItem` composable.

Let us head over to the `PetListItem.kt` file. We need to add a `testTags` modifier to our composable. This is because we are using tags to identify our composables. In the `PetListItem` composable, modify the composable contents to be as follows:

```
ElevatedCard(
    modifier = Modifier
        .fillMaxWidth()
        .padding(6.dp)
        .testTag("PetListItemCard"),
) {
    Column(
        modifier = Modifier
            .fillMaxWidth()
            .padding(bottom = 10.dp)
            .testTag("PetListItemColumn")
            .clickable {
                onPetClicked(cat)
            }
    ) {
        AsyncImage(
            model = "https://cataas.com/cat/${cat.id}",
            contentDescription = "Cute cat",
            modifier = Modifier
                .fillMaxWidth()
                .height(200.dp),
            contentScale = ContentScale.FillWidth
        )
        Row(
            modifier = Modifier
```

```
                .padding(start = 6.dp, end = 6.dp)
                .fillMaxWidth(),
            verticalAlignment = Alignment.CenterVertically,
            horizontalArrangement = Arrangement.SpaceBetween
        ) {
            FlowRow(
                modifier = Modifier
                    .padding(start = 6.dp, end = 6.dp)
            ) {
                repeat(cat.tags.size) {
                    SuggestionChip(
                        modifier = Modifier
                            .padding(start = 3.dp, end = 3.dp),
                        onClick = { },
                        label = {
                            Text(text = cat.tags[it])
                        }
                    )
                }
            }
            Icon(
                modifier = Modifier
                    .testTag("PetListItemFavoriteIcon")
                    .clickable {
                        onFavoriteClicked(cat.copy(isFavorite = !cat.
isFavorite))
                    },
                imageVector = if (cat.isFavorite) {
                    Icons.Default.Favorite
                } else {
                    Icons.Default.FavoriteBorder
                },
                contentDescription = "Favorite",
                tint = if (cat.isFavorite) {
                    Color.Red
                } else {
                    Color.Gray
                }
            )
        }
    }
}
```

Notice we have added the testTag() modifier to our components. With this, we are able to use the Finders APIs in Jetpack Compose to find our composables. Once we use the finders, we can perform actions and assert on our composables. Let us now create a new file in our androidTest directory called PetListItemTest.kt and add the following code:

```
class PetListItemTest {
    @get:Rule
    val composeTestRule = createComposeRule()

    @Test
    fun testPetListItem() {
        with(composeTestRule) {
            setContent {
                PetListItem(
                    cat = Cat(
                        id = "1",
                        owner = "John Doe",
                        tags = listOf("cute", "fluffy"),
                        createdAt = "2021-07-01T00:00:00.000Z",
                        updatedAt = "2021-07-01T00:00:00.000Z",
                        isFavorite = false
                    ),
                    onPetClicked = { },
                    onFavoriteClicked = {})
            }
            // Assertions using tags
            onNodeWithTag("PetListItemCard").assertExists()
            onNodeWithTag("PetListItemColumn").assertExists()
            onNodeWithTag("PetListItemFavoriteIcon").assertExists()

            // Assertions using text
            onNodeWithText("fluffy").assertIsDisplayed()
            onNodeWithContentDescription("Favorite").
assertIsDisplayed()
            onNodeWithContentDescription("Cute cat").
assertIsDisplayed()

            // Actions
            onNodeWithTag("PetListItemFavoriteIcon").performClick()
        }
    }
}
```

Here is a breakdown of the preceding code:

- We have created a class called `PetListItemTest`. We will use this class to test our `PetListItem` composable. Inside this class, we have created a rule called `composeTestRule`. This rule will be used to create our composables. Through this rule, we can set Compose content or access our activity.

- We have the `testPetListItem()` function, which is annotated with the `@Test` annotation. Several things are happening in this function:

  - We have used the `with` scoping function to be able to use `composeTestRule`. We then set the content of our composable. In this case, it is the `PetListItem` composable that we want to test. We pass a `cat` object to our composable.

  - We are using the `onNodeWithTag()` function to find our composables. We then use the `assertExists()` function to assert that the composables exist. This will find our composables using the tags that we added earlier.

  - We are using the `onNodeWithText()` function to find our composables. We then use the `assertIsDisplayed()` function to assert that the composables exist. We have also used the `onNodeWithContentDescription()` function to find our composables. These two functions help us find composables whose text or content description matches the text or content description that we pass to the function.

  - Lastly, we are using the `performClick()` function to perform an action on our composables. In this case, we are performing a click action on our `PetListItemFavoriteIcon` composable.

Click on the green *run* icon next to our test class to run our tests. We should see the following output in the **Run** window:

Figure 12.9 – Jetpack Compose UI tests

Our test runs successfully. Additionally, the test is also run on the device that we are working on. We are also able to see the components being displayed and actions being performed.

We have seen how to write UI tests in Jetpack Compose. To learn more about testing in Jetpack Compose, check out the official documentation (`https://developer.android.com/jetpack/compose/testing`). With the knowledge that we have gained in this chapter, we can add more tests to the different layers of our app. You can try adding more tests to test your knowledge.

Summary

In this chapter, we have learned how to add tests for the different layers in our MVVM architecture. We have learned about the importance of adding tests to our apps and how to add unit tests, integration tests, and instrumentation tests.

In the next chapter, we will learn step-by-step how to publish a new app in the Google Play Store. We will walk through how to create a signed app bundle and the things required for us to publish our first app to the Play Store. Additionally, we will learn about some of the Google Play Store policies and how to always stay compliant to avoid our apps from being removed or accounts from being banned.

Part 4:
Publishing Your App

Having successfully developed your app, the next phase unfolds in this part. You will discover the intricacies of publishing your app to the Google Play Store, navigating through crucial Google Play Store policies to ensure a seamless release. You will also dive into the realm of **continuous integration and continuous deployment** (**CI/CD**), unlocking the potential to automate routine tasks integral to Android development. You will learn how to seamlessly integrate tests and code analysis tools from *Part 3* into your CI/CD pipelines, streamlining development workflows. To conclude this part, you will elevate your app's performance by incorporating crash reporting tools and enhancing user engagement through the implementation of push notifications, and learn some useful tips on how to secure your app.

This section contains the following chapters:

- *Chapter 13, Publishing Your App*
- *Chapter 14, Continuous Integration and Continuous Deployment*
- *Chapter 15, Improving Your App*

13

Publishing Your App

Once our remarkable applications have been developed, the subsequent phase involves delivering these apps to our intended audience. This is accomplished by releasing our apps on the Google Play Store. This chapter will focus on the process of doing so.

In this chapter, we will learn step-by-step how to publish a new app in the Google Play Store. We will walk through how to create a signed app bundle and things such as answering questions about the content of our app, creating releases, setting up how users will access our app – either via controlled testing tracks or publicly, and much more. All this is required for us to publish our first app to the Play Store. Additionally, we will learn about some of the Google Play Store policies and how to always stay compliant to avoid our apps being removed or our accounts being banned.

In this chapter, we're going to cover the following main topics:

- Preparing our app for release
- Releasing our app to the Google Play Store
- Google Play Store policies overview

Technical requirements

To follow the instructions in this chapter, you will need to have Android Studio Hedgehog or later (`https://developer.android.com/studio`) downloaded.

You can use the previous chapter's code to follow the instructions in this chapter. You can find the code for this chapter on GitHub (`https://github.com/PacktPublishing/Mastering-Kotlin-for-Android/tree/main/chapterthirteen`).

Preparing our app for release

Before we upload our app to the Google Play Store, we have to do several things to prepare it for release. I have a **checklist** that I go through every time I release an app. We will be going through the checklist in this section. The checklist helps ensure that we do not forget anything as we release our app and that the app is functional. We will be tackling some of the checklist items later, in *Chapter 15* of this book, but they are worth mentioning here.

Here is the checklist:

- Add analytics to your app
- Add crash reporting to your app
- Turn off logging and debugging
- Internationalize and localize your app
- Improve error messages
- Test your app on different devices
- Provide proper feedback channels
- Reduce the size of your app
- Use Android App Bundle
- Enable minification and obfuscation

Now, let us learn about each of these items in greater detail.

Add analytics to your app

Adding **analytics** to an app helps in getting metrics on how the app is performing once it is released. This helps in making decisions on how to improve the app. Platforms such as Firebase Analytics, Google Analytics, Flurry, and Mixpanel offer such services. We are going to add Firebase Analytics to our app in *Chapter 15* of this book.

Add crash reporting to your app

Crash reporting libraries help us get crash reports for our apps. This helps in fixing the bugs that cause crashes. This is very helpful in catching crashes and stack traces when users are using our apps. We are going to add Firebase Crashlytics to our app as our crash reporting library in *Chapter 15* of this book. There are other crash-reporting tools that can be used, such as Sentry, Bugsnag, and Raygun. It's always good to weigh which tool works best you our use case.

Turn off logging and debugging

To ensure that we do not expose any sensitive information about our app to other users, we have to ensure that our release builds do not have **logs** or **debugging** enabled.

Internationalize and localize your app

If an app targets different countries, we have to ensure that we localize and internationalize the app. This means that we have to translate the app to the languages of the countries that we are targeting. Through internationalization, a well-structured code base enables seamless integration of accessibility features and supports diverse languages. Unicode support ensures compatibility with characters from various languages, enhancing accessibility. Localization adapts content, language, and cultural nuances, making our app more accessible to users with language-related needs. Adapting date, time, and numerical formats, as well as visual elements, contributes to both the accessibility and usability of our app. We have to ensure that apps work well in the different countries that we are targeting.

Improve error messages

As we release our app, we have to ensure that we display **error messages** in a way that is easy for our users to understand. We have to avoid displaying error messages that are meant for developers. With analytics in place, we can always log the technical details of errors and be able to know what is causing the errors.

Test your app on different devices

This is a very important checklist item. Since end users normally don't have the same devices and operating systems, it is important that we test the app on different devices. This helps us ensure that our app works well on different devices, including different screen sizes and different operating systems. We can always leverage services such as Firebase Test Lab to test apps on different devices. Firebase Test Lab (`https://firebase.google.com/docs/test-lab`) provides a variety of physical and virtual devices that we can use to test apps.

Provide proper feedback channels

At times, even with all these checklist items done, users might run into unexpected issues that we might not have anticipated. We have to ensure that we provide proper **feedback channels** for our users to reach out to us. This helps in ensuring that we get feedback from users and are able to fix any issues that they might be facing. This also makes users feel that we care about them and we are ready to help them. The feedback channels can be via email, social media, a phone number, or any other channel that we can use to respond to users.

Reduce the size of your app

We have to ensure that our app is not too big, reducing the size as much as possible. This helps in ensuring that our app is downloaded and installed faster. We do this by removing any unused resources from our app. We can also compress any audio or images that are bundled with our app. For images, we can strive to use vector images as much as possible. These are very small in size and scale well on different screen sizes.

Use the Android App Bundle

Android App Bundle (**AAB**) is a publishing format that includes all the compiled code and resources of an app but defers **Android Package Kit** (**APK**) generation and signing to Google Play. This helps in reducing the size of the app. With Android App Bundle, we benefit from a smaller app, are able to deliver some features on demand, and can deliver instant app experiences to our users.

Android Studio provides a way to create a signed Android App Bundle. Android requires all AABs to be signed with a certificate before they can be uploaded to the Google Play Store. Signing a bundle allows for size optimization and dynamic delivery, and simplifies the app signing process.

To create a signed Android App Bundle, we have to navigate to **Build | Generate Signed Bundle or APK**, as shown here:

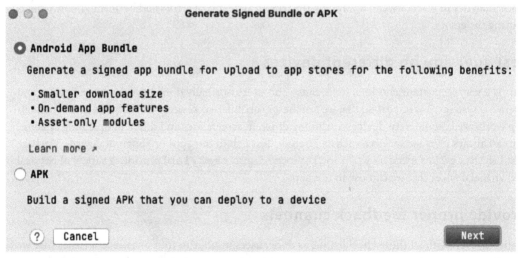

Figure 13.1 – Generate a signed bundle

As seen in the preceding screenshot, AAB offers a variety of benefits as we have already discussed. Click **Next** to continue with the process:

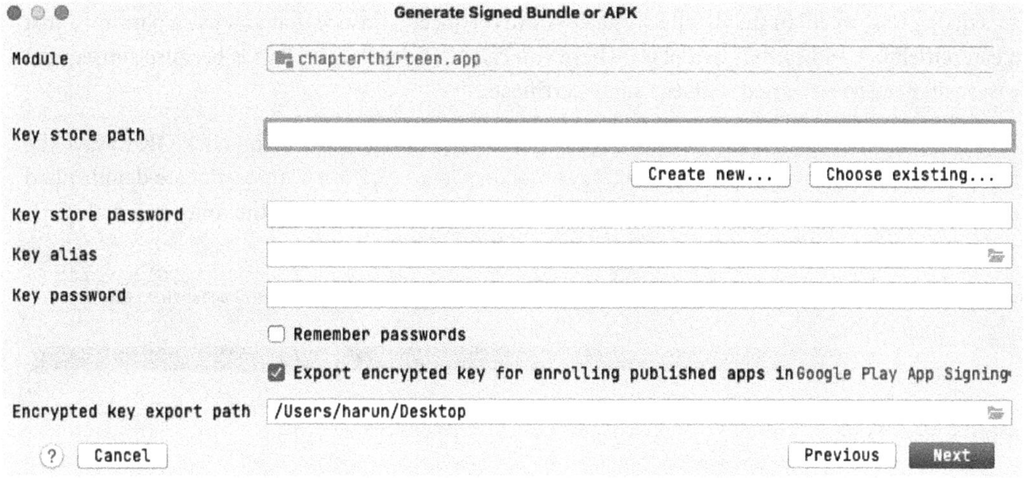

Figure 13.2 – Selecting your keystore certificate

In this step, we choose to either create a keystore certificate or use an existing one. Click **Create new...** to create a new keystore certificate. Then, you will be presented with the following dialog box:

Figure 13.3 – Creating a new keystore certificate

In this dialog box, we fill in the details of the keystore certificate. Ensure that you use a password that you can remember and store it in a place where you can always access it. This is because subsequent releases will need to be signed with the same certificate.

Also, ensure to save it with the .jks extension. Once done filling in the form, click **OK** to save the certificate. This brings you back to the dialog shown in *Figure 13.2* but with certificate details filled in now. Click **Next** to continue with the process. You will be presented with the following dialog:

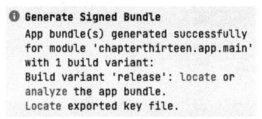

Figure 13.4 – Selecting the build variant

Here, we are going to select the build variant that we want to sign. We are going to select the **release** build variant. Click **Create** to create the signed Android App Bundle. Gradle will build the signed Android App Bundle. Once the process is done, you will be presented with the following notification:

> ℹ **Generate Signed Bundle**
> App bundle(s) generated successfully
> for module 'chapterthirteen.app.main'
> with 1 build variant:
> Build variant 'release': locate or
> analyze the app bundle.
> Locate exported key file.

Figure 13.5 – Signed bundle generated notification

You can either choose **analyze** to analyze the bundle or **locate** to locate the folder the bundle is located in. We are going to use this bundle later on when we upload our app to the Google Play Store.

Enable minification and obfuscation

Minification and obfuscation help in reducing the size of an app. Minification removes any unused code in the app. Obfuscation helps in making code unreadable. Minification involves reducing the size of the code base by removing unnecessary characters and renaming variables, leading to smaller APK sizes and improved app performance. Obfuscation, on the other hand, focuses on renaming classes, methods, and fields to obscure their original names, enhancing the security of the app and protecting against reverse engineering. Together, these techniques contribute to smaller, faster, and more secure Android applications by optimizing the code size and making it hard for hackers to reverse engineer the app. We do this for release builds.

Let us head over to our app-level `build.gradle.kts` file and modify the `buildTypes` block as shown here:

```
buildTypes {
    release {
        isMinifyEnabled = true
        isShrinkResources = true
        setProguardFiles(
            listOf(
                getDefaultProguardFile("proguard-android.txt"),
                "proguard-rules.pro"
            )
        )
    }
    debug {
        isMinifyEnabled = false
        isShrinkResources = false
    }
}
```

We have enabled minification and obfuscation for our release build. We have also disabled minification and obfuscation for our debug build. This is because we want to be able to debug our app when we are developing it. After doing this, it is recommended to run the release build locally before we upload it to the Google Play Store.

This is because some of the code might be removed when we enable minification and obfuscation. This might cause our app to crash. We have to check and see if we need to add rules on how our code is obfuscated.

We do this by adding rules in the `proguard-rules.pro` file. For example, for Retrofit to still do serialization of our JSON responses, we have to ensure that our model classes are not obfuscated.

Now, let us navigate to the `proguard-rules.pro` file and add the following rules:

```
-keep class com.packt.chapterthirteen.data.Cat.** { *; }
-keep class com.packt.chapterthirteen.data.CatEntity.** { *; }
# With R8 full mode generic signatures are stripped for classes that are not
# kept. Suspend functions are wrapped in continuations where the type rgument
# is used.
-keep,allowobfuscation,allowshrinking class kotlin.coroutines.
```

```
Continuation
-keep,allowobfuscation,allowshrinking interface retrofit2.Call
-keep,allowobfuscation,allowshrinking class retrofit2.Response
```

With these rules in place, when our code is shrunk, the classes that we have specified will not be obfuscated. Since our app is not that big, we do not have a lot of rules. For large apps, ensure you test thoroughly and check your dependencies documentation for any rules that you need to add.

On the **Build Variants** tab, select the **release** build variant and run a release build as shown here:

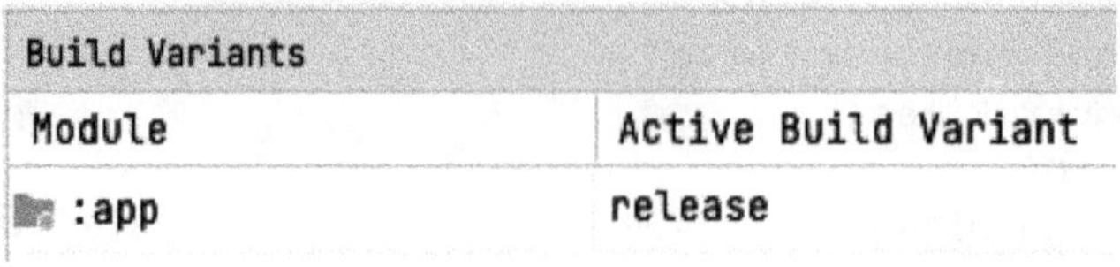

```
Build Variants

Module                    Active Build Variant

📁 :app                   release
```

Figure 13.6 – Release build variant

After choosing the release build variant, we need to set up the key signing certificate that we created earlier on so that our release variant can run. To do so, let us add the following in our app-level build.gradle.kts file:

```
signingConfigs {
    create("release") {
        storeFile = file("../keystore/packt.jks")
        storePassword = "android"
        keyAlias = "packt"
        keyPassword = "android"
    }
}
```

In the preceding code, we have created a new config in our signingConfigs block called release. We have specified keyAlias, keyPassword, storeFile, and storePassword. The keystore file is in the root directory of this project, as seen in the code snippet. If you saved it in a different location, be sure to change the path.

Click the **Sync Now** button to sync the project. Next, we need to add this new signingConfig to our release build type. To do so, let us add the following to our release build type:

```
signingConfig = signingConfigs.getByName("release")
```

Now we can run the release build locally. However, the release build takes longer to build than the debug build. After the app runs, we should be able to see our cute cat images in the app:

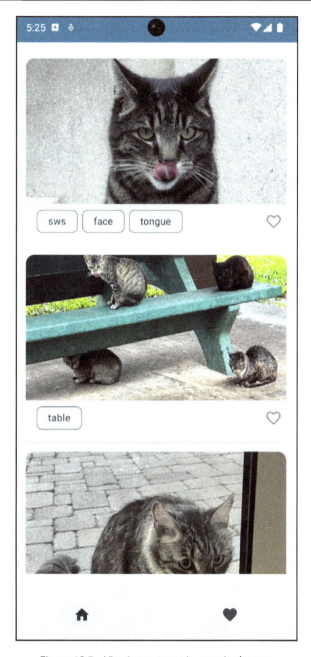

Figure 13.7 – Viewing cute cat images in the app

Our checklist is complete and we already have a signed AAB. In the next section, we will upload our app to the Google Play Store.

Releasing our app to the Google Play Store

Before you can publish apps to the Google Play Store, you need to have a developer account. You can get one by signing up on Google Play (`https://play.google.com/console/signup`).

You can either create an account for yourself or your organization as shown here:

 Google Play Console

To get started, choose an account type

Who are you creating an account for? Learn more about which account type to choose

Yourself

Choose if you're creating an account for an individual, rather than an organization. For example, if you're an amateur developer, student, or hobbyist. You'll still be able to earn money on Google Play, and invite others to join your account.

Get started →

An organization

Choose if you're creating an account for an organization or business. For example, if you're involved in commercial, industrial, professional, or governmental activities. You'll need to verify your organization.

Get started →

Figure 13.8 – Creating a developer account

Choosing the **Yourself** option shows the instructions for creating an account for yourself:

What you'll need to create a developer account for yourself

To create this account, you'll need:

⑦ **An email address for Google Play users**
This will be shown on Google Play so that users can contact you. You'll need to verify it by receiving a code. Learn more about developer verifications

@ **A contact phone number and email address for Google**
These will only be used by Google to contact you if we need to, and won't be shown on Google Play. You'll need to verify them by receiving a code.

▤ **A form of payment**
To pay the one-time USD 25 registration fee

You'll need to verify your identity to publish apps

Back   Continue

Figure 13.9 – Creating a developer account for yourself

As shown in the preceding screenshot, you need an email address where users can reach out to you and another one where Google Play can reach out to you. You also need to pay a lifetime registration fee of USD 25 for the Google Play account. If you don't have an account, you can proceed with the purchase as it is a very straightforward process.

Once you open a Google Play Console account, you will be presented with the following screen:

Figure 13.10 – Google Play Console landing page

This shows a list of all your apps if you already have some. It shows the developer account name and account ID as well. On the left, we have a navigation drawer that presents us with several options related to our developer account. At the top right, we have a button where we can create an app. Let us click the **Create app** button. We will then see a page with some fields to fill in:

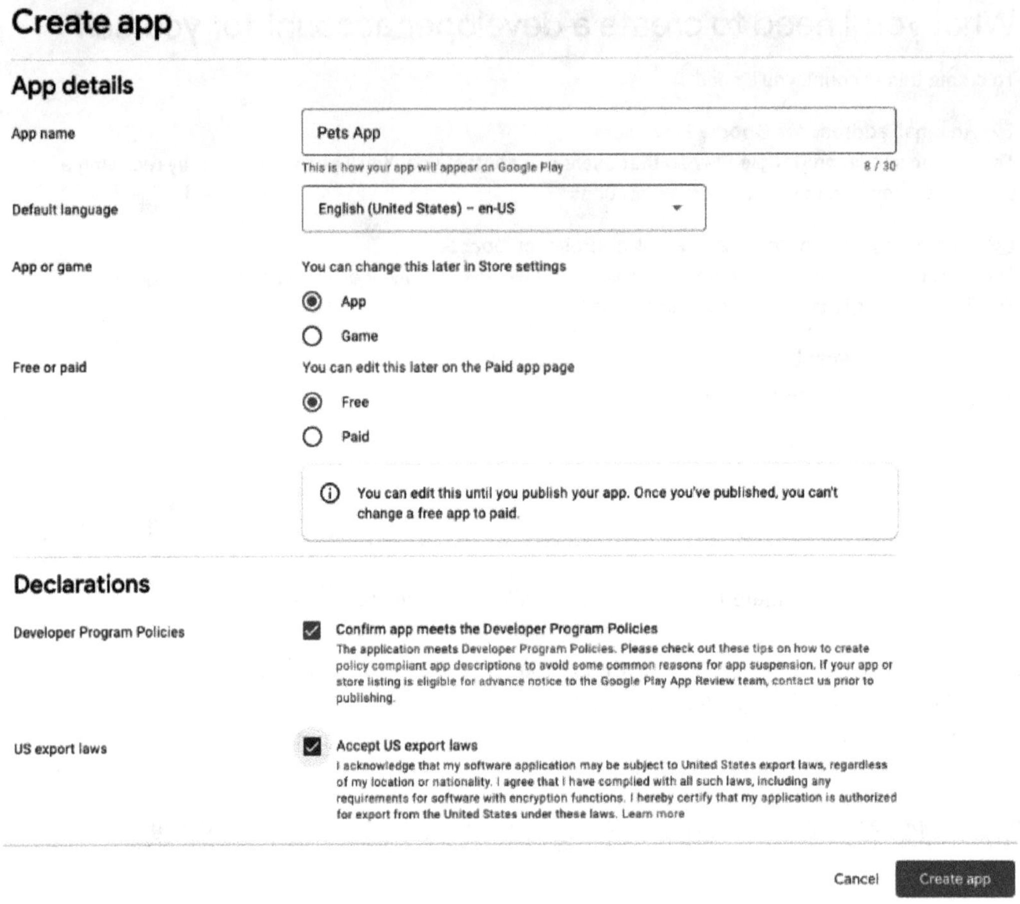

Create app

App details

App name

> Pets App
>
> This is how your app will appear on Google Play   8 / 30

Default language

> English (United States) – en-US   ▼

App or game

You can change this later in Store settings

- ◉ App
- ○ Game

Free or paid

You can edit this later on the Paid app page

- ◉ Free
- ○ Paid

> ⓘ   You can edit this until you publish your app. Once you've published, you can't change a free app to paid.

Declarations

Developer Program Policies

☑ **Confirm app meets the Developer Program Policies**
The application meets Developer Program Policies. Please check out these tips on how to create policy compliant app descriptions to avoid some common reasons for app suspension. If your app or store listing is eligible for advance notice to the Google Play App Review team, contact us prior to publishing.

US export laws

☑ **Accept US export laws**
I acknowledge that my software application may be subject to United States export laws, regardless of my location or nationality. I agree that I have complied with all such laws, including any requirements for software with encryption functions. I hereby certify that my application is authorized for export from the United States under these laws. Learn more

Cancel   Create app

Figure 13.11 – Creating your app

Here, we are supposed to fill in the app name and set the default language. We also select whether our app is an app or a game and specify whether it will be a free or paid app.

Lastly, we accept the declarations shown. Let us finish by clicking **Create app** at the bottom. This creates a new app. However, the app cannot be accessed by users on the Google Play Store yet. This is because we still have a number of pending tasks to complete, as seen on the app dashboard that is shown after creating the app.

Dashboard

Get started setting up your app. Show more

Start testing now

Release your app early for internal testing without review

Share your app with up to 100 internal testers to identify issues and get early feedback

View tasks ⌄

Set up your app

Provide information about your app and set up your store listing

Let us know about the content of your app, and manage how it is organized and presented on Google Play

View tasks ⌄

Figure 13.12 – Setting up your app

As seen in *Figure 13.12*, the first section involves setting up app details. Alternatively, you can also opt to test the app with a group of internal testers. Each step has its own tasks, which are listed, and the Play Console shows us the progress for each task. The second section involves creating a release for our app. It is in this section that we use the app bundle that we created earlier on:

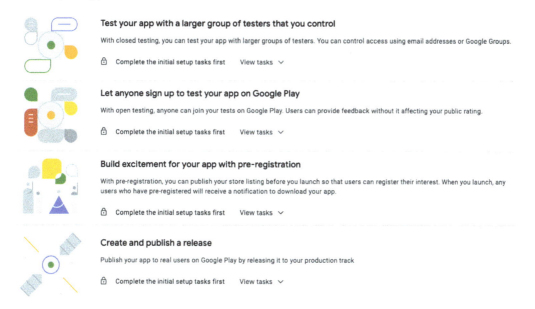

Figure 13.13 – Set up a release

As seen in *Figure 13.13*, this section has different subsections that involve creating and publishing our release, testing our app with many users, and options such as creating a pre-registration step for our app. All steps have a list of tasks that guide us on how to approach them.

Since it is our first app, let us expand the tasks by clicking the **View tasks** button in the **Set up your app** step:

Set up your app

Provide information about your app and set up your store listing

Let us know about the content of your app, and manage how it is organized and presented on Google Play

Hide tasks ∧

LET US KNOW ABOUT THE CONTENT OF YOUR APP

- ○   Set privacy policy ›
- ○   App access ›
- ○   Ads ›
- ○   Content rating ›
- ○   Target audience ›
- ○   News apps ›
- ○   COVID-19 contact tracing and status apps ›
- ○   Data safety ›
- ○   Government apps ›
- ○   Financial features ›

MANAGE HOW YOUR APP IS ORGANIZED AND PRESENTED

- ○   Select an app category and provide contact details ›
- ○   Set up your store listing ›

Figure 13.14 – Tasks listed under the Set up your app step

This provides us with a list of tasks that we need to complete. All these tasks provide more details regarding the content of our app. It is here that we provide the privacy policy of our app, specify whether users need special access to use features of our app, specify whether we have ads on our app, fill in content rating questionnaires and data safety forms, and specify our target audience, alongside other tasks. We will go through the tasks one by one:

1. **Set privacy policy**

    In this section, we add a privacy policy link to provide information on how we use data that we collect from our users. Failure to add a privacy policy to your app can lead to the app being removed from the Google Play Store.

    Privacy policies should be done by legal teams. However, many online tools can help generate a privacy policy. One such tool is `https://app-privacy-policy-generator.firebaseapp.com/`. We will use this tool to generate a privacy policy for our app. Once we have the privacy policy, we should have it on a public link and add the link to the privacy policy in the **Privacy policy URL** field as shown here:

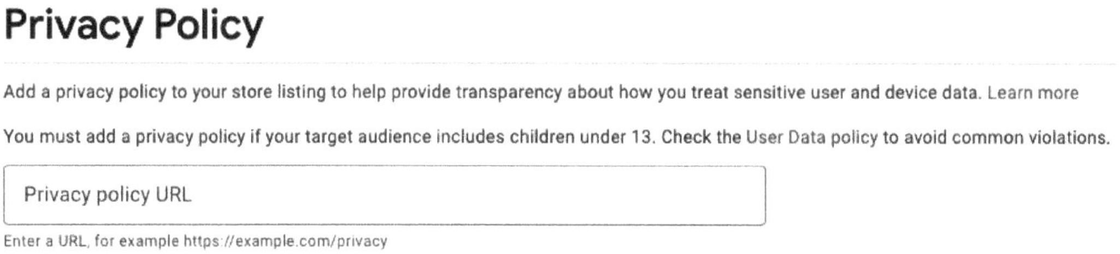

Privacy Policy

Add a privacy policy to your store listing to help provide transparency about how you treat sensitive user and device data. Learn more

You must add a privacy policy if your target audience includes children under 13. Check the User Data policy to avoid common violations.

> Privacy policy URL

Enter a URL, for example https://example.com/privacy

Figure 13.15 – Privacy Policy section

Click **Save** to add your changes. You can then go back to the main list of tasks to proceed with the next section.

2. **App access**

    In this section, we specify whether users need special access to use features in our app. If they do, we must provide the login credentials or instructions on how to be able to access the features.

    They are needed since the review process of apps involves testing all the functionality of the apps. Failure to provide the instructions may see our app being removed from the Google Play Store. Since our app does not need special access, we choose **All functionality in my app is available without any access restrictions** and save the answer.

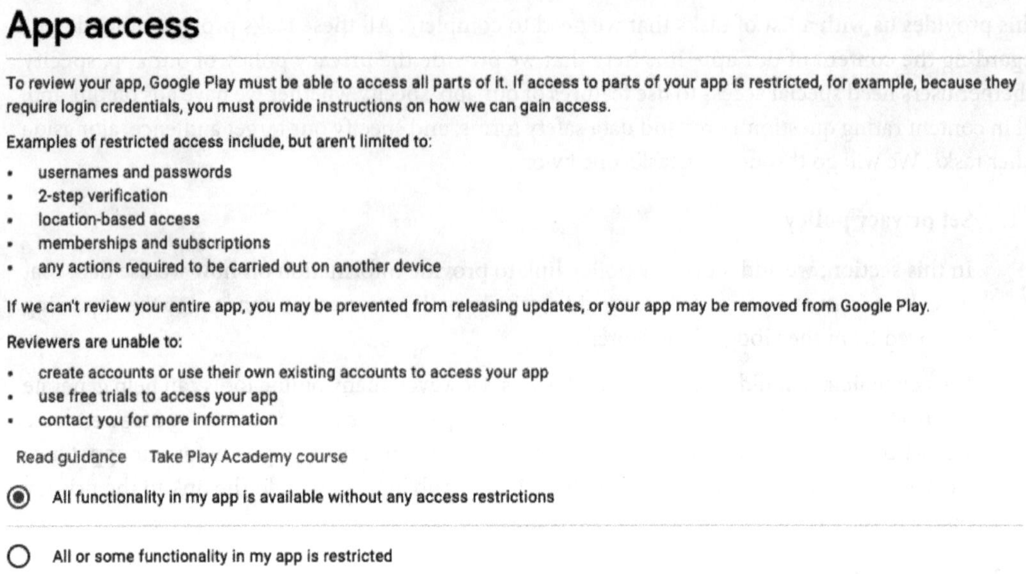

App access

To review your app, Google Play must be able to access all parts of it. If access to parts of your app is restricted, for example, because they require login credentials, you must provide instructions on how we can gain access.

Examples of restricted access include, but aren't limited to:

- usernames and passwords
- 2-step verification
- location-based access
- memberships and subscriptions
- any actions required to be carried out on another device

If we can't review your entire app, you may be prevented from releasing updates, or your app may be removed from Google Play.

Reviewers are unable to:

- create accounts or use their own existing accounts to access your app
- use free trials to access your app
- contact you for more information

Read guidance   Take Play Academy course

◉ All functionality in my app is available without any access restrictions

○ All or some functionality in my app is restricted

Figure 13.16 – App access section

3. **Ads**

In this task, we specify whether our app contains ads. Apps with ads have a **Contains ads** label on the Play Store. Since our app does not have ads, we choose the **No, my app does not contain ads** option and save the answer.

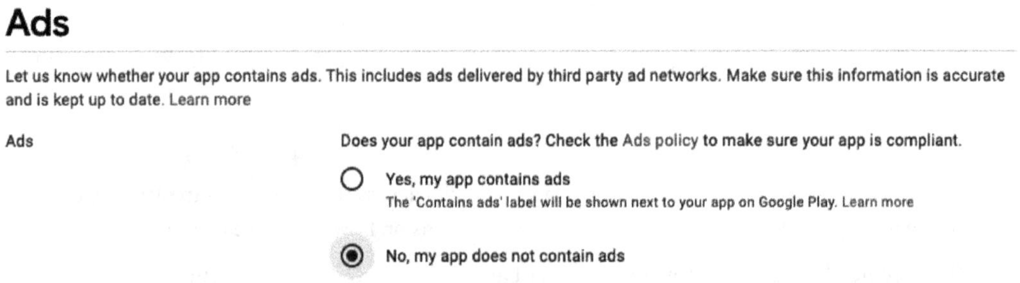

Ads

Let us know whether your app contains ads. This includes ads delivered by third party ad networks. Make sure this information is accurate and is kept up to date. Learn more

Ads   Does your app contain ads? Check the Ads policy to make sure your app is compliant.

○ Yes, my app contains ads
The 'Contains ads' label will be shown next to your app on Google Play. Learn more

◉ No, my app does not contain ads

Figure 13.17 – Ads section

4. **Content ratings**

In this task, we answer several questions that determine our app's content rating.

Content ratings

Receive ratings for your app from official rating authorities

Complete the content rating questionnaire to receive official content ratings for your app. Ratings are displayed on Google Play to help users identify whether your app is suitable for them.

Figure 13.18 – Content ratings section

Click the **Start questionnaire** button to start the questionnaire. You will be presented with the questions in three steps. The first step is about the category of the app:

Content ratings

1 Category   **2** Questionnaire   **3** Summary

Category

Email address

This will be used to contact you about your content ratings. It may be shared with rating authorities and IARC.

Category

○ Game
The app is a game or betting app. Examples include: Candy Crush Saga, Temple Run, Mario Kart, The Sims, Angry Birds, casino games, or daily fantasy sports.

○ Social or Communication
The primary purpose of this app is to meet or communicate with people. Examples include Facebook, Twitter, Skype, and SMS.

○ All Other App Types
Any app that isn't a game, social networking app, or communication app. Examples include entertainment products, consumer stores, news apps, lifestyle apps, streaming services, utilities, tools, emoji sets, fitness apps, magazines, and customizations.

Figure 13.19 – Content ratings category

Here, we specify an email address that can be used to reach us about the content rating and the category of our app. We have three categories, and each category has a description and an example to guide us in choosing the correct category. We'll choose **All Other App Types** and click **Next** at the bottom of the page to proceed to the next step, as shown:

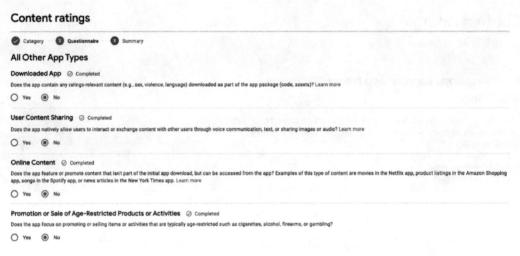

Figure 13.20 – Content ratings questionnaire

This section has many questions about the app's content. We must be careful when answering this to ensure we answer them correctly. Once we complete this step, we click **Next** to proceed to the next step, which shows a summary of our answers and the content rating of our app:

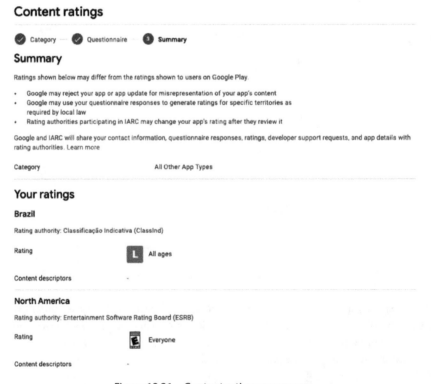

Figure 13.21 – Content ratings summary

We can also see the rating of our app in different regions of the world. We can save the rating and go back to the main list of tasks.

5. **Target audience**

    This section has several questions about our app's target audience. If we are targeting people under the age of 18, we must ensure that our content is safe for people in that age bracket.

Target audience and content

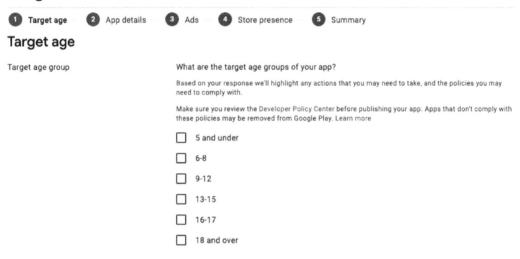

Figure 13.22 – Target audience and content section

Our app targets people above the age of 18 years. The next question is whether the app would unintentionally appeal to children.

Target audience and content

✅ Target age ── ② App details ── ③ Ads ── **④ Store presence** ── ⑤ Summary

Store presence

You've declared your target audience doesn't include children under 13. Google will review your store listing to make sure that it doesn't unintentionally appeal to children under 13.

The following question asks if you think your store listing could unintentionally appeal to children. Learn more

Answer 'Yes' if you think certain elements of your store listing may appeal to children, for example young characters or animations. The 'Not designed for children' label may be shown next to your app on Google Play.

Answer 'No' if you're unsure, prefer not to answer, or think your store listing doesn't unintentionally appeal to children.

Appeal to children	Could your store listing unintentionally appeal to children?
	⭘ Yes
	The 'Not designed for children' label may be shown next to your app on Google Play. Learn more
	⦿ No
	If Google disagrees with your answer, you won't be able to update your app.

Figure 13.23 – Appeal to children

We chose the **No** option. This will skip the ads section in this section since we said our app does not have ads.

Let us click **Next** to proceed to the next step, which shows a summary of our answers:

Target audience and content

✅ Target age ── ② App details ── ③ Ads ── ✅ Store presence ── **⑤ Summary**

Here's what you've told us

Changes you make here may cause your Data safety form to become out of date. If you make changes, check your Data safety form to make sure that it accurately represents how your app collects and shares data.

Target age	The target age group for your app is: 18 and over
Store presence	Your app doesn't appeal to children. If Google disagrees with your answer, you won't be able to update the app. If this happens, there are a number of ways you can resolve it. Learn more

Figure 13.24 – Target audience summary

As we can see in *Figure 13.24*, in case the review team does not agree with our answers in this section, we won't be able to update our app. So, we must be careful when answering the questions. We can save the answers and go back to the main list of tasks. After going back, we can see the progress in the various tasks:

Set up your app

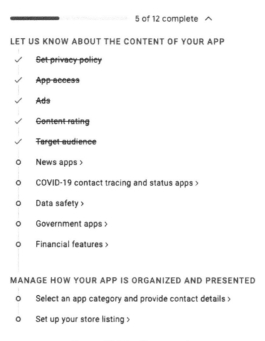

Provide information about your app and set up your store listing

Let us know about the content of your app, and manage how it is organized and presented on Google Play

5 of 12 complete ∧

LET US KNOW ABOUT THE CONTENT OF YOUR APP

✓ ~~Set privacy policy~~

✓ ~~App access~~

✓ ~~Ads~~

✓ ~~Content rating~~

✓ ~~Target audience~~

○ News apps ›

○ COVID-19 contact tracing and status apps ›

○ Data safety ›

○ Government apps ›

○ Financial features ›

MANAGE HOW YOUR APP IS ORGANIZED AND PRESENTED

○ Select an app category and provide contact details ›

○ Set up your store listing ›

Figure 13.25 – Setup tasks progress

6. **News apps**

    In this section, we specify whether our app is a news app. Note that we must comply with Google Play Store guidelines on news policy, which we can read more about when publishing a news app. Here, we choose the **No** option and save the answer. We can go back to the main list of tasks.

News apps

Let us know whether your app is a news app. This helps us make sure you comply with the Google Play News policy. Learn more

News apps   Is your app a news app?

⦿   No

○   Yes
     I confirm my app complies with the Google Play News policy

Figure 13.26 – News apps section

7.   **COVID-19 contact tracing and status apps**

This section is for apps that are related to COVID-19.

COVID-19 contact tracing and status apps

To help us understand whether your app is a COVID-19 contact tracing or status app, select all of the statements below that apply to your app.

☐ My app is a publicly available COVID-19 contact tracing app
For example, an app that tracks or monitors infected or exposed individuals for the purpose of COVID-19 response or mitigation

☐ My app is a publicly available COVID-19 status app
For example, an app that verifies an individual's current infection status, vaccination status, or history of infection for the purposes of determining the individual's eligibility for travel or entry into public spaces.
Learn more

☑ My app is not a publicly available COVID-19 contact tracing or status app

Figure 13.27 – COVID-19 apps section

We'll choose the **My app is not a publicly available COVID-19 contact tracing or status app** option and save the answer.

8.   **Data safety**

In this section, we disclose the kind of data our app collects and how we are using the data. There are several questions about the collection, security, data types, and usage of this data. If our app collects personal or sensitive data, we must provide a privacy policy and answer questions in this section.

Data safety

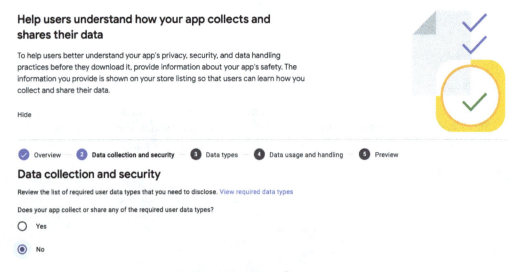

Help users understand how your app collects and shares their data

To help users better understand your app's privacy, security, and data handling practices before they download it, provide information about your app's safety. The information you provide is shown on your store listing so that users can learn how you collect and share their data.

Hide

✓ Overview   ② **Data collection and security**   ③ Data types   ④ Data usage and handling   ⑤ Preview

Data collection and security

Review the list of required user data types that you need to disclose. View required data types

Does your app collect or share any of the required user data types?

◯ Yes

◉ No

Figure 13.28 – Data safety section

We choose the **No** option since we are not collecting any data in our app, and save the answer. After filling in the form, we can proceed to preview the answers that we provided and cross-check that everything is in order, as shown in the following figure:

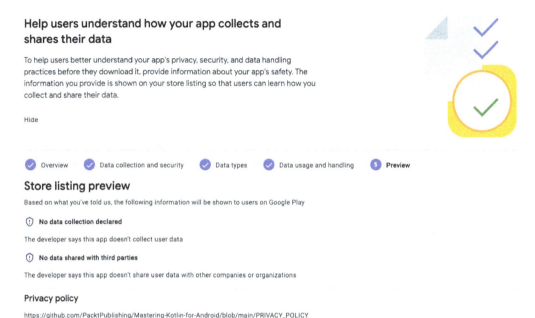

Figure 13.29 – Data safety summary

As shown in *Figure 13.29*, we can see a summary of our answers and the privacy policy link. You must ensure we answer this section properly, especially if you are publishing an app that collects personal or sensitive data.

9. **Government apps**

   This section is for apps that are related to the government.

Government apps

Figure 13.30 – Government apps section

We choose the **No** option since our app is not a government app, and save the answer.

10. **Financial features**

This section is for apps that have financial features. If our app provides personal loans, banking services, or other financial services, we must answer the questions in this section.

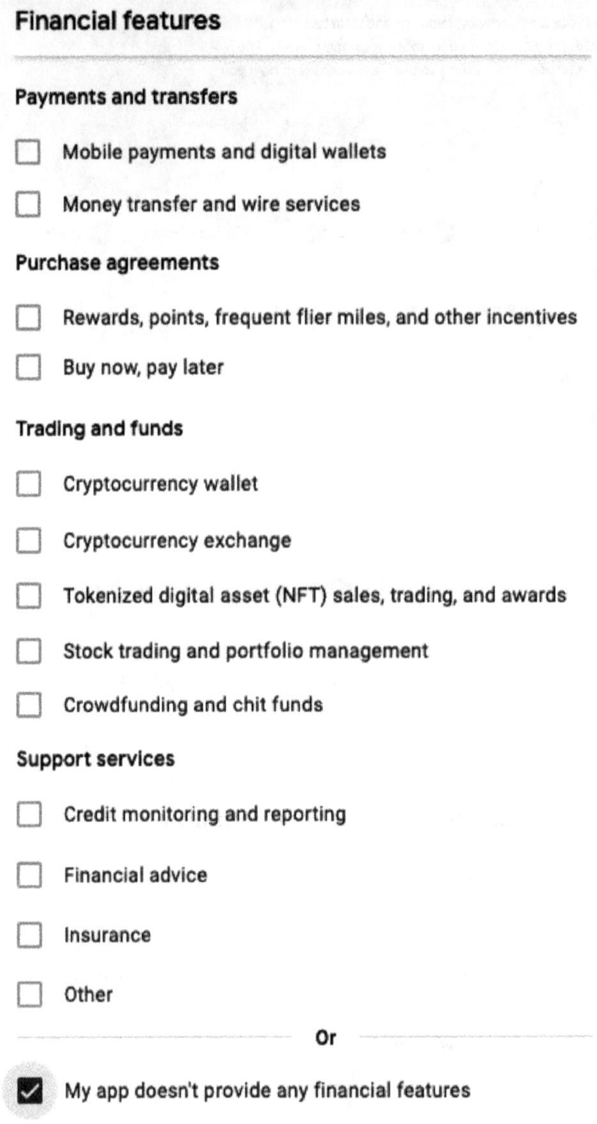

Financial features

Payments and transfers

☐ Mobile payments and digital wallets

☐ Money transfer and wire services

Purchase agreements

☐ Rewards, points, frequent flier miles, and other incentives

☐ Buy now, pay later

Trading and funds

☐ Cryptocurrency wallet

☐ Cryptocurrency exchange

☐ Tokenized digital asset (NFT) sales, trading, and awards

☐ Stock trading and portfolio management

☐ Crowdfunding and chit funds

Support services

☐ Credit monitoring and reporting

☐ Financial advice

☐ Insurance

☐ Other

―――――――――――――――― Or ――――――――――――――――

☑ My app doesn't provide any financial features

Figure 13.31 – Financial features section

We choose the **My app doesn't provide any financial features** option since our app does not provide any of the services, and save the answer.

11. **Store settings**

In this section, we provide contact details such as **Email address**, **Phone number**, and **Website**. The **Email address** field is the only mandatory field.

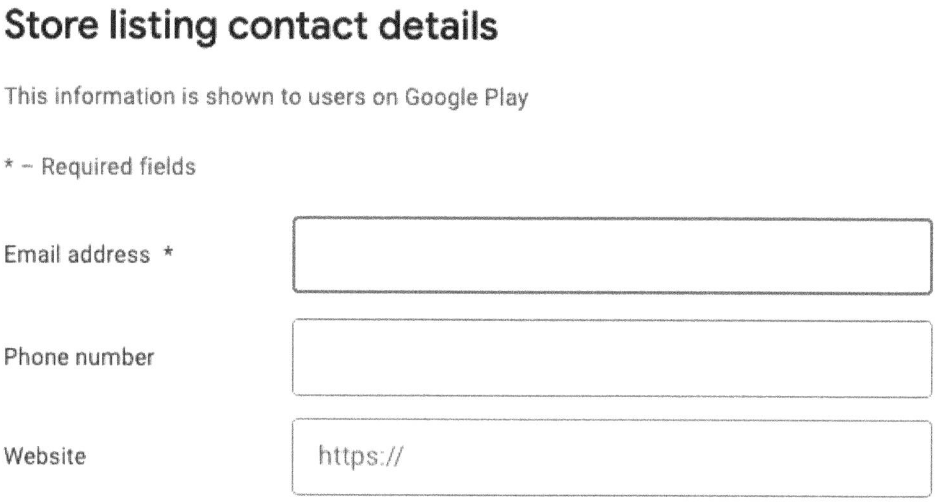

Store listing contact details

This information is shown to users on Google Play

* – Required fields

Email address *

Phone number

Website   https://

Figure 13.32 – Store listing contact details

After filling in the contact details, we also need to specify the category.

App category

Choose an application type, category, and tags that best describe the content or main function of your app. These help users discover apps on Google Play.

* – Required fields

App or game *   App   ▼

Category *   Education   ▼

Figure 13.33 – App category

Choose the category that best describes what your app does.

12. **Store listing**

In this section, we complete the details of our app. We provide a short and full description of what our app does. We also provide different graphics for our app. We must add an app icon, phone and tablet screenshots, and a feature graphic. This information is displayed on the Google Play page of our app. For all graphics, we have the required dimensions provided for us.

Main store listing

Default – English (United States) – en-US   Manage translations ▾

App name *

Pets App

This is how your app will appear on Google Play   8 / 30

Short description *

A short description for your app. Users can expand to view your full description.   0 / 80

Full description *

0 / 4000

Graphics

Manage your app icon, screenshots, and videos to promote your app on Google Play. Review the content guidelines before uploading new graphics. If you add translations for your store listing without localized graphics, we will use the graphics from your default language.

App icon *

Drop a PNG or JPEG file here to upload

⬆ Upload

Your app icon must be a PNG or JPEG, up to 1 MB, 512 px by 512 px, and meet our design specifications

Figure 13.34 – Store listing section

After filling out all these sections, we are now ready to push our first release to the Google Play Store. If we need to edit any of the preceding sections, we can always head over to the **App content** section and the **Store settings** sections and edit the section that we want to edit. Also, note that several sections may have been added since this chapter's writing. The Google Play Store team always sends updates to developers on any changes that they make.

Now, let us create our first release in the next section.

Creating our first release

The Google Play Store offers the following types of releases:

- **Internal app sharing**: This allows us to quickly share our app with internal team members for testing. They access the app via a link that we share with them. This is extremely useful when we want to test our app with a small group of people before we release it to the public.

- **Internal app testing**: This allows us to add a group of testers – a maximum of 100 people who are able to opt in to test our app. The testers can be a group of people from our organization or external testers.

- **Closed testing**: This allows us to create one or more testing tracks to test pre-releases of our app with a larger group of testers.

- **Open testing**: This allows anyone to opt in to test the app. There is no limit on the number of testers.

- **Production release**: This is the final release of our app. This is the release that is available to all users on the Google Play Store.

For all these releases, we must upload an Android App Bundle. We already have an Android App Bundle that we created earlier on. Let us head over to the **Testing** section and select the **Internal testing** option to create our first release. We are going to create an *internal testing release*:

1. *Adding testers*

   We need to create a new email list with the emails of our testers.

Create email list

Figure 13.35 – Create email list

Only people in this email list can access the app with a special opt-in link provided by Google Play. You can always access the link after you save the email list, as shown here:

Testers

Up to 100 testers can join your internal tests. You can choose more than 100 testers, but only the first 100 to join will be successful.

Testers	List name	Users
	☑ Pet App Testers	1 →

Create email list

Feedback URL or email address

Let testers know how to provide you with feedback   0 / 512

How testers join your test

Join on the web   Testers can join your test on the web

                         🔗 Copy link

Figure 13.36 – Testing the opt-in link

2. *Creating a release*

    In this section, we upload the AAB that we created earlier on. Before the upload, we can see we have a warning to choose the signing key, as shown in *Figure 13.37*:

Create internal testing release

Internal testing releases are available to up to 100 testers that you choose

① **Create release** — ② Preview and confirm

App integrity

ⓘ Releases not signed by Google Play

Google Play's integrity and signing services help you to ensure your apps and games are experienced the way you intend

Get integrity protection   **Choose signing key**

App bundles

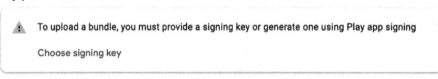

⚠ To upload a bundle, you must provide a signing key or generate one using Play app signing

Choose signing key

Figure 13.37 – Signing key warning

We must choose the Play signing one in addition to our own. This ensures we can recover our signing key if it is lost. Once we choose, we are able to upload our AAB. After we choose our signing key, we can proceed to create our release.

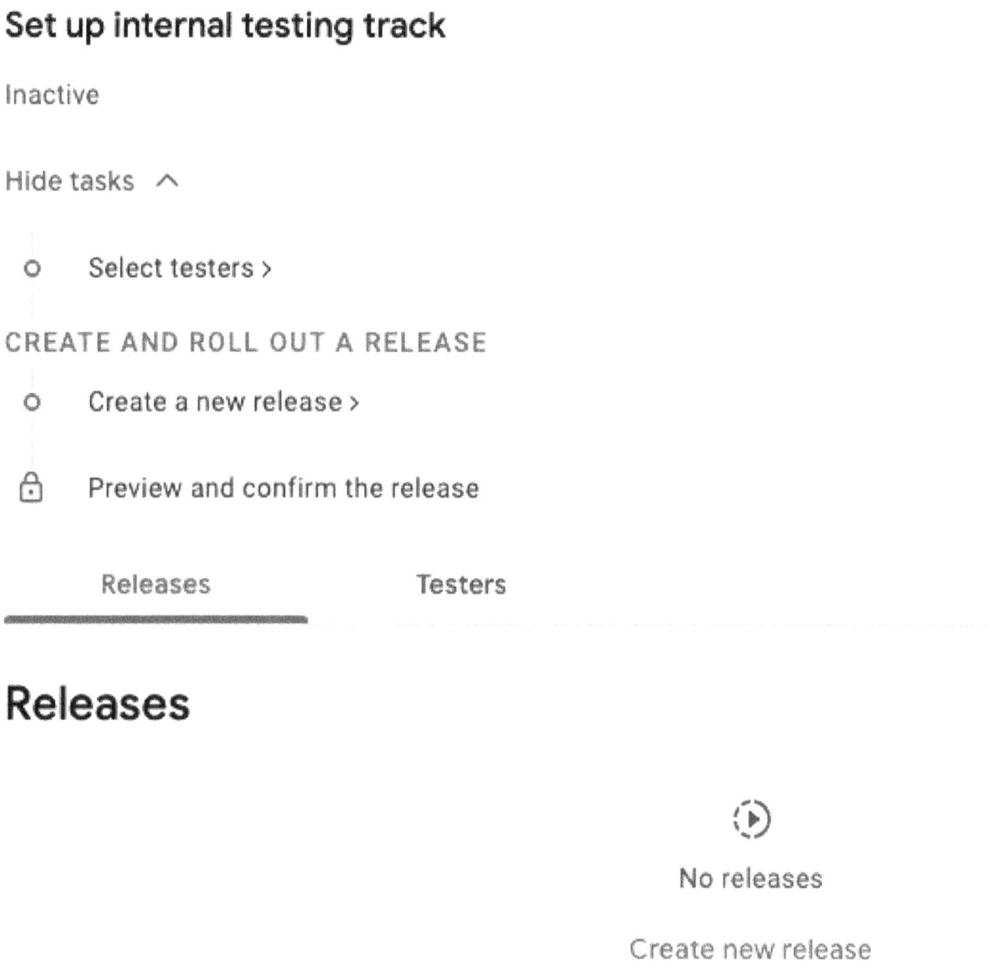

Set up internal testing track

Inactive

Hide tasks ∧

○   Select testers >

CREATE AND ROLL OUT A RELEASE

○   Create a new release >

🔒   Preview and confirm the release

Releases   Testers

Releases

No releases

Create new release

Figure 13.38 – Set up release track

For first-time releases, ensure that the **app id** is correct since you cannot change that once you upload the AAB. Once our bundle is uploaded successfully, we can see the release details being populated:

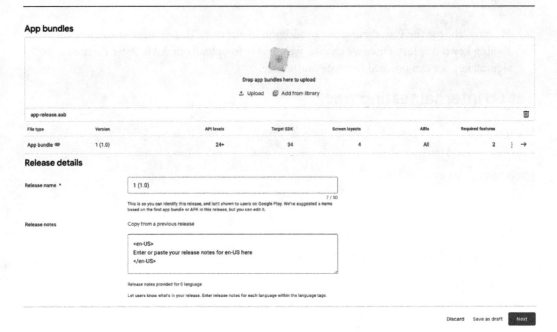

Figure 13.39 – Bundle details

Click **Next** to continue with the process. You will be presented with the following screen:

Figure 13.40 – Release summary

This shows a summary of our release and all the details that we have provided. Clicking **Save** creates the release as shown:

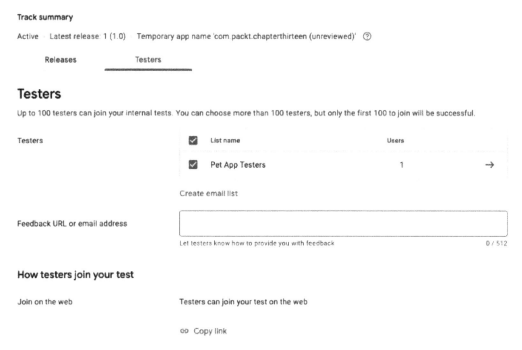

Track summary   Pause track

Active · Latest release: 1 (1.0) · Temporary app name 'com.packt.chapterthirteen (unreviewed)' ⑦

Releases   Testers

Releases

1 (1.0)   View release details

⊘ Available to internal testers · 1 version code · Released on Nov 21 1:00 AM · Not reviewed

Show summary ⌄   Promote release ▾

Figure 13.41 – Internal testing track summary

We can click the **Testers** tab where we can see the testers we added and an opt-in link that we can share with our testers.

Track summary

Active · Latest release: 1 (1.0) · Temporary app name 'com.packt.chapterthirteen (unreviewed)' ⑦

Releases   Testers

Testers

Up to 100 testers can join your internal tests. You can choose more than 100 testers, but only the first 100 to join will be successful.

Testers	☑	List name	Users	
	☑	Pet App Testers	1	→

Create email list

Feedback URL or email address

Let testers know how to provide you with feedback   0 / 512

How testers join your test

Join on the web   Testers can join your test on the web

ເວ Copy link

Figure 13.42 – Viewing the testers

We can always add more testers and create more releases in the same way as described in this section. All the other tracks have the same process, but the audience is different.

Congratulations on your first release! You have been able to release your first app to the Google Play Store. You can always go back and edit the details of your app.

Now you can promote this release to production so that your app will be live on the Google Play Store as shown:

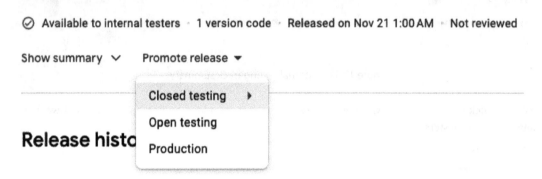

Releases

1 (1.0)

⊘ Available to internal testers · 1 version code · Released on Nov 21 1:00 AM · Not reviewed

Show summary ∨   Promote release ▼

Closed testing   ▶

Open testing

Release histo

Production

Figure 13.43 – Promote release

In the next section, let us look at some of the policies to be kept in mind as you are developing your app.

An overview of Google Play Store policies

Google Play policies are part of our releases. As such, we developers must be aware of most of them, if not all. This is because if we violate any of the policies, our app could be removed from the Google Play Store. We also need to be aware of them since some of them influence how we develop our apps.

In this section, we will look at some of the policies we need to be aware of as we develop our apps:

- **Background location access**: Apps are restricted from accessing the user's location in the background unless they are delivering a high-quality, beneficial user experience. This is to ensure that apps do not drain the battery of the user's device. If your app needs to access location in the background, you must provide a compelling reason why it needs to access location in the background. You also must provide a privacy policy that explains how you are using the location data that you are collecting.

- **Data safety**: With newer Android versions, there has been an emphasis on data safety. As mentioned, when filling out the **Data safety** section, we must ensure our app complies with the policies. We must provide privacy policies, terms, and conditions and share with our users how we use their data.

- **Financial apps**: Different countries have different rules for financial apps. We must ensure we are aware of the rules of the country we are targeting. Some countries provide licenses and Google Play requires us to upload these licenses as proof of compliance. If we are developing a financial app, we must ensure we are compliant and have the necessary licenses.

- **Restricted content**: Google Play has several types of restricted content. We must check that our app does not have any restricted content.

- **Intellectual property**: We must ensure our app does not infringe on any intellectual property. We must ensure we have the necessary rights to use any content in our app.

- **Use of SMS or call log permission groups**: Apps that use SMS or call log permission groups are required to be approved by Google Play. This is to ensure that apps do not misuse the permissions. If our app uses any of these permissions, we must submit a permission declaration form.

- **Health content and services**: Google Play does now allow apps that expose users to harmful health-related content. We must ensure our app does not expose users to such content.

To learn more about these policies, you can read more on the Google Play Console help page (`https://support.google.com/googleplay/android-developer/answer/13837496?hl=en`). This page provides an extensive overview of the policies with in-depth examples of violations. You can also check Google Play Academy (`https://playacademy.withgoogle.com/`) to learn more about Google Play.

Summary

In this chapter, we have learned step-by-step how to publish a new app in the Google Play Store. We walked through how to create a signed app bundle and the things required for us to publish our first app to the Google Play Store. Additionally, we learned about some of the Google Play Store policies and how to always stay compliant to avoid our apps being removed or accounts being banned.

In the next chapter, we will learn how to use GitHub Actions to automate some manual tasks such as deploying new builds to the Play Store. We will learn how to run tests on **Continous Integration and Continous Delivery (CI/CD)** pipelines and push builds to the Google Play Store using GitHub Actions.

14

Continuous Integration and Continuous Deployment

After we complete the development and first deployment of our app, we must think of how to make the process smoother for consecutive deployments, and that's where **Continuous integration/Continuous delivery (CI/CD)** comes in.

In this chapter, we will learn how to use GitHub Actions to automate some of the manual tasks, such as deploying new builds to the Google Play Store. We will learn how to run tests on CI/CD pipelines and push builds to the Play Store using GitHub Actions.

In this chapter, we're going to cover the following main topics:

- Setting up GitHub Actions
- Running lint checks and tests on GitHub Actions
- Deploying to Play Store using GitHub Actions

Technical requirements

To follow the instructions in this chapter, you will need to have Android Studio Hedgehog or later (`https://developer.android.com/studio`) downloaded.

You can use the previous chapter's code to follow the instructions in this chapter. You can find the code for this chapter at `https://github.com/PacktPublishing/Mastering-Kotlin-for-Android/tree/main/chapterfourteen`.

Setting up GitHub Actions

Before we can understand GitHub Actions, we need to understand what CI/CD is. This is a process that allows us to automate the building, testing, and deployment of our code to production. CI/CD not only automates these processes but also integrates them into a single coherent pipeline. This ensures that code changes are more reliable and stable when deployed. The definition should emphasize the role of CI/CD in facilitating frequent and reliable updates. This is an especially important process as it aims to improve the speed, efficiency, and reliability of how we deliver our software.

Benefits of CI/CD

Let's go through some of the benefits of CI/CD:

- **Fast release cycles**: CI/CD allows us to release our software faster and more frequently. This is because we are automating the process of building, testing, and deploying our code.

- **Increased collaboration**: Since a lot of the processes are automated, we can focus on the code and the features we are building. This allows us to collaborate more effectively with our team.

- **Less manual work**: We are reducing the amount of manual work we do due to automation. This means we can focus on the code and the features we are building.

- **Improved quality**: Automating the process allows us to test our code more frequently and more effectively. This means we can catch bugs and errors earlier in the process.

Now we have learned about the benefits of CI/CD, let us look at how CI/CD works in detail.

How CI/CD works

Let us go through how CI/CD works:

- **CI**: This is the process of automating the building and testing of our code. This is done every time we push our code to our repository. This allows us to catch bugs and errors earlier in the process. In this step, once we push or commit code to our remote repository, which can be hosted in GitHub, Gitlab, Bitbucket, and so on, we run checks and tests against these changes to ensure they are functional and meet the code quality standards. If the tests pass, we can merge the code into the main branch. If the tests fail, we can fix the code and run the tests again.

- **CD**: This is the process of automating the deployment of our code to production. This is done every time we push our code to our repository. This allows us to release our software faster and more frequently. This happens after the CI step. Once the changes are merged to the main or development branch, we can deploy the code to production or whichever environment it needs to be deployed to. This step aims at pushing minor changes to production more frequently. This allows us to release our software faster and more frequently.

With this background, we can now look at GitHub Actions (`https://docs.github.com/en/actions`). GitHub Actions is a CI/CD tool that allows us to automate the building, testing, and deployment of our code. It is built into GitHub and is free to use up to certain limits. It is also extremely easy to use and set up.

In the next section, we are going to set up GitHub Actions for our project that is in this repository: `https://github.com/PacktPublishing/Mastering-Kotlin-for-Android`

Setting up GitHub Actions

To enable GitHub Actions in our project, follow these steps:

1. Go to the **Actions** tab of our repository, as shown in the following screenshot:

Figure 14.1 – GitHub Actions tab

This step will bring us to the GitHub Actions landing page:

Get started with GitHub Actions

Build, test, and deploy your code. Make code reviews, branch management, and issue triaging work the way you want. Select a workflow to get started.

Skip this and set up a workflow yourself →

Q Search workflows

Suggested for this repository

Publish Java Package with Gradle
By GitHub Actions

Build a Java Package using Gradle and publish to GitHub Packages.

Configure   Java ●

Java with Gradle
By GitHub Actions

Build and test a Java project using a Gradle wrapper script.

Configure   Java ●

Deployment   View all

Deploy Node.js to Azure Web App
By Microsoft Azure

Build a Node.js project and deploy it to an Azure Web App.

Configure   Deployment ●

Deploy to Amazon ECS
By Amazon Web Services

Deploy a container to an Amazon ECS service powered by AWS Fargate or Amazon EC2.

Configure   Deployment ●

Build and Deploy to GKE
By Google Cloud

Build a docker container, publish it to Google Container Registry, and deploy to GKE.

Configure   Deployment ●

Terraform
By HashiCorp

Set up Terraform CLI in your GitHub Actions workflow.

Configure   Deployment ●

Deploy to Alibaba Cloud ACK
By Alibaba Cloud

Deploy a container to Alibaba Cloud Container Service for Kubernetes (ACK).

Configure   Deployment ●

Deploy to IBM Cloud Kubernetes Service
By IBM

Build a docker container, publish it to IBM Cloud Container Registry, and deploy to IBM Cloud Kubernetes Service.

Configure   Deployment ●

Tencent Kubernetes Engine
By Tencent Cloud

This workflow will build a docker container, publish and deploy it to Tencent Kubernetes Engine (TKE).

Configure   Deployment ●

OpenShift
By Red Hat

Build a Docker-based project and deploy it to OpenShift.

Configure   Deployment ●

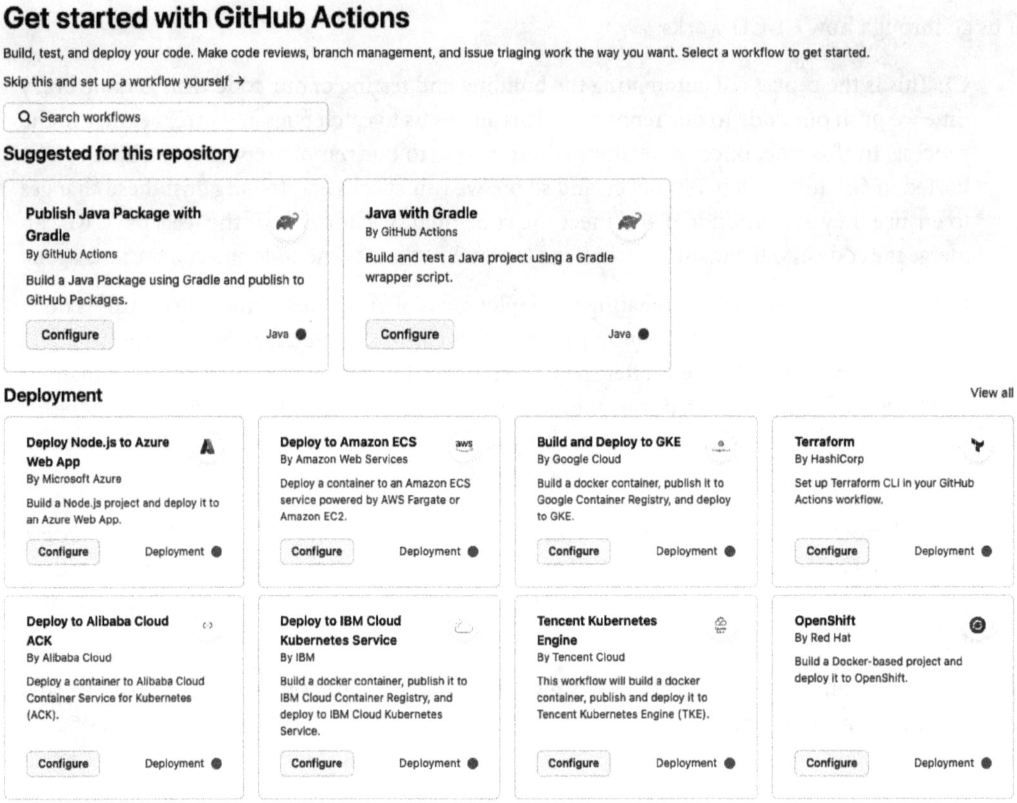

Figure 14.2 – GitHub Actions landing page

2. As seen in the preceding image, we have some suggested actions that we can use in our repository. For now, we will set the actions by ourselves, so let us click on the **set up a workflow yourself** option. This brings us to the following page:

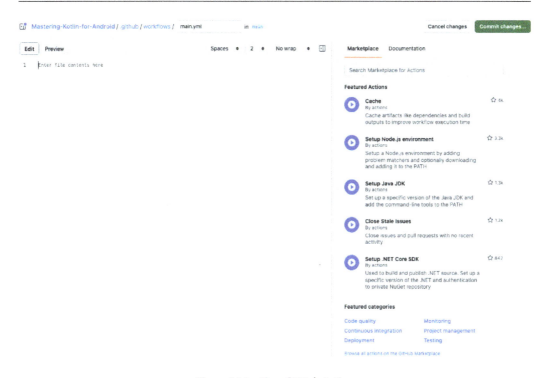

Figure 14.3 – New GitHub Action

As you can see in the preceding image, we have an editor for writing our workflow. Notice at the top we now have a new folder called .github. This is where we will store our workflow files. The editor saves the workflow file in the .github/workflows folder. By default, our workflow is named main.yml. On the right, we have templates that we can use to easily create our workflow.

3. For now, we are going to create our own workflow, so let us add the following code to our workflow:

```
name: Push

on:
  push:
    branches: ["main" ]
  workflow_dispatch:

jobs:
  build:
    name: Build
    runs-on: ubuntu-latest
    steps:
        - run: echo "The job was automatically triggered by a
${{ github.event_name }} event."
```

Let's understand the different fields in the preceding workflow file:

- `name`: This is the name of our workflow. This will be displayed on the GitHub Actions page.

- `on`: This is the event that will trigger our workflow. In our case, we are triggering our workflow when we push code to the main branch.

- `workflow_dispatch`: This is a manual trigger that we can use to trigger our workflow from the GitHub Actions page. This is useful when we want to trigger our workflow manually.

- `jobs`: This is the job that will be run when our workflow is triggered. In our case, we have a job called `build`. This job will run on the latest version of Ubuntu as specified by the `runs-on` field.

- `steps`: This field contains the steps that will be run in our job. In our case, we have a single step that will run a command. This command will print out the event that triggered our workflow. A step can contain a shell command or an action from GitHub Marketplace.

4. Click on the **Commit changes...** button. This will commit our workflow file to our repository and trigger our workflow. We can see the workflow running in the **Actions** tab, as shown in the following screenshot:

Figure 14.4 – First GitHub Action

In the preceding image, we can see the commit that triggered the workflow and the workflow itself. We can also see the job that was run and the step that was run. We can also see the output of the step. Additionally, we can see the time it took to run the workflow. If we tap the action, we can see more details:

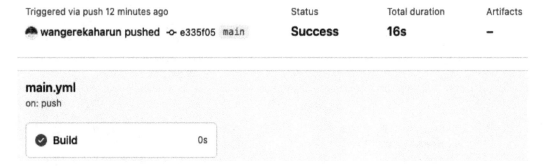

Figure 14.5 – Github Action details

This shows the steps that were run and the time the job took to run. It also shows the total duration of the workflow.

This was a simple workflow that just printed out the event that triggered the workflow. We can also do more complex things in our workflow.

Let us see how we can set up Android-related actions in our workflow:

1. Head to the newly created `.github/workflows` folder and edit the `main.yml` file.

2. Let us add the following code to our workflow below the previous command we ran in *step 3* of the previous section:

```
- name: Checkout
  uses: actions/checkout@v3

- name: Set up JDK 17
  uses: actions/setup-java@v3
  with:
    java-version: '17'
    distribution: 'zulu'
    cache: gradle
- name: Grant execute permission for gradlew
  run: chmod +x gradlew
  working-directory: ./chapterfourteen

- name: Build with Gradle
  run: ./gradlew assembleDebug
  working-directory: ./chapterfourteen
```

Let us understand the preceding code:

- We have created another step called `Checkout`. This step will `checkout` our code from our repository. This is done using the `checkout` action, which we specify using the `uses` field. This action is fetched from GitHub Marketplace.

- We have created another step called `Set up JDK 17`. This step will set up JDK 17. **Java Development Kit** (**JDK**) is a development environment for building applications and components using the Java programming language. 17 is the version of JDK that we use. We use this version since the **Android Gradle Plugin** (**AGP**) from version 8.0.0 requires JDK 17 to work. Our project runs on AGP 8.2.1.

- This is done using the `setup-java` action, which we specify using the `uses` field. We specify the version of Java we want to use using the `java-version` field. We specify the distribution of Java we want to use using the `distribution` field. We also specify that we want to cache Gradle using the `cache` field.

- We have created another step called `Grant execute permission for gradlew`. This step will grant execute permission for gradlew. This is done using the `run` command. We specify the command we want to run using the `run` field. We also specify the working directory we want to run the command in using the `working-directory` field. In this case, we want to run the command in the `chapterfourteen` folder since we have a number of folders in our repository. Note that this step is platform-dependent since it is only necessary for Unix-based systems but might be redundant for Windows-based systems. Therefore, it may not be required in all CI/CD setups.

- Lastly, we have created another step called `Build with Gradle`. This step will build our project using Gradle. Here, we run the `./gradlew assembleDebug` command. This command generates a debug Android APK for our project. We also specify the working directory in which we want to run the command.

One thing to note is that `.yml` files are overly sensitive to indentation. So, we need to ensure that we indent our code correctly.

3. Commit to the changes and the action will automatically run. We can see the workflow results and, looking at the job build, we can see all the steps that were run, as shown in the following screenshot:

Figure 14.6 – GitHub Action steps

We now know what GitHub Actions are, have created our first action, and have seen how we can run Android-specific workflows on GitHub Actions. In the next section, we will run lint checks and tests in our workflow.

Running lint checks and tests on GitHub Actions

In *Chapter 11*, we learned how to run lint checks on our project using shell commands on the terminal. We have also learned how to write tests for our code base. In this section, we are going to run the format, lint checks, and tests on our newly created actions and we will do all of this step by step:

1. First, we will add the `ktlintCheck` step:

    ```
    - name: Run ktlintCheck
      run: ./gradlew ktlintCheck
      working-directory: ./chapterfourteen
    ```

    In this code, we have added a step called `Run ktlintCheck`. This step will run the `ktlintCheck` command, which will check whether our code is formatted correctly. This step fails if our code is not formatted correctly.

2. Next, we add the `detekt` step:

    ```
    - name: Run detekt
      run: ./gradlew detekt
      working-directory: ./chapterfourteen
    ```

    In this step, we run the `detekt` command, which will run the detekt checks on the code that we set up earlier in *Chapter 11*. This step fails if our code does not pass the detekt checks.

3. Next, we add the test step:

    ```
    - name: Run unit tests
      run: ./gradlew testDebugUnitTest
      working-directory: ./chapterfourteen
    ```

    This step will run all the unit tests in our project. This step fails if any of the tests fail.

4. Lastly, we add the step to run our instrumented tests:

    ```
    - name: Run connected tests
      uses: ReactiveCircus/android-emulator-runner@v2
      with:
        working-directory: ./chapterfourteen
        api-level: 33
        target: google_apis
        arch: x86_64
        disable-animations: true
        script: ./gradlew connectedCheck
    ```

This step uses the `android-emulator-runner` action to run our instrumented tests on an emulator. This action sets up an emulator to run our instrumented tests in the CI environment. In the action configuration, we set up the following:

- `working-directory`: This is where our project is located.

- `api-level`: This is the API level of the platform system image for our emulator.

- `target`: This is the target for the system image of the emulator.

- `architecture`: We specify the architecture of the emulator we want to run our tests on.

- `disable-animations`: We disable animations in the emulator.

- Lastly, we specify the command we want to run using the script field. In this case, we run the `connectedCheck` task, which will run our instrumented tests.

5. After making the preceding changes, commit the changes and the action will run. We can see the results of the action in the **Actions** tab, as shown in the following screenshot:

Figure 14.7 – More Github Actions steps

We've expanded our workflow by incorporating additional steps to perform lint checks and tests. We can see the results of each step. We can also see the time it took to run each step. The `Run connected test` step takes the longest time to run. This is because it must set up the emulator and run the tests.

We need to modify when the **Push** workflow on the `main.yml` file runs. Currently, our workflow runs when we push code to the main branch. We are going to change this to also run when we create a pull request to the main branch. This is because we want to run our checks before we move our code to the main branch. To do this, we are going to add the `pull_request` event just above the `workflow_dispatch` event:

```
on:
  push:
    branches: ["main" ]
  pull_request:
  workflow_dispatch:
```

After making this change, we can commit the changes and the action will run. Let us now create a pull request to test the changes. Ensure that you pull all the changes that we made in our browser locally before proceeding with the following steps:

1. First, let us create a new branch called `test`.

2. Open the terminal in Android Studio and run the following command:

    ```
    git checkout -b test
    ```

    This command creates a new branch called `test` and switches to the newly created branch.

3. Next, let us modify the app's `versionName` and `versionCode` in our app-level `build.gradle.kts` file:

    ```
    versionCode = 2
    versionName = "1.0.1"
    ```

4. Tap **Sync Now** to sync these changes to our project.

5. After making the `versionName` and `versionCode` changes, we can commit the changes and push them to our remote repository. We can do this by running the following command in the terminal:

    ```
    it add .
    ```

    This command stages all the changes we have made.

6. Next, we run the following command:

    ```
    git commit -m "Update app version name and code"
    ```

    This command commits the changes we have made.

7. Next, we run the following command:

```
git push origin test
```

This command pushes the changes to our remote repository.

8. Next, head to our repository in a browser, open the **Pull requests** tab, and click on the **New pull request** button. This will open the following page:

Figure 14.8 – Create a new pull request

On this page, we set the `base` branch and the `compare` branch. The `base` branch is the branch we want to merge our changes to. In our case, we want to merge our changes to the `main` branch. The `compare` branch is the branch that has recent changes. In our case, we want to merge changes from the `test` branch to the `main` branch. We can see the changes we have made as soon as we set the `compare` branch.

9. Finalize the pull request by clicking on the **Create pull request** button. After creating the pull request, we can review the pull request details:

Update app version name and code #2

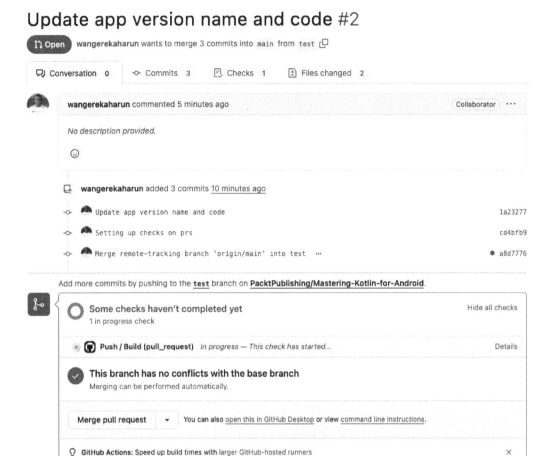

Figure 14.9 – Pull request checks

As seen in the preceding image, the workflow checks have started running since we created a pull request and we specified that our workflow should run when we create a pull request. The **Merge pull request** button is disabled since the workflow is still running.

Once the workflow is done running, we can merge the pull request. We can enforce even further rules per the checks but for now, we are good to go with the default behavior. Once the workflow completes and all checks pass, we should see the following:

Figure 14.10 – Pull request checks complete

We have now learned how to run lint checks and tests on GitHub Actions. In the next section, we are going to learn how to deploy our app to Google Play Store using GitHub Actions.

Deploying to Play Store using GitHub Actions

In *Chapter 13*, we learned how to deploy our app to Google Play Store using Google Play Console. However, in that chapter, we did it manually. In this chapter, we are going to learn how to deploy our app to Google Play Store using GitHub Actions. We are going to use the Google Play Publisher action to deploy our app to Google Play Store. This action is available in GitHub Marketplace.

Before we can write our workflow, we need to do some setup. We need to create a service account on our Google Play Store account. We can do this by following these steps:

1. Configure the service account in Google Cloud Platform by following these steps:

    I.   Navigate to `https://cloud.google.com/gcp`.

    II.   Navigate to **IAM and admin** | **Service accounts** | **Create service account**.

    III. Pick a name and add appropriate permissions, for example, owner permissions.

    IV.   Open the newly created service account, click on the **Keys** tab, and add a new JSON type key.

    V.   When the key is successfully created, a JSON file will be automatically downloaded to your machine.

    VI.   Store the content of this file in your GitHub repository secrets. You can do this by going to the **Settings** tab in your repository, clicking on the **Secrets and variables** section, and selecting the **Actions** option.

    VII. Create a **New Repository Secret** and upload the JSON file. You can name the secret `GOOGLE_SERVICES_JSON`. This is the name we will use in our workflow to access the JSON file.

2. Add a user to Google Play Console by following these steps:

    VIII. Open `https://play.google.com/console` and pick your developer account.

    IX.   Open **Users and permissions**.

    X.   Click on **Invite new user** and add the email of the service account created in step 1.

    XI.   Grant permissions to the app to which you want the service account to deploy in-app permissions.

    If you need more details on how to do this, you can check out the following link: `https://developers.google.com/android/management/service-account`

Like how we created the `GOOGLE_SERVICES_JSON` variable in our repository secrets, we need to add the details of our signing certificate to our variables so that we can use them on our CI/CD pipeline. The first step is to generate a `base64`-encoded version of our signing certificate. We can do this by running the following command in the terminal:

```
openssl base64 < packt.jks | tr -d '\n' | tee packt.jks.base64.txt
```

You should run this command in the directory where you saved your keystore file. You could change the name to match the filename of the keystore file if you named yours differently. This command will generate a `base64`-encoded version of our keystore file. We can then copy the contents of the file and add it to our repository secrets. We need to also add the following secrets to our repository:

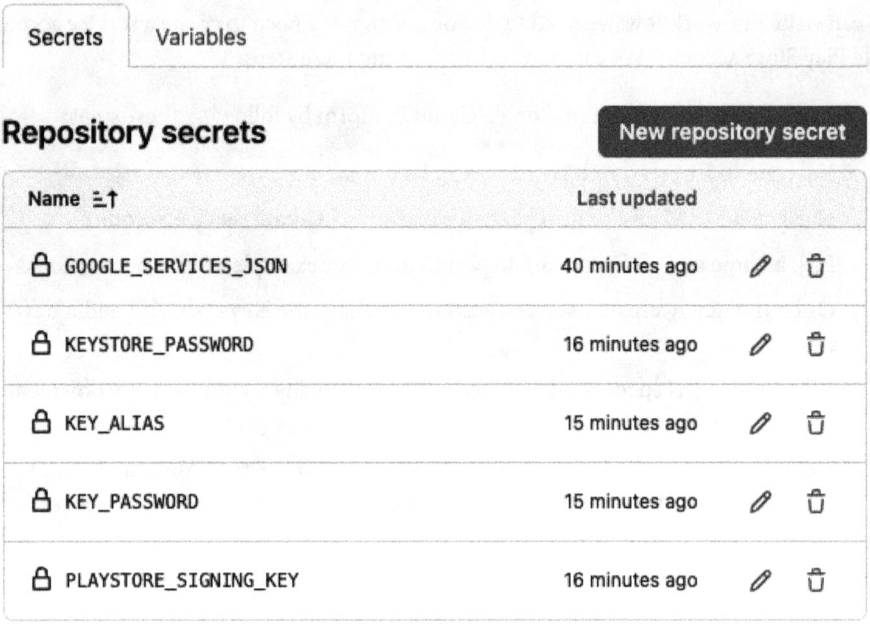

Secrets	Variables

Repository secrets

New repository secret

Name ⇅↑	Last updated		
🔒 GOOGLE_SERVICES_JSON	40 minutes ago	✏️	🗑️
🔒 KEYSTORE_PASSWORD	16 minutes ago	✏️	🗑️
🔒 KEY_ALIAS	15 minutes ago	✏️	🗑️
🔒 KEY_PASSWORD	15 minutes ago	✏️	🗑️
🔒 PLAYSTORE_SIGNING_KEY	16 minutes ago	✏️	🗑️

Figure 14.11 – Repository secrets

The newly created secrets are explained as follows:

- `KEYSTORE_PASSWORD`: This is the password of our keystore file
- `KEY_ALIAS`: This is the alias of our keystore file
- `KEY_PASSWORD`: This is the password of our keystore file alias

All these details should be like the ones we used when we created our keystore file. Now, let us write our workflow. Before writing the workflow, ensure that you have completed the publishing of our app steps in *Chapter 13*, since this is needed for this action to work. Let us head to the `.github/workflows` folder, create a new file called `deploy-to-playstore.yml`, and add the following code:

```
name: Deploy to Playstore
on:
  push:
    branches: [ "main"]

jobs:
  build:
    runs-on: ubuntu-latest

    steps:
      - uses: actions/checkout@v3
```

```
    - name: set up JDK 17
      uses: actions/setup-java@v3
      with:
        distribution: 'zulu'
        java-version: '17'

    - name: Bump version
      uses: chkfung/android-version-actions@v1.1
      with:
        gradlePath: chapterfourteen/build.gradle.kts
        versionCode: ${{github.run_number}}
        versionName: ${{ format('1.0.{0}', github.run_number ) }}

    - name: Assemble Release Bundle
      working-directory: chapterfourteen
      run: ./gradlew bundleRelease

    - name: Deploy to Internal Testing
      uses: r0adkll/upload-google-play@v1.1.1
      with:
        serviceAccountJsonPlainText: ${{ secrets.GOOGLE_SERVICES_
JSON }}
        packageName: com.packt.chapterthirteen
        releaseFiles: chapterfourteen/build/outputs/bundle/release/
app-release.aab
        track: internal
        whatsNewDirectory: whatsnew/
        status: completed
```

The workflow is remarkably similar to the one we created earlier on in the *Setting up GitHub Actions* and *Running lint checks and tests in GitHub Actions* sections with only slight differences. We have a step that bumps the versionName and versionCode for us instead of us having to do this manually every time. Versioning serves as a structured identifier for different software iterations. Employing semantic versioning aids in communicating the impact of changes, distinguishing major backward-incompatible updates, minor backward-compatible feature additions, and patch-level bug fixes. It plays a crucial role in dependency management, facilitating compatibility between different components. Additionally, versioning supports rollbacks, hotfixes, and efficient testing, ensuring the stability of the application. Release notes and communication are streamlined, providing users and stakeholders with clear insights into each release. Ultimately, versioning contributes to a reliable and predictable user experience, fostering trust and transparency throughout the software development life cycle.

We have another step that builds a signed **Android App Bundle** (**AAB**). We also have another step that deploys the signed AAB to the Google Play Store **Internal testing** track. We use the `upload-google-play` action, which automates and makes the process easier. We do the configurations on this action, such as specifying our service account, the package name of our app on Play Store, the directory where our signed AAB will be found, and lastly, the track that we want to deploy to. Pushing the changes to the main branch will trigger the actions again and once the `deploy-to-playstore` workflow is complete, we should see a new internal testing release on our Play Store page, as shown in the following:

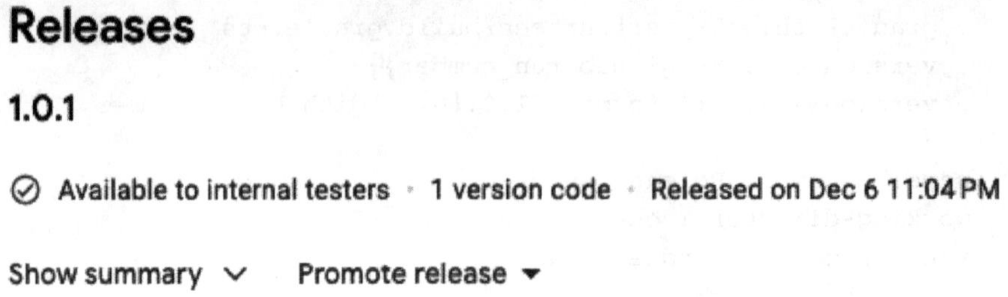

Releases

1.0.1

⊘ Available to internal testers · 1 version code · Released on Dec 6 11:04 PM

Show summary ∨   Promote release ▼

Figure 14.12 – New internal testing release

We have completed putting in place our CI/CD process. We only do this setup once and we can always use it to make deployments and automated testing easier, faster, and more reliable for us.

Summary

In this chapter, we learned how to use GitHub Actions to automate some manual tasks, such as deploying new builds to the Play Store. Additionally, we learned how to run lint checks and tests on CI/CD pipelines and push builds to Google Play Store using GitHub Actions.

In the next chapter, we will learn about techniques to improve our apps by adding analytics, using Firebase Crashlytics, and using cloud messaging to increase user engagement in our apps. Additionally, we will learn some tips and tricks for securing our apps.

15

Improving Your App

After we complete the development and publishing of our app, it is important to always be on the lookout when using things that help improve our apps, such as Firebase Messaging or Crashlytics. We are going to be learning how to use Firebase Messaging and Crashlytics in this chapter.

In this chapter, we will learn step-by-step techniques on how to improve our apps by adding analytics—Firebase Crashlytics—and how to use cloud messaging to increase user engagement. We will learn how to send notifications to our apps from the Firebase console. Additionally, we will learn some tips and tricks for securing our apps to ensure that user data is not compromised.

In this chapter, we're going to cover the following main topics:

- Using Firebase Crashlytics to detect crashes
- Improving app engagement with Firebase Messaging
- Securing your app

Technical requirements

To follow the instructions in this chapter, you will need to have Android Studio Hedgehog or a later version (`https://developer.android.com/studio`) downloaded.

You can use the previous chapter's code to follow the instructions in this chapter. You can find the code for this chapter on GitHub at `https://github.com/PacktPublishing/Mastering-Kotlin-for-Android/tree/main/chapterfifteen`.

Using Firebase Crashlytics to detect crashes

Crashes can happen in our apps for a variety of reasons, including common coding issues such as null pointer exceptions, memory leaks, and improper data handling. Device fragmentation caused by different device hardware configurations and different Android operation systems introduces compatibility issues that may at times cause crashes too. Network issues, insufficient resources, or mismanagement of external dependencies, such as third-party libraries, can cause crashes too. Sometimes, we can anticipate and handle them gracefully. Other times, they are unexpected and we need to know about them so we can fix them. Our app is already on Google Play Store, so at times, we might not have the luxury to debug on the devices that are having issues. Tools such as **Firebase Crashlytics** can help us detect crashes in our apps and provide us with the information we need to fix them. In this section, we will be setting up Firebase Crashlytics in our app and seeing how we can use it to detect crashes.

Android Studio has a built-in Firebase tool to help us quickly add Firebase to our app. We can access it from **Tools | Firebase**, which should open a side panel on the right, as shown in the following figure:

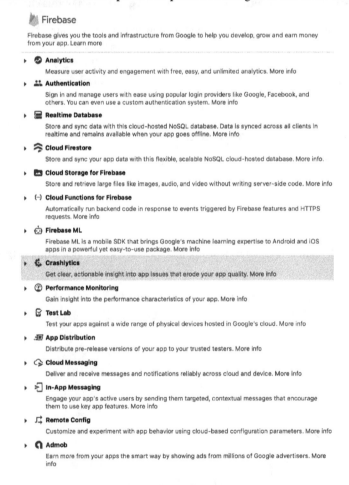

Figure 15.1 – Firebase setup

As seen in *Figure 15.1*, we can set up a variety of Firebase SDKs from this tool. We are interested in setting up **Crashlytics**. Tap on the **Crashlytics** option and we will see the following options:

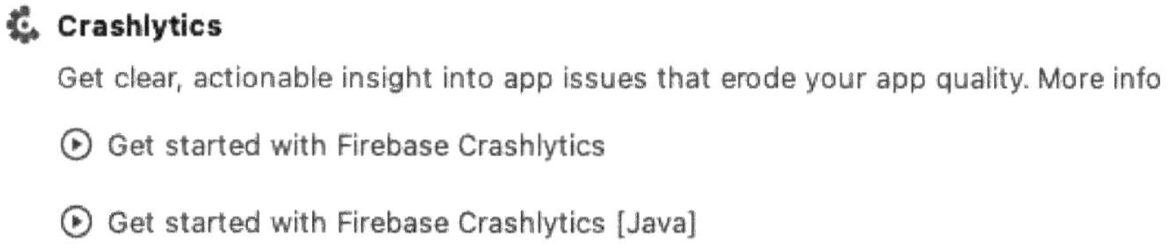

Crashlytics

Get clear, actionable insight into app issues that erode your app quality. More info

⊙ Get started with Firebase Crashlytics

⊙ Get started with Firebase Crashlytics [Java]

Figure 15.2 – Firebase Crashlytics setup

Since our project is written in Kotlin, we are going to select **Get started with Firebase Crashlytics** as an option. This will open a new window with the following instructions:

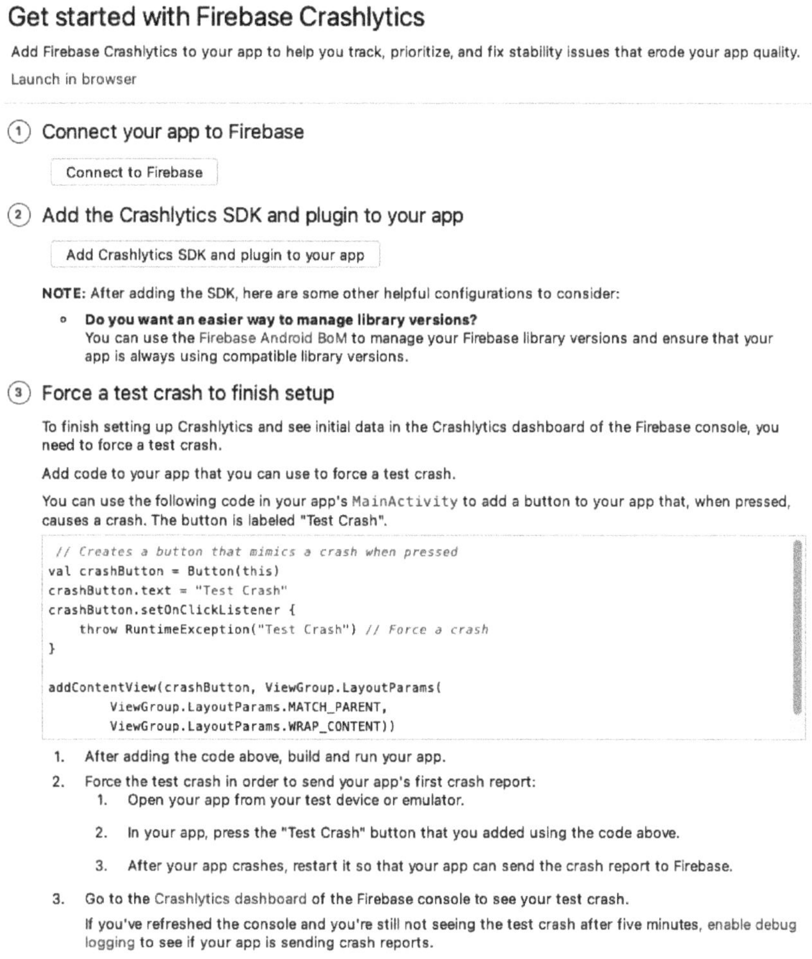

Get started with Firebase Crashlytics

Add Firebase Crashlytics to your app to help you track, prioritize, and fix stability issues that erode your app quality.

Launch in browser

① Connect your app to Firebase

> Connect to Firebase

② Add the Crashlytics SDK and plugin to your app

> Add Crashlytics SDK and plugin to your app

NOTE: After adding the SDK, here are some other helpful configurations to consider:

○ **Do you want an easier way to manage library versions?**
You can use the Firebase Android BoM to manage your Firebase library versions and ensure that your app is always using compatible library versions.

③ Force a test crash to finish setup

To finish setting up Crashlytics and see initial data in the Crashlytics dashboard of the Firebase console, you need to force a test crash.

Add code to your app that you can use to force a test crash.

You can use the following code in your app's `MainActivity` to add a button to your app that, when pressed, causes a crash. The button is labeled "Test Crash".

```
// Creates a button that mimics a crash when pressed
val crashButton = Button(this)
crashButton.text = "Test Crash"
crashButton.setOnClickListener {
    throw RuntimeException("Test Crash") // Force a crash
}

addContentView(crashButton, ViewGroup.LayoutParams(
        ViewGroup.LayoutParams.MATCH_PARENT,
        ViewGroup.LayoutParams.WRAP_CONTENT))
```

1. After adding the code above, build and run your app.
2. Force the test crash in order to send your app's first crash report:
   1. Open your app from your test device or emulator.
   2. In your app, press the "Test Crash" button that you added using the code above.
   3. After your app crashes, restart it so that your app can send the crash report to Firebase.
3. Go to the Crashlytics dashboard of the Firebase console to see your test crash.
   If you've refreshed the console and you're still not seeing the test crash after five minutes, enable debug logging to see if your app is sending crash reports.

Figure 15.3 – Steps to set up Crashlytics

As seen from *Figure 15.3*, it provides all the steps necessary for us to set up Firebase Crashlytics in our app. Let us tap the **Connect to Firebase** option. This opens a new tab in our browser with the Firebase console opened (see *Figure 15.4*). It shows all the Firebase projects that we have on our console (if we have any). Use the **Create a project** option and specify your preferred project name:

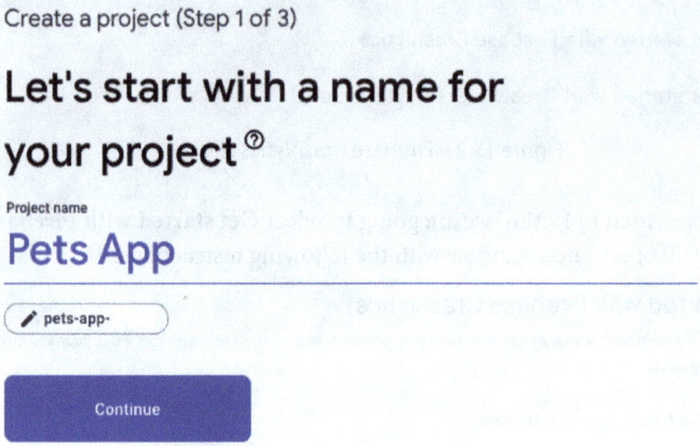

Create a project (Step 1 of 3)

Let's start with a name for your project ⊙

Project name

Pets App

✎ pets-app-

Continue

Figure 15.4 – New Firebase project

Click **Continue** to proceed to the next step. This will take us to the following screen:

Create a project (Step 2 of 3)

Google Analytics
for your Firebase project

Google Analytics is a free and unlimited analytics solution that enables targeting, reporting, and more in Firebase Crashlytics, Cloud Messaging, In-App Messaging, Remote Config, A/B Testing, and Cloud Functions.

Google Analytics enables:

🧪 A/B testing ⑦   🐞 Crash-free users ⑦

⊛ User segmentation & targeting across ⑦   🔔 Event-based Cloud Functions triggers ⑦
   Firebase products
                                                     ᵢᵢI Free unlimited reporting ⑦

✓ Enable Google Analytics for this project
   Recommended

Previous   Continue

Figure 15.5 – Google Analytics setup

In this screen, we configure Google Analytics for our app. It also shows the functionalities that Google Analytics provides for our app. Google Analytics collects usage and behavior data for our apps. We use it for tracking user events, system events, or errors, analyzing app performance, collecting user properties such as language preference and geographic location, and so on.

Click **Continue** to proceed to the next step:

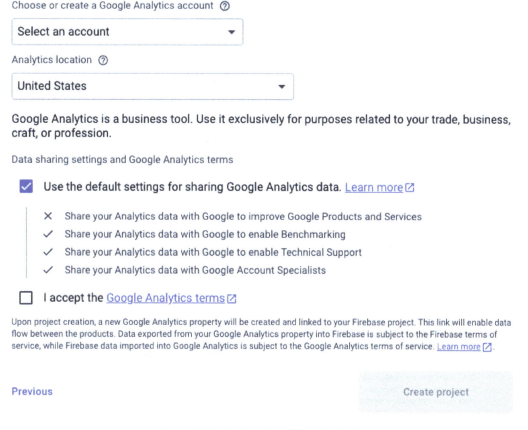

Figure 15.6 – Configuring Google Analytics

In this step, we configure more options for Google Analytics. We must select a Google Analytics account. Selecting the default account hides the other questions if you have already configured other projects. When done, click **Create project** to finalize creating the project and you will see the following dialog:

Your Firebase Android app has been created in Firebase.

It's ready for you to connect to your Android Studio project!

Connect

Figure 15.7 – Finalizing setup dialog

Clicking **Connect** after our project is created finalizes the setup of Firebase Crashlytics with Android Studio. Let us head back to Android Studio and see what has changed. We can see that the Firebase Crashlytics option is now checked:

Get started with Firebase Crashlytics

Add Firebase Crashlytics to your app to help you track, prioritize, and fix stability issues that erode your app quality.
Launch in browser

(1) Connect your app to Firebase

✓ Connected

(2) Add the Crashlytics SDK and plugin to your app

Add Crashlytics SDK and plugin to your app

NOTE: After adding the SDK, here are some other helpful configurations to consider:

○ **Do you want an easier way to manage library versions?**
You can use the Firebase Android BoM to manage your Firebase library versions and ensure that your app is always using compatible library versions.

Figure 15.8 – App connected

The next step is to add the Firebase Crashlytics SDK to our app. We can do this by clicking the **Add Crashlytics SDK and plugin to your app** button. This will add the necessary dependencies to our app. You can check the Gradle files to see these changes.

With all the steps complete, we can now **force-crash** our app to see if the Firebase Crashlytics setup is working. We can do this by adding the following code to our `MainActivity.kt` file inside the `onCreate()` function:

```
throw RuntimeException("Test Crash")
```

Now, run the app. The app will crash with the following stack trace:

```
E  FATAL EXCEPTION: main
   Process: com.packt.chapterthirteen, PID: 15987
   java.lang.RuntimeException: Unable to start activity ComponentInfo{com.packt.chapterthirteen/com.packt.chapterfifteen.MainActivity}: java.lang.RuntimeException: Test Crash
       at android.app.ActivityThread.performLaunchActivity(ActivityThread.java:3645)
       at android.app.ActivityThread.handleLaunchActivity(ActivityThread.java:3782)
       at android.app.servertransaction.LaunchActivityItem.execute(LaunchActivityItem.java:101)
       at android.app.servertransaction.TransactionExecutor.executeCallbacks(TransactionExecutor.java:135)
       at android.app.servertransaction.TransactionExecutor.execute(TransactionExecutor.java:95)
       at android.app.ActivityThread$H.handleMessage(ActivityThread.java:2307)
       at android.os.Handler.dispatchMessage(Handler.java:106)
       at android.os.Looper.loopOnce(Looper.java:201)
       at android.os.Looper.loop(Looper.java:288)
       at android.app.ActivityThread.main(ActivityThread.java:7872) <1 internal line>
       at com.android.internal.os.RuntimeInit$MethodAndArgsCaller.run(RuntimeInit.java:548)
       at com.android.internal.os.ZygoteInit.main(ZygoteInit.java:936)
   Caused by: java.lang.RuntimeException: Test Crash
       at com.packt.chapterfifteen.MainActivity.onCreate(MainActivity.kt:47)
       at android.app.Activity.performCreate(Activity.java:8305)
       at android.app.Activity.performCreate(Activity.java:8284)
       at android.app.Instrumentation.callActivityOnCreate(Instrumentation.java:1417)
       at android.app.ActivityThread.performLaunchActivity(ActivityThread.java:3626)<12 more...>
```

Figure 15.9 – Crash stack trace

We can head over to our newly created project in the Firebase console and see if the crash has been reported. In the Firebase console, Crashlytics is normally found under the **Release and Monitor** section on the navigation drawer, which is on the left side of the screen. It shows the following screen:

Figure 15.10 – Firebase console crash overview

We can see that the crash has been reported. We can click on the `MainActivity.onCreate` crash to see more details about it. It shows the following screen:

Figure 15.11 – Firebase console crash details

As seen in *Figure 15.10*, we have the following details from the Firebase console:

- **Stack trace**: This shows the stack trace of the crash.

- **Device**: This shows the device that the crash happened on. We can see the device model, the OS version, and the device state.

- **App version**: This shows the version of the app that crashed. It also shows the total number of crashes that have happened for that version.

This information is very helpful when debugging crashes. Android Studio Hedgehog and more recent versions also have a useful tool, **App Quality Insights**, that helps us view the Firebase crashes right from Android Studio. We can access it from the bottom tool tabs, as shown:

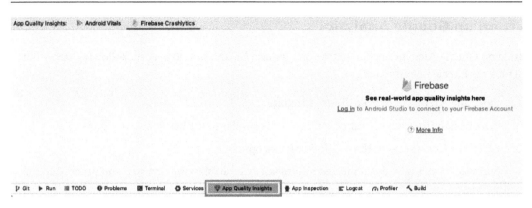

Figure 15.12 – App Quality Insights

As seen in *Figure 15.11*, we need to log in to our Firebase account that has the project we are working on. We can do this by clicking on the **Log in** button and completing the login process on our browser. Once logged in, we can see the crashes that have happened in our app:

Figure 15.13 – App Quality Insights crash details

This shows all the details, as we saw earlier in our Firebase console. We can see the stack trace too. The beauty of this is that we can easily navigate to the file and line causing the crash without having to switch context and go to the browser.

With Firebase Crashlytics set up, we can now detect crashes in our app and fix them. This will help us improve the quality of our app and make our users happy.

> **Important note**
> Remember to remove the code that we added to force a crash in our app.

Next, let us set up **Firebase Analytics**, which also gathers useful information about our app. This will help us understand how our users are using our app and help us make informed decisions on how to improve it.

Setting up Google Analytics

Setting up Google Analytics is like setting up Firebase Crashlytics. Repeat the following steps that you took for Firebase Crashlytics:

1. Open the Firebase tool from **Tools | Firebase**.

2. Select **Analytics** from the list of options that is similar to the list we saw in *Figure 15.1*.

3. Select the **Get started with Google Analytics** option.

4. Since our app is already connected to Firebase, we can skip the first step and proceed to the next step.

5. Tap the **Add Analytics to your app** button to add the necessary dependencies to our app.

6. Once Gradle sync is complete, we have finalized setting up Firebase Analytics in our app.

With that set, we can always view the analytics from the Firebase console. We can access it from the navigation drawer under the **Analytics** section. It shows the following screen:

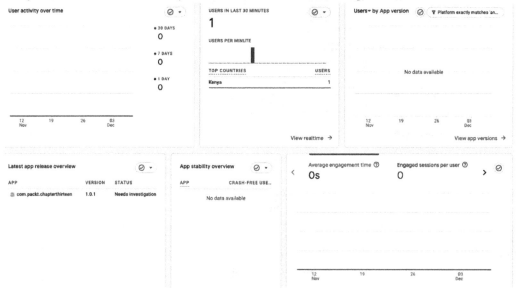

Figure 15.14 – App analytics

We have learned how to set up Firebase Crashlytics and Firebase Analytics in our app. We can now detect crashes in our app and gather useful information about our app. This will help us improve the quality of our app and make our users happy.

In the next section, we will learn how to use Firebase Cloud Messaging to send notifications to our app.

Improving app engagement with Firebase Messaging

When users install our app, they might not use it again after they finish what they want to do. This can lead to a decline in the number of active users, which can have different impacts on different apps.

We can leverage **Firebase Cloud Messaging** to send notifications to our users to remind them of our app. This will help us improve our app's engagement and increase the number of active users. In this section, we will be setting up Firebase Cloud Messaging in our app and see how we can use it to send notifications to our app users.

First, we need to set up the Firebase Cloud Messaging SDK on our app. This allows us to use the SDK within our project and enables our app to receive Firebase notifications once the setup is complete. We will do it the same way we did for Firebase Crashlytics and Firebase Analytics. Repeat the following steps:

1. Open the Firebase tool from **Tools | Firebase**.

2. Select **Cloud Messaging** from the list of options that is similar to the list we saw in *Figure 15.1*.

3. Select the **Setup Firebase Cloud Messaging** option.

4. Since our app is already connected to Firebase, we can skip the first step and proceed to the next step.

5. Tap the **Add FCM to your app** button to add the necessary dependencies to the app.

6. Once Gradle sync is complete, the FCM SDK is already set up in our app.

We need to create a new service to handle notifications when they are received and to also get the device token. Let us create a new package called `firebase`. Inside this package, let us create a new file called `FirebaseMessagingService.kt`. This will be our service that will handle notifications that are received.

Let us add the following code to it:

```
class FirebaseNotificationService: FirebaseMessagingService() {
    override fun onNewToken(token: String) {
        super.onNewToken(token)
        Log.d("Firebase Token", token)
    }

    override fun onMessageReceived(remoteMessage: RemoteMessage) {
        super.onMessageReceived(remoteMessage)
        sendNotification(remoteMessage)
    }

    private fun sendNotification(remoteMessage: RemoteMessage) {
        val notification = NotificationCompat.
Builder(applicationContext, "Pets Apps")
```

```
            .setContentTitle(remoteMessage.notification?.title)
            .setTicker(remoteMessage.notification?.ticker)
            .setContentText(remoteMessage.notification?.body)
            .setContentInfo(remoteMessage.notification?.body)
            .setStyle(NotificationCompat.BigTextStyle().
bigText(remoteMessage.notification?.body))
            .setSmallIcon(R.drawable.ic_launcher_background)

        if (Build.VERSION.SDK_INT >= Build.VERSION_CODES.O) {
            createChannel(notification, "Pets Apps")
        }
    }

    @RequiresApi(Build.VERSION_CODES.O)
    private fun createChannel(notificationBuilder: NotificationCompat.
Builder, id: String) {
        notificationBuilder.setDefaults(Notification.DEFAULT_VIBRATE)
        val channel = NotificationChannel(
            id,
            "Pets Apps",
            NotificationManager.IMPORTANCE_HIGH
        )
        channel.description = "Pets Apps"
        val notificationManager: NotificationManager =
            getSystemService(Context.NOTIFICATION_SERVICE) as
NotificationManager
        notificationManager.createNotificationChannel(channel)
    }
}
```

The following is a breakdown of the preceding code:

- We have created a class called `FirebaseNotificationService` that extends `FirebaseMessagingService`. This is the service that will handle notifications that are received.

- We have overridden the `onNewToken()` function. This function is called when a new token is generated. We can use this token to send notifications to our app. We have added a log message to log the token to our Logcat. Alternatively, we can send the token to our backend server to be used to send notifications to our app if we have such a requirement.

- We have overridden the `onMessageReceived()` function. This function is called when a notification is received. We have called the `sendNotification()` function and passed the `RemoteMessage` object to it.

- The `sendNotification()` function creates a notification and shows it to the user. We have used the `NotificationCompat.Builder` class to create the notification. We have also used the `RemoteMessage` object to get the notification `title`, `body`, and `ticker`. We have also set up a small icon to be used for the notification. We additionally set the notification channel if the device is running on Android Oreo or more recent versions.

- Lastly, we have created the `createChannel()` function, which creates the notification channel using the `NotificationChannel` class. We have also set the channel description and the importance of the channel. Additionally, we have set the default vibration for the channel. Finally, we have created the notification manager and used it to create the channel.

With the service created, we need to register it in our `AndroidManifest.xml` file. Let us add the following code to it:

```
<service
    android:name=".firebase.FirebaseNotificationService"
    android:exported="false">
    <intent-filter>
        <action android:name="com.google.firebase.MESSAGING_EVENT" />
    </intent-filter>
</service>
```

With the service registered, we can now receive notifications in our app. Run the app with the recent changes.

Next, let us test this by sending a notification from the Firebase console. We can do this by going to our Firebase console and selecting the **Cloud Messaging** option from the navigation drawer, which is in the **Engage** category. It shows the following screen:

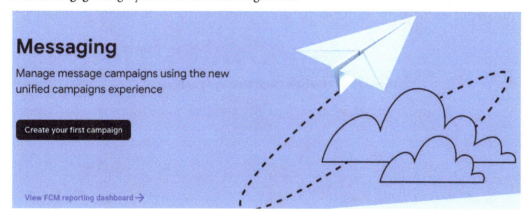

Figure 15.15 – Firebase Cloud Messaging landing page

This is our first time using Cloud Messaging, so we need to create a new campaign. Tap the **Create your first campaign** button. This opens a new dialog with the following options:

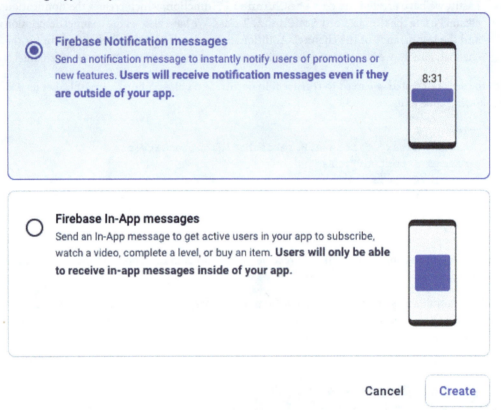

Firebase Messaging Onboarding

Message type and platform

◉ **Firebase Notification messages**
Send a notification message to instantly notify users of promotions or new features. **Users will receive notification messages even if they are outside of your app.**

8:31

○ **Firebase In-App messages**
Send an In-App message to get active users in your app to subscribe, watch a video, complete a level, or buy an item. **Users will only be able to receive in-app messages inside of your app.**

Cancel   Create

Figure 15.16 – Firebase Cloud Messaging options

We can send either **Firebase Notification messages** or **Firebase In-App messages**. Firebase notifications are designed to reach users outside of the app, delivering messages through push notifications even when our app is inactive. In contrast, Firebase in-app messages are tailored to engage users actively using our app by displaying content directly within the app's interface. Firebase notifications are suitable for sending timely updates or promotions, while in-app messages are effective for delivering contextual content and enhancing the user experience within our app. We are interested in **Firebase Notification messages**. Select the **Firebase Notification messages** option and tap **Create**. This brings us to the following screen:

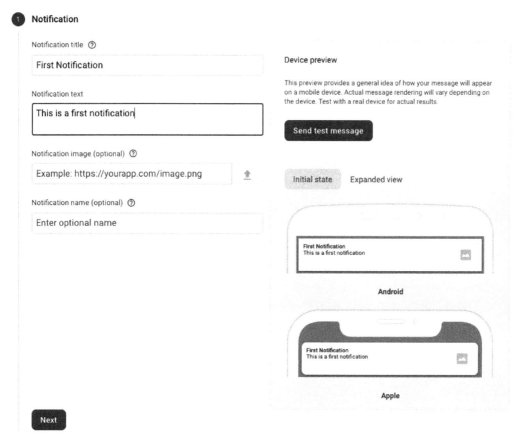

Figure 15.17 – Creating a new notification

In this screen, we add the title and text for our notification. Once you fill in these details, tap **Next** to proceed to the next steps:

Figure 15.18 – Target and Scheduling settings

As seen in *Figure 15.17*, we set the target app for our notification. In this case, it is the app that we created earlier in the *Using Firebase Crashlytics to detect crashes* section of this chapter. We then set the schedule for our notification. We have set the scheduling setting to **Send now**. Tap the **Review** button, which shows a dialog with the information we have set:

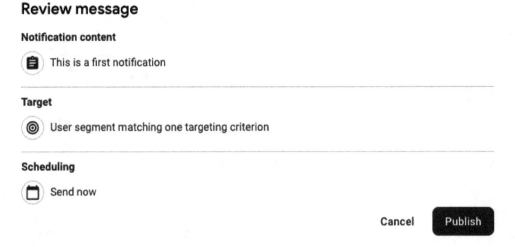

Figure 15.19 – Review message dialog

Tap the **Publish** button to publish the notification. This will send a notification to our app. We can now see the notification from our app:

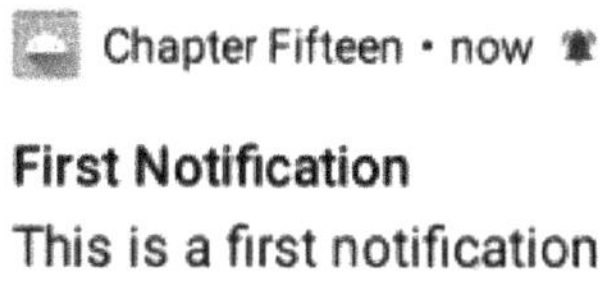

Chapter Fifteen • now 🔔

First Notification
This is a first notification

Figure 15.20 – First notification

> **Important note**
> Ensure that you always test using a real device to see your notifications.

We learned how to set up Firebase Cloud Messaging in our app and how to send notifications to it. In the next section, we will cover yet another critical topic—securing our app.

Securing your app

Ensuring your apps are secure is particularly important. We need to ensure that our users' data is safe and secure. We also need to ensure that our app is not vulnerable to attacks. Attacks such as malware, man-in-the-middle attacks, and data interception pose risks to sensitive information, while vulnerabilities such as SQL injection and privilege escalation can lead to unauthorized access and manipulation of databases or app functionalities. Cross-site scripting and code injection present avenues for attackers to execute malicious scripts or commands within the app, potentially compromising user sessions and data. Insecure data storage practices may expose sensitive information, and denial-of-service attacks can disrupt app services.

In this section, we are going to see some tips and tricks for securing our app. The following are some of the things that we can do to secure our app:

- **HTTPS**: We should always use HTTPS for all our network requests, which adds an extra layer of security to our app.

- **Code minification and obfuscation**: We should always minify and obfuscate our code to make it harder for attackers to reverse engineer our app. We already did this in *Chapter 13* for our release build.

- **Encryption**: We should always encrypt sensitive data that we store in our app.

- **Passwords and private keys**: Never store passwords and private keys in Shared Preferences. We can always store them in other secure alternatives, such as the Android Keystore system used for storing cryptographic keys.

- **Minimizing logged information**: We should always minimize the information that we log. We should never log sensitive information such as passwords and private keys.

- **Internal storage**: We should always use internal storage for sensitive data. This is because internal storage is private to our app and other apps cannot access it.

- **WebView**: We use WebView to display web content in our app. This can introduce security issues on our app, so we should be careful when using WebView.

- **Dependencies**: We should always keep all our dependencies up to date. This is because new versions of dependencies might have security fixes that we need to apply to our app. We use tools such as Dependabot (`https://github.com/dependabot`) to automate dependency updates.

- **Emulators or rooted devices**: For payment or banking apps, ensure that they do not work on emulators or rooted devices. With emulators and rooted devices, it is easy to change your code or view the data that is being sent to the server or stored in our app. This can lead to security issues.

- **Permissions**: We should always use the necessary permissions in our app. We should not use permissions that we do not need. This is because permissions can be used to access sensitive data in our app.

As you develop your apps, always keep security in mind. This will help you ensure that your app is secure and that your users' data is safe. You can learn more about Android security from the official Android documentation at `https://developer.android.com/privacy-and-security/security-tips`.

Summary

In this chapter, we have learned techniques for improving our apps by adding analytics—in this case, Firebase Crashlytics—and how to use cloud messaging to increase user engagement in our apps. Additionally, we learned some tips and tricks for securing our apps.

We have come to the end of this chapter and book. We hope that you've enjoyed following along with the chapters and that you're now in a position to develop Android apps with the knowledge gained from this book. What are the next steps? Here are some of the things that you can do:

- Secure your app using the tips and tricks we went over in this chapter.

- Inspect, improve, and monitor the performance of your app. You can learn more about this from the official documentation at `https://developer.android.com/topic/performance/overview`.

- Learn more about **Modern Android Development** (**MAD**). MAD is a set of tools and libraries that help us develop Android apps faster and better. You can learn more about M.A.D from the official documentation at `https://developer.android.com/modern-android-development`.

- Learn more about Google Play Vitals and how you can use the information at `https://play.google.com/console/about/vitals/` to improve the quality of your app.

- Keep learning about Kotlin and Android. Build more apps and share them with the world. You can also contribute to open source projects.

Index

B

background tasks
scheduling, with WorkManager 181-185
baseline profiles 88
billion-dollar mistake 4
Bill of Materials (BOM) 61
breakpoints 213-215
bundles keyword 97

C

canonical layouts 72
Cat as a Service API
URL 102
checklist 272
Chucker 220
network requests, inspecting with 220-227
code smell 231
cold streams 105
companion objects 236
composable functions 35-37
composables
creating 84-86
UI tests, adding 264-267
compose destinations
navigating to 120-125
continuous Integration/Continuous
    Delivery (CI/CD) 305
benefits 306
working 307
coroutines 235
crash reporting 272
Create, Read, Update, and
    Delete (CRUD) 87

D

dangerous permissions 193
data
saving, and reading from
    local database 158-166
Data Access Object (DAO) 160
database layer
testing 258-261
data binding 81
debugging tips and tricks
breakpoints 213-215
Logcat 208-210
stack trace 210-213
debug mode 213
declarative UIs
versus imperative UIs 32-35
declarative UI toolkit 32
density-independent pixel 38
dependency injection 88-90
destinations
arguments, passing to 125-129
detekt
code smells, detecting with 241, 242
customizing 244-247
setting up 242-244
dynamic color 62

E

error messages 273
extension functions 233

Subscribe to our online digital library for full access to over 7,000 books and videos, as well as industry leading tools to help you plan your personal development and advance your career. For more information, please visit our website.

Why subscribe?

- Spend less time learning and more time coding with practical eBooks and Videos from over 4,000 industry professionals

- Improve your learning with Skill Plans built especially for you

- Get a free eBook or video every month

- Fully searchable for easy access to vital information

- Copy and paste, print, and bookmark content

Did you know that Packt offers eBook versions of every book published, with PDF and ePub files available? You can upgrade to the eBook version at packtpub.com and as a print book customer, you are entitled to a discount on the eBook copy. Get in touch with us at customercare@packtpub.com for more details.

At www.packtpub.com, you can also read a collection of free technical articles, sign up for a range of free newsletters, and receive exclusive discounts and offers on Packt books and eBooks.

Other Books You May Enjoy

If you enjoyed this book, you may be interested in these other books by Packt:

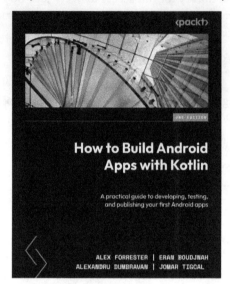

How to Build Android Apps with Kotlin

Alex Forrester, Eran Boudjnah, Alexandru Dumbravan, Jomar Tigcal

ISBN: 978-1-83763-493-4

- Create maintainable and scalable apps using Kotlin
- Understand the Android app development lifecycle
- Simplify app development with Google architecture components
- Use standard libraries for dependency injection and data parsing
- Apply the repository pattern to retrieve data from outside sources
- Build user interfaces using Jetpack Compose
- Explore Android asynchronous programming with Coroutines and the Flow API
- Publish your app on the Google Play store

Kickstart Modern Android Development with Jetpack and Kotlin

Catalin Ghita

ISBN: 978-1-80181-107-1

- Integrate popular Jetpack libraries such as Compose, ViewModel, Hilt, and Navigation into real Android apps with Kotlin
- Apply modern app architecture concepts such as MVVM, dependency injection, and clean architecture
- Explore Android libraries such as Retrofit, Coroutines, and Flow
- Integrate Compose with the rest of the Jetpack libraries or other popular Android libraries
- Work with other Jetpack libraries such as Paging and Room while integrating a real REST API that supports pagination
- Test Compose UI and the application logic through unit tests

Packt is searching for authors like you

If you're interested in becoming an author for Packt, please visit authors.packtpub.com and apply today. We have worked with thousands of developers and tech professionals, just like you, to help them share their insight with the global tech community. You can make a general application, apply for a specific hot topic that we are recruiting an author for, or submit your own idea.

Hi!

I am Harun Wangereka author of *Mastering Kotlin for Android 14*. I really hope you enjoyed reading this book and found it useful for increasing your productivity and efficiency using Kotlin.

It would really help me (and other potential readers!) if you could leave a review on Amazon sharing your thoughts on this book.

Go to the link below or scan the QR code to leave your review:

https://packt.link/r/1837631719

Your review will help me to understand what's worked well in this book, and what could be improved upon for future editions, so it really is appreciated.

Best Wishes,

Harun Wangereka

Download a free PDF copy of this book

Thanks for purchasing this book!

Do you like to read on the go but are unable to carry your print books everywhere?

Is your eBook purchase not compatible with the device of your choice?

Don't worry, now with every Packt book you get a DRM-free PDF version of that book at no cost.

Read anywhere, any place, on any device. Search, copy, and paste code from your favorite technical books directly into your application.

The perks don't stop there, you can get exclusive access to discounts, newsletters, and great free content in your inbox daily

Follow these simple steps to get the benefits:

1. Scan the QR code or visit the link below

https://packt.link/free-ebook/9781837631711

2. Submit your proof of purchase
3. That's it! We'll send your free PDF and other benefits to your email directly